Network Leadership

Across organisations and communities there are leaders who manage to get things done through their ability to understand how a network of individuals connect, who to talk to and how to bring people together in the right constellation of effort. These are "network leaders".

Network Leadership enables readers to identify and make the most of informal social and organisational networks in order to challenge the status quo effectively and facilitate greater engagement and productivity. Not only will the research in these chapters help you become a better leader and manager of your own team or department, it will also help make you a better network leader, effecting positive change across teams, and departmental and organisational boundaries. Leaders who facilitate action do so through four key practices: they understand the social systems in which they work; they have convening power, uncovering and connecting underlying movements and giving voice to something that is worth listening to; they lead beyond their formal authority; and they possess the power of restless persuasion and a capacity to thrive in complexity and crises.

This book is invaluable reading for those who have mastered the basics of leadership but wish to take the next steps. It is particularly relevant to organisations and managers dealing with the geographic separation of business units, change, innovation, matrix management, project or portfolio management and other cross-departmental projects.

James Whitehead is a Senior Lecturer in Strategic Management at Cardiff Metropolitan University, Wales, and an Associate of PSA Training and Development, where he worked as senior lead consultant for six years before taking up his current post. Prior to that he was an officer in the British Army, specialising in leadership and management education and influence operations in Afghanistan.

Mike Peckham is Managing Partner at Gadhia Consultants, Managing Director of PSA Training and Development and Chairman of Airbox Systems.

"We only truly grow up when we know what it is to be fully human. In our hands we are being given technology tools that are transforming what we can do and how we grow. But just because we can do it, doesn't make it good for us. The world needs leaders who thrive on living in this tension and use tools for growing transparency of truth. That's good for all of us."

***Ruth Dearnley* OBE, CEO, STOP THE TRAFFIK**

"Mike and James have produced a timely gem of a handbook for leaders at all levels. Leading amidst the profound shifts in how we live, work and relate to one another demands we evolve how we lead, and *Network Leadership* shows us how."

Neil Ventura, Executive Vice President, Strategy & Innovation (De Beers Group)

"In *Network Leadership*, James and Mike connect the dots beautifully in laying out what it means to be an agile and resilient leader in a rapidly changing world. I hope that you will find in *Network Leadership* tangible ideas to help you elegantly navigate your networks and galvanise action towards the change you believe in."

Demi Edosomwan, Managing Director, TotalEnergies Ventures

Network Leadership

Navigating and Shaping Our Interconnected World

James Whitehead and Mike Peckham

Routledge
Taylor & Francis Group
LONDON AND NEW YORK

Cover image: © Getty Images

First published 2022
by Routledge
4 Park Square, Milton Park, Abingdon, Oxon OX14 4RN

and by Routledge
605 Third Avenue, New York, NY 10158

Routledge is an imprint of the Taylor & Francis Group, an informa business

British Library Cataloguing-in-Publication Data
A catalogue record for this book is available from the British Library

Library of Congress Cataloging-in-Publication Data
Names: Whitehead, James (Senior lecturer), author. | Peckham, Mike, author.
Title: Network leadership: navigating and shaping our interconnected world / James Whitehead and Mike Peckham.
Description: Abingdon, Oxon; New York, NY: Routledge, 2022. | Includes bibliographical references and index.
Identifiers: LCCN 2021046988 (print) | LCCN 2021046989 (ebook)
Subjects: LCSH: Leadership. | Business networks—Social aspects. | Organizational resilience.
Classification: LCC HD57.7 .W475 2022 (print) | LCC HD57.7 (ebook) | DDC 658.4/092—dc23
LC record available at https://lccn.loc.gov/2021046988
LC ebook record available at https://lccn.loc.gov/2021046989

ISBN: 978-0-367-54414-0 (hbk)
ISBN: 978-0-367-55254-1 (pbk)
ISBN: 978-1-003-09258-2 (ebk)

DOI: 10.4324/9781003092582

Typeset in Goudy
by codeMantra

Contents

Illustrations

Figures

Tables

About the Authors

Mike Peckham FRGS, FRSA, MA

Mike is Managing Partner at Gadhia Consultants, Managing Director of PSA Training and Development and Chairman of Airbox Systems.

He works internationally with senior leaders from the public, private and third sector. His work with outstanding leaders in a rapidly changing context has shaped his thinking about how leaders must shift how they think about what they do. His clients include Virgin Money, De Beers Diamonds, Starbucks, Total Exploration and Production and EDF. He has worked extensively in West and sub-Saharan Africa.

He is a Trustee of the Armed Forces charity Hire a Hero; Chair of the trauma recovery charity SAFE; and founding Trustee of the Virgin Money Foundation. He is a member of the Advisory Board to Kina, a specialist firm providing Environmental, Social and Governance consultancy to businesses across Africa. He is a Visiting Fellow at the Business School of the University of South Wales. He is a Fellow of the Royal Geographical Society and the Royal Society of Arts and a member of the Royal United Services Institute.

Mike – a personal perspective on Network Leadership and why "restless persuasion" matters

Almost as long as I have been a consultant, I have been told that the world is more uncertain, volatile and chaotic than it has ever been. Thirty years ago, in 1989, I can recall Tom Peters invoking, indeed goading, us to "thrive on chaos" and how everything was moving at an exponential rate. Bennis and Nanus (1985) term VUCA or a world of volatility, uncertainty, complexity and ambiguity has been dusted off and is being used to describe the world we live in. Indeed, there have been ever increasing challenges from management gurus to face "wicked problems" and to live in the "Age of Unreason" etc. I have no doubt that if you are reading this you will be able to recant any number of book titles or aphorisms that broadly say the same thing.

The paradox for me is that if we have been saying this for at least the last 30 years, shouldn't we just stop sensationalising it and say – *this is the business reality and move on*. Business leaders today know that this is the case and don't see anything other than the need to get on in a world that has a tempo and rhythm that they have adapted to. The Hungarian scientist Hans Selye's first used the term "general adaptation syndrome" to identify three distinct stages as the body and brain adapt to stress, moving from alarm to resistance and ultimately, without adaptation, exhaustion. In the long term, if we don't adapt, we become exhausted. However, our bodies can become habituated to higher levels of stress. Arguably, people working "in" business have adapted but people working "on" business are still in the stage of alarm and resistance.

Network Leadership isn't a response to a new business reality, it's not a consultant inspired fad but an uncovering of a way of working that has existed below the surface of organisations as they struggle to make sense of how to act. As our impatience grows and we push the world to speed up, to collapse boundaries and become more interconnected and interdependent it is imperative to know how to act. Network Leadership provides an answer.

David Goodhart's (2017) book *The Road to Somewhere* was the first to identify the tribal lines of the "anywheres" and the "somewheres". The educated "anywheres" dominate the social and cultural debate and are defined by their portable career and educational achievements, whilst the "somewheres" are defined by the location they are rooted in. The rise of political populism could represent the first two stages of the "general adaptation syndrome" – alarm and resistance and a demand for heroic leaders to save the day.

The "heroic" leadership model, in which we pin our hopes and aspirations on a single omniscient and omnipotent individual to lead the way, becomes problematic when the challenges are bigger than a single brain can cope with. Network Leadership is an alternative model that draws on a web of connections to get things done. My understanding of Network Leadership is a result of working closely with hundreds of leaders across organisations globally, working closely with them through organisational change and upheaval and observing what enables them to act and mobilise those around them.

So how do I define and characterise "Network Leadership"? Network Leadership is the ability and capacity to bring together people, ideas and resources to solve problems, create opportunities and deliver for a constituency. Network Leaders recognise that they don't know the answer but those around them do; that they don't own all of the resources to deliver for their constituents but others within their network do; that their power comes from the ability to work across boundaries to connect ideas with action and people with resources. They are net contributors to their network in terms of connecting, energising and mobilising others to act.

In the overly simplistic characterisation of leadership styles, heroic leaders are defined by their sense of destination; the trinity of "vision, mission and values" captures what they do, where we are going and how we will behave towards each other. The Network Leader works in a more subtle way informed by purpose and belief; open to possibility and opportunity; working without authority but being influential; prepared to shift and reconfigure in order to deliver.

Network Leadership is not to be confused with distributed leadership; it's not diluting the authority of the leader across others but using singular authority to enlist others in their sense of purpose. Network Leaders have a mental "manifesto" that describes what they believe in, what they stand for and what they are trying to achieve. Mission, vision and values is replaced with manifesto thinking informed by a sense of restless persuasion.

Network Leaders at the top use their power to bring people together from across, within and between organisations. Assembling cross hierarchical groups to solve problems, re-forming them as a project unfolds; always being open to possibility and opportunity.

Network Leaders within organisations have an intuitive grasp of the social system within their organisation: how decisions are made, how resources are allocated and who determines who is listened too. They are frequently the "go to" people, the problem unlockers, and are sought out for their advice.

Network Leadership challenges the orthodoxy of the conventional schools of leadership by asking leaders to think about themselves in relation to others inside and outside their organisation, over which they may have no authority; to ensure purpose and values are of equal importance and present in all they do. "Restless persuasion" is how Network Leadership is executed day to day.

Dr James Whitehead FRSA, PhD, MSc, MEd

James is a Senior Lecturer in Strategic Management at Cardiff Metropolitan University and an Associate of PSA Training and Development, where he worked as senior lead consultant for six years before taking up his current post. Prior to that he was an officer in the British Army, specializing in leadership and management education, and influence operations in Afghanistan.

He has played a leading role in supporting individual and organisational learning in a wide variety of settings, both in the UK and abroad, and has an extensive background in operational and strategic planning in large multinational contexts. He has worked as a facilitator, coach and mentor in the public, private and third sector, and has taught sociology and psychology in Further Education.

His Doctoral thesis examined change leadership in the contested cultural environment of Northern Ireland, while his current research focuses on social networks and their contribution to understanding social capital and network leadership in organisational and community settings. He is a Fellow of the Royal Society of Arts.

James – a personal perspective on Network Leadership and why networks matter

In May 2008, while preparing for my first operational tour in Afghanistan, I was invited to the Ministry of Defence (MOD) in London to be shown how US forces had tracked down and caught Saddam Hussein. I was taken to a windowless room in MOD Main Building and shown a large projected image of interconnected dots and lines, which my host called a network diagram, specifically Saddam's network. He pointed to various dots, identifying them as specific individuals in Saddam's inner circle, and to the lines that connected them, amongst a host of other individuals and links. The diagram had been created using data collected from tracking cell phones and Saddam's capture had resulted, in part, from following one outlying connection, which led them to his hiding place in Tikrit.

I, however, was going to the International Security and Assistance Force (ISAF) Headquarters in Kabul, Afghanistan, and my interest was not in finding Osama Bin Laden. I wanted my host to explain how the same approach might be used to map terrorist networks, insurgent groups, criminal gangs and drug cartels in Afghanistan. How we might use this technology to identify the key players in Afghanistan and how they operated. The obvious use was in targeting, identifying individuals for kill or capture by stand-off missiles or Special Forces, but as an influence operative (social marketing is the closest civilian term) I was more interested in how information and ideas spread through social networks. If ISAF could identify the key nodes in the network of the broader population, perhaps we could target information at influential people and better spread our narrative and messages through key indigenous audiences.

Once in theatre, however, I found that the network approach, what I later came to know as Social Network Analysis, was largely unheard of. Undaunted, my international colleagues and I focused instead on key but under exploited groups such as female politicians and businesswomen and, most fruitfully, university students. Students are influential because as graduates they go back to their towns and villages with enhanced prestige and are listened to.

At the same time I realised that the network approach to influence could be applied in the Headquarters. ISAF was extremely hierarchical and bureaucratic. To get things done at speed you needed a good network; you needed to be able to work across the chain of command not just laboriously up, across and down. Gradually, this network coalesced organically around a group of about a dozen colleagues, both military and civilian, and we called our group SECSI (Synergistic Exchange of Contacts, Stories and Information) and soon lots more people wanted to join. Who doesn't want to be SECSI?

We met at least once a week, connecting those who needed connections and support, within and outside ISAF, with those who could offer it. And it was through a female Afghan university student, who, unusually, approached me (a male foreigner) during a conference, that I was able to put the network to use.

At Kabul University, she told me that female students are housed separately from the male students in a walled and gated enclosure. Their parents will only let them attend if the sexes live in rigidly separate accommodation blocks. To get to the University buildings, however, the young women had to walk down half a kilometre of road, which at night was unlit, because the streetlights had all been damaged years previously during the civil war. She asked if I could help.

Seeing this as an opportunity to achieve something tangible and demonstrate ISAF's positive message, I set about trying to fix the problem using my network. First, I got an introduction to the Vice-Chancellor of the University through a contact at the Ministry of Higher Education, who, in turn, was known to a member of SECSI. The next obvious step was to approach the reconstruction team in ISAF. Again, using contacts within SECSI I got an introduction to the German commanding officer, but it turned out he had no money for reconstruction as there was no Provincial Reconstruction Team (PRT) in the capital, but he suggested I approach the French who controlled Kabul. I did this through a French colleague, but they had already allocated their budget for the year and Kabul was not a priority.

So I changed tack. Again using SECSI, I contacted an American engineering company that worked in Afghanistan, including with British Forces at the Kajaki Dam in Helmand province, and offered apprenticeships to local young men. They were interested in the project, seeing it as an interesting and worthwhile assignment for these apprentices. I visited the University with their Canadian chief engineer and we agreed on a plan. All we needed were metal poles to replace the existing streetlights, which were peppered with bullet holes. Fortunately, the CEO of the engineering company, based in the United States, also liked the idea and, following a telephone call, he agreed to supply the metal poles. All I had to do was arrange for them to be shipped to Afghanistan by the US Air Force.

It was not to be. The US Air Force was not allowed to fly "civilian equipment" on military planes. I tried through ISAF's own logistics chain and I had a plan to get the US Commander of ISAF involved through his German Chief of Staff, whose deputy was a friend of mine. But I was nearing the end of my tour and just ran out of time. But that was not the end of the story. I passed the project to the SECSI network and eventually the University did get its streetlights but powered by solar panels not electric cables. I wished I had thought of that.

My own failure, apart from an inability to see beyond my own assumptions, was a consequence of rotational tours of duty, which exposed a further network issue. Extended military operations in Afghanistan necessitated the rotation of personnel on a six-monthly basis. When this is charted hierarchically, it appears that such rotations have minimal effect. One individual leaves theatre and another qualified individual immediately fills that space in the org chart. There is no indication of the actual impact on the organisation. However, if instead we visualise ISAF as a network, we can see the damage that rotations of personnel can cause.

As an "individual augmentee" (military speak for anyone posted to an operational theatre and not part of a larger deploying unit), I arrived in Afghanistan and took over my job in ISAF headquarters. Despite having a short handover with the person I was replacing, at first the only people I really knew were my boss and a handful of colleagues in our dusty office. In a network diagram I would have shown up as a small node with few connections. As time passed, however, I made new connections and found British colleagues in other jobs throughout Afghanistan. Gradually, I developed further connections with other military organisations, UK and allied government agencies, host-nation agencies, non-government organisations (NGOs) and so forth. On a network map, you would have seen me growing from a tiny node to a more significant connective hub.

Yet, when I left, just as clearly you would have seen that large hub instantaneously replaced by my replacement – a small node with few connections – and so it went on. When combined with the departure of numerous other hubs, this undoubtedly had a huge impact on the performance of ISAF against an indigenous and largely static enemy and was behind US pressure to extend European operational tours from six months to the US rotation pattern of one year. From a personal perspective, I left Afghanistan and later the British Army with a profound sense of the power of networks and our critical need to understand them.

Acknowledgements

I have had the good fortune to work with outstanding leaders from around the world, often as a consultant, sometimes as a teacher and frequently as a coach. I have seen them flourish and struggle as they lead through shifting and complex times. Each of those leaders has shaped what I know and have been instrumental in the creation of this book. I am grateful to my good friends and colleagues Dame Jayne-Anne Gadhia and Darcy Willson-Rymer who have shaped my thinking through demonstrating the practices of Network Leadership and engaging in the ongoing debate. As we were writing the early drafts of the book, we ran our first 'Introduction to Network Leadership' programme for the energy company Total and we are grateful to the first cohort of international leaders from North and South America, Europe, Africa and Asia for their insight and bringing their world to us for scrutiny. My work in sub-Saharan Africa and with Rosalind Kainyah of Kina Advisory provided an African perspective on network leadership and embodies the spirit of Ubuntu – "I am because we are". I am especially indebted to my co-author James for the many hours of conversation, challenge and debate and for sustaining the considerable effort of committing ideas to paper so that we could fashion it into a coherent accessible framework.

Mike Peckham

As an army officer, educator and consultant I have had the opportunity to work for and with some exemplary leaders and in writing this book they have been at the forefront of my thinking, reflecting on how they inspired me and helped me understand the different worlds in which I worked. I have also had the privilege of leading people and learnt immeasurably from them all, not least in how not to do it. From such a diverse array of experience, it is difficult to select the key personalities without feeling bad for those who would inevitably be missed, so let me instead thank the key networks of which I have been a part and are therefore a part of me. The staff of the Royal Military Academy Sandhurst, where I first began to consider what it meant to be a leader; my colleagues in the Royal Army Educational Corps, as it was known, where I learnt to be an educator; my international colleagues in Afghanistan who helped me fully appreciate the power of networks; and the network managers of the Royal National Institute of Blind People who helped me understand what I was trying to say. The only individual I will thank specifically is my co-author Mike, whose coaching and mentoring helped me as a consultant to understand and appreciate the many and varied challenges faced by the organisations we worked with and how to lead beyond the military. Thank you to you all.

James Whitehead

Introduction

Across organisations and communities, there are some leaders who manage to get things done through their sheer ability to understand how the network of individuals connect on the ground, who to talk to and how to bring together people in just the right constellation of effort that can make things happen. Our work with leaders in the public, private and third sector over many years has helped to identify these as what we now term "Network Leaders", which we define as those with:

> The capability to work across social boundaries, connecting ideas with action and people with resources, in pursuit of shared goals. Leaders who, while open to possibility and opportunity, remain true to the core beliefs of alignment, synergy and restless persuasion.

For us, Network Leadership has four components: two leadership components – convening power and leading beyond authority – bookended by two enabling components – understanding the system and restless persuasion. Understanding the system is about identifying the nodes (individuals and groups) in your network, who they connect with and why and discerning where the knowledge, capacity and resources lie. Convening power is about harnessing those components by attracting the right constellation of people around you, by having something to say that is worth listening to, which then requires you to lead beyond authority, turning your ideas into action with and without resort to formal hierarchical power and positional authority. Finally, restless persuasion is about having the energy and resilience to keep going despite setbacks and naysayers. It recognises that when you step beyond your formal authority, things get messy and slow.

Network Leaders can see across organisations and communities and make the sum of the parts greater than the whole. They are leaders who know that opportunities and threats do not come neatly parcelled to fit within the hierarchical structure of teams, departments and divisions into which we have organised

DOI: 10.4324/9781003092582-1

ourselves. They are leaders who take responsibility for problems other than their own and recognise that the best way to get things done is not to mind who gets the credit for doing them. Crucially, Network Leadership is relevant at all levels of an organisation, whether you formally lead a team or contribute as an individual technical expert.

Network Leaders identify and make the most of the informal networks that inevitably exist within all teams, organisations and communities to get things done. Effective Network Leadership facilitates the exchange of accurate information about who does what, who knows what and who needs what in order to:

- Better target scarce resources.
- Challenge the silo mentality.
- Restructure the formal organisation to complement the informal.
- "Rewire" faulty networks to achieve goals.
- Deepen the quality of relationships.
- Reduce transactional costs (e.g. micromanaging and second guessing).
- Be more innovative.

And they do this through an implicit understanding of networks – how to navigate them and how to shape them.

Network Leaders recognise the interconnected world we live in, they understand the social system of organisations, they bring people together, they can lead informally but know when to use their formal or positional power and are relentless in what they want to achieve for their organisation or community. The purpose of this book is to explore the origins of this approach to leadership, to examine network thinking, social networks and network business models, in order to define the characteristics of Network Leadership and Network Leaders, the likes of which we need more than ever.

In the modern world, the challenges we face – from global warming to terrorism and inequality – flow through interlocking webs of connection and causation, leading to volatility, uncertainty, complexity and ambiguity. Simultaneously, the power of networks is growing. In science, technology, health, environment and civil society, networks are becoming a way to uncover the hidden architecture of complexity and unlock people's capacity to think and act in different ways.

But focused network change in organisations and communities will not happen without leadership. Left to their own devices, networks develop naturally through proximity and homophily: natural human inclinations to associate with people who are near us and/or like us. While such bonds often contribute to a group's strength, they can also inhibit communication with other groups.

An understanding of networks helps identify the tribes, cliques, silos and gaps in connectivity, but effective collective action – improving productivity and responsiveness, smoothing channels of communication and impelling change and innovation – requires some to lead and others to follow. Direction, however gentle or subtle, is always required. Formal, positional leadership will remain important, but in a networked world, leaders will increasingly be asked to lead without positional authority, across internal and external organisational boundaries.

Unlike conventional top-down leadership, Network Leadership is more about influencing and enabling than directing. It is leadership understood first and foremost as a social process that creates direction, alignment and commitment without recourse to the traditional mantra of positional authority: "because I say so". Network Leaders recognise that leadership is not something you get but something you give.

However, as American lawyer and political scientist Anne-Marie Slaughter observed in her 2017 book, *The Chessboard and the Web*,[1] we do not yet know how to handle this networked world at the strategic, operational or tactical level. The network provides a metaphor, not an analytical tool, and we need to understand how to connect for specific purposes. We need a "playbook". And the purpose of this book is to provide the beginnings of that "playbook" by asking what leadership actions and styles will be effective in getting others aligned and what new structures, tools and processes will enable broader coordination and keep progress on track. Essentially, we set out to write the book we wanted to read.

It is the product of more than 60 years of combined experience as leaders and followers, managers and employees, entrepreneurs and consultants, army officers, teachers and academics. But its genesis lies in our shared dissatisfaction with the formal organisational hierarchy as a way of understanding organisations and the related perception that leadership stems from your position in that hierarchy. In our experience, this is not how stuff actually gets done. For us, leadership is not about your position in the pecking order; most of what gets done happens in the informal networks of connection and collaboration that exist behind the veil of the organogram. This is where real leadership happens. Robbed of positional authority, a leader in this space, a Network Leader, must depend on and cultivate aspects of leadership that encourage people to follow them not because they have to, but because they want to.

We use the term Network Leader in part because it resonates with the spirit of our age and the fact that networks are increasingly becoming common linguistic currency, but in truth, Network Leadership is far more ancient than that. It is primeval, long predating the internet and social media. It is leadership in the raw and its attributes have been in existence for as long as people have gathered in groups, since our primate forebears first huddled together. We are social animals and part of that inheritance is that we exist in groups with leaders and followers. And in the first instance, leaders emerged from the group on their own merit. Only then, once they had stepped up and assumed the mantle of leadership, did we confer titles and positions of authority upon them. What we now call formal and traditional authority came after the assumption of power through personal authority.

This then is a book for leaders who have mastered the basics of good leadership but wish to take the next step. A step that takes them outside their formal and positional authority, beyond leadership of like-minded people and toward leadership that crosses boundaries. Leadership that harnesses the collective will of different teams and departments toward shared organisational goals. Leadership that inspires people of all types to follow you, not because they must, but because they want to – because they believe in you and your goals.

Leadership Questions

Each part of the book concludes with a summary and Leadership Questions (LQs) for you to consider. We use LQs in all our leadership programmes, specific questions that attendees are expected to write up and present at the next workshop. We do this because learning requires that we reflect on not just absorbing the information we receive. Not only does actively thinking about what we are told aid retention, it also allows us to place our learning in context. The key metric for any leadership programme, aside from individual development, should be its impact on the organisation or business in which the leader operates. And our approach in this book is no different. We hope that you use this book as a process of enquiry, reflecting on what you read and applying it to your own context. Network Leaders are after all, as we shall explain, reflective practitioners in and on the art of leadership.

Note

1 Slaughter, A. (2017). *The Chessboard and the Web: Strategies of Connection in a Networked World*. New Haven, CT and London: Yale University Press, p. 13.

Part I

The Leadership Stage

We have identified Network Leadership as an emerging response by leaders to the challenge of making things happen in an increasingly complex world. In some respects, it contrasts with the previous thinking about leadership that has studied the leader separate from their context, either through studying what leaders do and distilling that essence into several aspirational traits or by linking it to delivering a vision with leadership as a form of destination management.

Essential to Network Leadership is the understanding of context and the role of the leader in shifting the context and mobilising individuals, teams and resources across organisations towards achieving a goal. In this section, therefore, we identify and describe some of the key influences that have informed Network Leadership and its practice by looking at some critical changes globally and within the world of work and the changing demands they place on leaders.

DOI: 10.4324/9781003092582-2

1 The World Is Changing

In the first half of 2020, the Covid-19 virus spread across the world. The pandemic was an extraordinary event in global history as a near simultaneous effect across the world, in a way that had never happened before. It reconfigured how we live our daily lives; the lockdown changed the daily working rhythm as people worked from home and adjusted to a new reality.

For many it forced them to work from home using remote working technology such as video conferencing and screen sharing; it challenged working rituals, most notably the morning commute and the standardised working day of 9–5, both legacies of early 20th-century labour laws. As home became the new workplace, individuals juggled caring for elderly relatives and home schooling with work calls and videoconferences. The boundary between work and home became more permeable than ever. These enforced changes to our ways of working and rituals accelerated some inevitable changes to our working and home lives as the choice to change was taken away from people.

Much has been written about how our world has been shaped by a series of catalytic inventions that ushered in periods of rapid, simultaneous and systemic transformation. The first industrial revolution took place in the second half of the 18th century, with the mechanisation of manufacturing using water and steam power. The second happened 150 years later, in the early 20th century, with mass production and assembly lines using electric power. The third happened in the 1980s, with the arrival of computers, robotics and the digital revolution. Some would argue that we are in the midst of the fourth or even the fifth industrial revolution.

The fourth industrial revolution has accelerated since the turn of the Millennium and is associated with mass data, computing and cloud power, the rise of Artificial Intelligence (AI) and machine learning; the emergence of technology connected and enhanced humans. The World Economic Forum has described it as representing:

DOI: 10.4324/9781003092582-3

> A fundamental change in the way we live, work and relate to one another. It is a new chapter in human development, enabled by extraordinary technology advances commensurate with those of the first, second and third industrial revolutions. These advances are merging the physical, digital and biological worlds in ways that create both huge promise and potential peril. The speed, breadth and depth of this revolution is forcing us to rethink how countries develop, how organisations create value and even what it means to be human.[1]

Some critiques of the fourth industrial revolution are concerned about how this new technology only serves self-interest rather than societal advancement and humanity.[2] At the start of 2020, the Blackrock boss Larry Fink challenged business to balance profit with purpose[3] and to reshape finance in the cause of solving pressing social and economic issues. At the 2020 Davos summit of world leaders, Marc Benioff of Salesforce[4] challenged the audience to think about how technology will make the world a better place. Some identified this as an emerging fifth industrial revolution in which technology serves humanity and businesses identify their wider social purpose in supporting and solving some of the world's greatest problems.

The fifth industrial revolution, like the previous revolutions, affects every sphere of human activity from the social, cultural and political to the economic and technological, with huge ramifications for how we organize our lives, how we work and consequently how we lead and manage.

Whether you agree with the idea of a fourth or fifth industrial revolution, we are sure most will agree that with each of the industrial revolutions, the underlying technology, speed, scale and sophistication increase. We are now at the point that no single person can know the answer. Indeed, with the onset of AI, we are possibly at the point when machines are certainly smarter than us.

This is a world that is increasingly characterised as complex and chaotic. The macroeconomic models of leading economists were not able to predict the market crash of 2008, because of our inability to understand the wider systemic risks incurred though the creation of new financial instruments.

Behavioural economics has emerged as a growing response to Adam Smith's "invisible hand" view of economics, in which "rational self-interest" alone is the basis for action. Behavioural economics combines cognitive, emotional, cultural and social factors with insights from psychology and human behaviour to understand and in some instances manage individual and institutional decision-making.

At the very moment when technology is more sophisticated and our world is ever more complex, our understanding of the wider political and economic machine is best understood through understanding the individual in context.

Our primordial instincts are collective; in pre-history the protection of the tribe was a necessity and even today we define ourselves through membership, be that through sport, religion or politics. Today, social media is part of the process of definition in an ever-complex world in which truth is very much in the eye of the beholder.

Simultaneous Trends and Accelerations

Each of these trends alone would be dislocation enough, but when combined they have an even greater impact. In his book, *Thank You For Being Late: An Optimist's Guide to Thriving in The Age of Accelerations*, Thomas L. Friedman[5] refers to the simultaneous accelerations we are experiencing in technology, globalisation and our impact on the planet, each of which affects the others in a complex web of interaction. But in Friedman's view, it is the gap between the speed of change in these three domains, particularly the technological, set against the slower pace of human adaptability that is causing a sociocultural angst: feelings of confusion, dislocation and a loss of control over our lives.

To give a sense of the pace of change, Ray Kurzweil, Google's Director of Engineering, believes that the rate of technological progress, stemming from what he calls the law of accelerating returns, where each advance accelerates the rate of future breakthroughs, means that humanity will experience the equivalent of 20,000 years of technological progress in the 21st century.[6]

On the one hand, Friedman recognises that advances in technology are reducing complexity to a simple click of a button: from calling a taxi to booking a room or buying home appliances. It is taking the complexity out of more and more industrial processes and human interactions. Technology has reduced friction and made the world faster, but the complexity is just hidden and the speed of these new developments can leave people floundering.

Similarly, when people feel their identities and sense of home being threatened, they will set aside their economic interests and choose "walls over webs and closed over open". Many Americans and Europeans feel overwhelmed by globalisation because the rapid expansion in digital flows, trade flows and immigration flows is outstripping our social technologies: our learning, adapting and cushioning tools, and therefore threaten the things that anchor us, our jobs, our local culture and our sense of home, community and nation.

To succeed now we have to continually refresh our stock of knowledge by participating in relevant flows of new knowledge. At an individual level, the future, Friedman argues, will belong to those who have the self-motivation to take advantage of all the free and cheap tools and flows coming out of the

Mid-2020 – A Working Day

A World Turned Upside Down is the title of a book written by the radical historian Christopher Hill to describe the upheaval of the short-lived English Republic of the mid-17th century. It is an extraordinary book because it describes how the culmination of the Civil War with the execution of Charles I went on to affect the lives of every person in England as they tried to make sense of the new reality. It is rare that one event changes the lives of everyone. The global pandemic is such an event and has certainly turned the world upside down.

As a consultant, Mike's pre-Covid routine typically involved travelling, staying in hotels, meetings and working long hours with clients; today, he replaces the travel with a commute to his desk, nights away with nights at home and meetings with Zoom calls. The only thing that has not changed is the long hours.

The cost of meeting has decreased as video calls become the de facto way of working. He misses the inadvertent and the spontaneous, the unplanned conversation and chance encounter. His rushing is no longer from one meeting place to another but between different video conferencing formats.

Whilst digital has triumphed as we work from home, there is a higher premium placed on being able to meet people in 3D. He has a longing for real person-to-person contact in a shared meeting room rather than via a digitally mediated face to face.

Digital has made geography and the physical almost meaningless. He shops, reads and consumes news and content online. Groceries, post and parcels arrive magically after a few clicks on his smartphone.

For some the world got smaller as their permission to travel was taken away from them; for him the world got bigger. No longer constrained by travel and the expectation of in-office meetings, a meeting with a client in Singapore, United States or Spain become equally important. The length of my day is no longer defined by trains and planes but time zones.

This is Mike's experience of 2020 and a "world turned upside down".

technological acceleration. In today's knowledge economy, the key assets will be human capital: talent, skills, empathy and creativity. The key is an agile mind-set that values learning over knowing, alongside educational systems that are retooled to maximise the fundamentals of writing, reading, coding, mathematics, creativity, critical thinking, communication, collaboration, grit, self-motivation, lifelong learning, entrepreneurship and improvisation.

But at an organisational and community level, Friedman is in no doubt that it requires leadership and addressing our collective anxiety is one of today's greatest leadership challenges. People are looking for navigational help and sense-making, for someone to apply the brakes or just give them a simple answer to make their anxiety go away. The problem is that few political leaders can understand or explain what is happening, let alone identify a way ahead.

Instead, Friedman argues, we need leadership that can promote inclusion and adaptation, leaders who recognise that rather than applying the traditional top-down, hierarchical command and control structures, success is better organised around small teams and local action groups, who form loosely coupled networks with other teams and groups from whom they can learn and seek support. In other words, Network Leadership. But to understand how leaders might achieve this transformation in the context of the organisation, we must first explore the impact of the next Industrial Revolution in the workplace.

Notes

1 World Economic Forum. (2021). Fourth Industrial Revolution. (online) Available at https://www.weforum.org/focus/fourth-industrial-revolution (accessed 17 April 2021).
2 Van Erden, J.A. (2020). Davos POV about a 5th Industrial Revolution. (online) Available at https://real-leaders.com/a-5th-industrial-revolution-what-it-is-and-why-it-matters/ (accessed 17 April 2021).
3 Fink, L. (2020). Letter to CEO's: A Fundamental Reshaping of Finance. (online). Available at https://www.blackrock.com/corporate/investor-relations/2020-larry-fink-ceo-letterr (accessed 17 April 2021).
4 Lachlan, S. (2019). The Fifth Industrial Revolution Is Coming – and It's about Trust, Values and Saving the Planet. (online) Available at https://diginomica.com/the-fifth-industrial-revolution-is-coming-and-its-about-trust-values-and-saving-the-planet (accessed 17 April 2021).
5 Friedman, T.L. (2017). *Thank You for Being Late: An Optimist's Guide to Thriving in The Age of Accelerations*. UK: Penguin Books.
6 Kurzweil, R. (2001). The Law of Accelerating Returns. (online) Available at https://www.kurzweilai.net/the-law-of-accelerating-returns (accessed 17 April 2021).

2 Work and Organisations Are Changing

As we recognise a fourth or fifth industrial revolution, we can start to identify how this is impacting the world of work, the shape of organisations and how we work every day. This includes the impact of technology, changes to organisational structure and service models, the impact of globalisation, demographics and social media and the changing nature of careers and aspirations and therefore the role of leaders and managers. A summary of those changes is offered in Figure 1.1 based upon the analysis of Stanley McChrystal and his colleagues in the book *Team of Teams*.[1]

Technology. Digital technology is disrupting and dividing the world. So far, the impact has been felt most by low and mid-skilled workers in rich economies. However, it is now increasingly threatening skilled workers in the knowledge economy. Artificial Intelligence (AI) and machine learning are proving to be powerful tools that can speed up routine knowledge-intensive tasks by processing large volumes of data far beyond the capacity of a single individual or specialist team.

When Covid-19 was identified in China in January 2020, the virus's entire genetic makeup or genome was published online within days in contrast to the Ebola outbreak in 2013 that took three months. The combination of big data and smart machines is thought likely to take over some occupations entirely, while others will change profoundly. Any job that requires the processing of data and decision-making will be impacted; this includes research, marketing, sales, medicine and the law.

Like previous industrial revolutions, this one is destroying jobs as well as creating them, and once again individuals will be required to embrace change and build resilience by continually learning new skills and knowledge. The difference this time is that machines can do cognitive as well as physical tasks. The knowledge economy is now subject to the same forces as the industrial and service sectors: routinisation, division of labour and contracting out. More and more of the routine parts of knowledge work can be parcelled out to machines.

DOI: 10.4324/9781003092582-4

Key Changes

	Factor	Old	New
Inside the organisation	Organisational unit	Department	Cross functional team
	Roles	Functional experts	Generalists
	Task	Optimise process (and repeat)	Innovate (and improvise)
Outside the organisation	Organisational structure	Hierarchy	Network
	Communication	Limited and linear	Frequent and omni-directional
	Decision making	Centralised	Distributed an empowered
	Perspective	Tactical	Strategic
The wider context	Environment	Complicated	Complex
	Knowledge	Finite and knowable	Infinite and unknowable
	Metaphor	Machine	Organism

Based on McChrystal, Fussell, Silverman, Collins (2015) Team of Teams: New Rules of Engagement for a Complex World; Penguin

Figure 1.1 Changing World of Work.

It therefore requires both manual and knowledge workers to change or evolve their roles as organisations and career paths are disrupted. Not all tasks, however, can be easily automated. Those requiring high levels of innovation and creativity may not be automated at all. Consequently, people with the ability to think around a completely new problem and generate moments of clarity and insight will still be at a premium. At the other end of the scale, low-skilled manual jobs such as fruit picking will still be needed.

The ubiquity of technology and computing power means that we have more computing power in our pockets via our phones that the NASA had in whole of the Apollo space missions.[2] In the future, AI and machine learning coupled with robotics will replace humans in some tasks and augment them in others. We will have to confront important questions, such as what are humans uniquely good at, what is our comparative advantage and what is our place alongside machines? We will be entering a new kind of partnership with machines that will build on our mutual strengths, resulting in new levels of human–machine collaboration.

The "Internet of Things" (IoT) and 5G will increase our ability to locate and track things as well as each other globally. It is widely expected that there will be 41.6 billion connected IoT devices by 2025. Every object, every interaction, everything we encounter will be converted into data, which will enable us to model social systems at extreme scales, helping us to uncover new patterns and relationships that were previously invisible; by 2025, we expect to have 4,900 data engagements per day – many of which will be unknown to us.[3]

Technology has reframed the shape of organisation and the meaning of work as an activity and not a place. Work being conducted across office space, home or a coffee shop and eroding the boundary between work and home and beyond 9am to 5pm; whether work is chosen or forced; whether work is for positive personal growth or a necessity; alongside the transient nature of work with employees, organisations and external collaborators engaging, disengaging and reengaging with each other in cycles of varying duration and permanence.

Organisations. Organisational structures will change as traditional hierarchies struggle and the size of organisations is likely to matter less. Instead, organisations will need the capabilities to establish agile, flexible purpose-specific structures that allow them to address current challenges and easily transition to other structures when necessary. In this environment of organisational fluidity, informal influence born of emotional and social intelligence will be the key. And as relationships continue to be important and since face-to-face and digital contact are equally vital, the challenge for organisations will be to facilitate them both, in order to facilitate the process of sharing work.

New service delivery models have changed how we shop: Amazon, eBay and online retailers continue to reconfigure the high street, whilst Airbnb and Booking.com have changed how we book hotels and holidays. These companies are examples of intermediary platform companies that connect demand with supply at a consumer level.

The growth of the digital economy has enabled tasks to be divided with platform companies now effectively creating digital production lines across the world, with freelance professionals selling their skills through websites like Fiverr and TaskRabbit through to people working on a portfolio of different assignments for a number of businesses. In the same way that Henry Ford combined moving assembly lines with mass labour to make building cars much cheaper and quicker, today's entrepreneurs are striving to do the same with services, bringing together computer power with freelance workers to supply luxuries that were once reserved for the wealthy. Uber provides chauffeurs, Handy supplies cleaners, Deliveroo delivers restaurant-quality meals to your home and Instacart stocks your fridge. But it goes further than luxuries to include the services of doctors, lawyers, consultants, programmers and designers.

Global Connection. Covid-19 has highlighted our dependency on global supply chains and the movement of goods and people to support how we live, from the annual movement of immigrant workers to the digital movement of capital across borders to support investment. The early stages of global outsourcing saw low-skilled digital jobs, such as call centres, being outsourced to less developed economies; this trend is being reversed as countries shorten supply chains and decrease their dependency on critical infrastructure beyond their borders.

Despite the advantages accruing from a globalised world, such as the spread of technology, ideas and innovation, lower costs for products and access to new markets and talent, governments are increasingly restricting immigration, imposing high tariffs, excluding foreign technology, censoring foreign ideas and turning their countries into fortresses. Some hope that the world will become a network of walled but friendly fortresses. In its most idealised form, there will be no immigration, no multiculturalism, no global elites, but also no global war. The problem is that walled fortresses have seldom proven friendly. Without some universal values and global organisations, rival nations will be unable to agree on common rules, and despite the changes that will potentially be wrought by Covid-19, no modern economy can survive without a global trade network.

Furthermore, humankind faces common problems that make a mockery of national borders and can only be solved through global cooperation: climate change, the threat of nuclear war and technological disruption, not least among them. Even if one country decides to pursue "killer robots" or genetically enhanced babies, then other countries will be forced to follow suit for fear of being left behind. To confront these dangers, we will need to encourage a sense of global identity and encourage people to be loyal to humankind and to planet earth in addition to their particular nation or community. That will not happen in isolationist fortresses.

Demography. The demographics of today's workforce are also changing dramatically, with baby boomers making way for millennials. At the same time, as we live longer and birth rates in the western world decrease, the median age of the population edges upwards with a greater proportion of 60+-year olds versus 16-year olds in contrast to the emerging economies where there are more 16-year olds than 60-year olds. As the baby boomers leave the workforce, they take with them experience and knowledge, whilst millennials bring increased technological fluency and a high expectation of corporate social responsibility and social purpose.

Globally, lifespans are extending and this will change the nature of careers and learning. Since the late 19th century, we have followed a three-stage life cycle of education, work and retirement. However, the longer working life means that this neat sequence may no longer apply. With people increasingly working past 65 in order to have adequate resources for retirement, individuals will need to rearrange their careers, family life and education to accommodate this demographic shift.

In *The 100-Year Life*, Lynda Gratton and Andrew Scott[4] suggest that the new life cycle stages might be education, exploration, individual producer/-entrepreneur, regular work/employment, portfolio work and retirement. For individuals, it will be important to recognise when these transitions are coming and navigate them successfully. Multiple careers will become commonplace and lifelong learning will see renewed growth as the knowledge economy continues to grow.

Social Media. Social media and its role in influencing opinion, alongside the reconfiguration of journalism, have created a new media ecology and sparked a debate about the very nature of truth. New communication technology is placing new demands on our attention and cognition and virtual networks are being integrated at an ever-faster pace into our lives, enabling new ways to create an online identity and new ways for groups to collaborate. At the same time, it is altering our attitudes towards reality and truth, with events seen from multiple angles and perspectives, each telling a different story of events appealing to different subjective experiences, which, in turn, has led to a concern that political misinformation is driven by maligned social media corporations that facilitate information sharing.

The disturbing acceptance of "fake news" and the idea of "post truth", in which half-truths are normalised online and at the same time scientific knowledge and evidential argument are dismissed and delegitimised unless they support narrow and factional interpretations of the truth. All of which is repeated and recycled by a limited number of big social media firms (Facebook, Google, Twitter and YouTube), using complex algorithms to personalise individual news feeds. Often these dominant firms represent themselves as defenders of free speech, whilst disguising their commercial interest in gathering our data for advertisers.

Workforce. Pressure on organisations is likely to push service companies to follow manufacturers and focus on their core competencies. A pattern seems to be emerging of knowledge workforces made up of full-time employees with deep experience of the business; younger employees working towards a full-time position, there or elsewhere; and high calibre individuals who choose to work on a flexible consultancy, project-based or part-time basis. As transaction costs fall, the attraction of using an outsider to fix something rather than keeping the function inside your company will only increase, and on-demand companies will increasingly act as middlemen, arranging these connections. But, as they don't employ full-time staff, with their associated pay and benefits, responsibility for pensions and health care and the associated risks are again pushed back onto individuals, increasing the need for self-reliance.

As the *Economist* points out,[5] optimists will argue that it ushers in a world where everybody can control their own lives, doing the work they want when they want, while pessimists will worry that everyone will be reduced to the status of 19th-century dock workers, crowded on the quayside at dawn waiting to be hired by a contractor. The winners will be consumers and taxpayers (as long as on-demand labour is used to reduce costs and improve the efficiency of public services) as well as workers who value flexibility over security, such as students, young mothers, elite workers and those who can afford to dip into and out of the labour market. The losers are likely to be workers who value security over flexibility, such as middle-aged professionals with children to educate and mortgages to pay.

The on-demand economy may well deliver enormous benefits, but not without a period of uncomfortable change. More worrying is the potential for greater inequality and social exclusion as well as the growing divide between a skilled elite and ordinary workers, which may provoke further anger among voters seeking scapegoats and further propel the rise of xenophobia and protectionism, which is a recipe for extremism and unrest. Governments can help by investing in housing close to sources of work and improving transport infrastructure, but they can also raise productivity and employability by funding and encouraging lifelong learning in the skills required for work in the future.

Fundamentally, we believe there is an intrinsic desire to make meaning from what we do, but that meaning is very personal. It can be instrumental/-transactional, working for a wage; it can be bureaucratic, working for the good of the organisation; it can be communal, working for the good of fellow workers; or it can be idealistic, working for a moral cause or purpose. The work of Robert Levering[6] identified "pride and meaning in what you do" as one of three key elements of a "Great Place to Work", the others being "trust between bosses and employees" and "enjoying being with co-workers".

Levering also identified what people don't want: work that is dehumanising, where they are treated like an animal or robot, or work that is deskilling, where they are given little scope for personal initiative or creativity. In these circumstances, people can find meaning in organisational subcultures which can subvert the organisation through humour, shirking or at an extreme, sabotage.

Emerging Leadership Skills

Changes in the way organisations work have always had an impact on the way people and teams function and therefore upon how they are managed and led, from the rigid hierarchies of the post-war period to the flatter more collaborative structures of the 1990s and the networks of diverse teams we see today. The established research and commentary about gender and leadership along with the drive for greater representation across businesses have challenged and broadened the inherent male connotation that is implicit in the very word "leadership". The "Reykjavik Index"[7] provides a global measure of how women are perceived in leadership roles and the extent to which men and women are perceived equally as suitable leaders. Whilst attitudes about men and women and their suitability for leadership roles vary across countries and sectors, sadly there are persistent stereotypes that show we are some way from gender not being an issue when debating leadership.

As the world changes and organisations become more fluid, leadership and management will become ever more complex, necessitating changes to the critical skills required of leaders. These new skills will include an interpretative ability to navigate complexity, provide context and provide sense to those around them; a social and emotional intelligence to adapt and connect individuals and teams; and an ability to innovate and a technical fluency to process large volumes of disparate data. Leaders will need to have both a depth of skills alongside a breadth of abilities to lead what will become a growing number of permanent and transient virtual teams.

Social Intelligence is the ability to connect to others, in order to stimulate the desired actions and interactions, and socially adept leaders who are able to assess the emotions of those around them and adapt accordingly. Furthermore, in an increasingly fluid world, leaders will need to operate in whatever environment they find themselves. Conversely, as organisations increasingly see diversity as a key driver of innovation, dealing with diversity will become a core competency for leaders, enabling them to build relationships and work together effectively.

Leaders will need the ability to think, innovate and come up with solutions and responses that move us beyond what has gone before, but also the ability and humility to seek out new ideas and ways of doing things. It is the ability to recognise and discriminate between problems and appropriate solutions; to identify when a problem is familiar and the solution is ready made, as opposed to when the solution is unknown or at an extreme when the problem is ill-defined or not understood.

As the amount of data we use increases, leaders will need the technical skills to be able to analyse and understand it as well as use it effectively in discussion and decision-making. The ability to discriminate and filter information for importance will be key. Conversely, leaders will need to be aware of the limitations of data and modelling and not become paralysed when they lack an algorithm to guide decision-making. They will also need the ability to develop content that uses new media forms and use these media for persuasive presentations and communication, while also having the capacity to critically assess the content of others' communication and presentations.

As technology enables global working as well as flexible working, virtual collaboration becomes the norm: the ability to work productively, drive engagement and demonstrate presence as a leader and a member of virtual teams. While connective technologies make it easier to work, share ideas and be productive despite physical separation, the virtual work environment also demands new competencies. Leaders of virtual teams will need to develop new strategies for engaging and motivating a dispersed group. Techniques that may, for instance, include features from gaming to engage large virtual communities, such as immediate feedback, clear objectives, and a staged series of challenges.

The ideal leader will be "T-shaped", able to bring to bear a deep understanding of their own field (the down bar), but also the ability to converse in the language of a broader range of disciplines (the cross bar) and place their own work in the broader, shared context of their organisation or community. Complex, multifaceted and ill-defined problems will necessarily require transdisciplinary solutions, which will require more than simply bringing together teams from different disciplines; it will need leaders who understand the language of those multiple disciplines. This, in turn, will require leaders with a sense of curiosity and enquiry to go on learning throughout their working lives. And it is to a deeper examination of how leadership is changing that we now turn.

Notes

1 McChrystal, S., Collins, T., Silverman, D. and Fussell, C. (2015). *Team of Teams: New Rules of Engagement for a Complex World*. London: Portfolio Penguin.

2 Puiu, T. (2020). Your Smartphone Is Millions of Times More Powerful Than the Apollo 11 Guidance Computers. (online) Available at https://www.zmescience.com/science/news-science/smartphone-power-compared-to-apollo-432/ (accessed 17 April 2021).

3 Reinsel, D., Gantz, J. and Rydning, J. (2018). The Digitization of the World from Edge to Core. (online) Available at https://www.seagate.com/files/www-content/our-story/trends/files/idc-seagate-dataage-whitepaper.pdf (accessed 17 April 2021).

4 Gratton, L. and Scott, A. (2020). *The 100-Year Life: Living and Working in an Age of Longevity*. London: Bloomsbury Publishing.

5 The Economist. (2015). Workers on Tap, The On-Demand Economy. January 3rd–10th, p. 67.

6 Levering, R. (1994). *A Great Place to Work: What Makes Some Employers So Good – And Most So Bad*. New York: Avon Books.

7 Reykjavik Index 2019. (2021). (online) Available at https://www.womenpoliticalleaders.org/the-reykjavik-index-for-leadership-2019/ (accessed 17 April 2021).

3
Leadership Is Changing

To be clear, we are not suggesting that Network Leadership is a new phenomenon; rather, it is a reformatting of leadership. It is about uncovering a way of working that has always existed below the surface of organisations as they struggle to make sense of and act in turbulent times. Yet it is a way of working that has been only vaguely understood within tribal pecking orders, military chains of command and neat organisational hierarchies and bureaucracies. For networks to emerge as a new way of seeing the world, it needed a language of its own: a language provided by the World Wide Web, social networks and social media. What follows, therefore, is an attempt to provide a framework in which we can locate Network Leadership in the extensive landscape of existing leadership theory and practice.

A Framework of Leadership

Fundamentally, leadership is having followers. And, broadly speaking, people follow leaders for three reasons. Because of the position they hold in an organisation, institution or community. Because of something intrinsic to that individual: their ideas, their character, their demeanour and so on. And alternatively, because of the way in which they lead, which might be broadly inclusive and collective, hierarchical and directive or individual and autocratic.

In most instances it will be a combination of all three elements, although the quantities will vary depending upon the personality and the context. But in all three cases people will only continue to follow so long as the leader, by and large, gets the results they desire and enables them to do things they could not otherwise have done themselves. It is our contention that leadership boils down to three ideal and diametrically opposed dimensions: Individual, Hierarchical and Collective (ideals in the sense that they are the extreme or ultimate representation of their kind, rather than something we should necessarily aspire

DOI: 10.4324/9781003092582-5

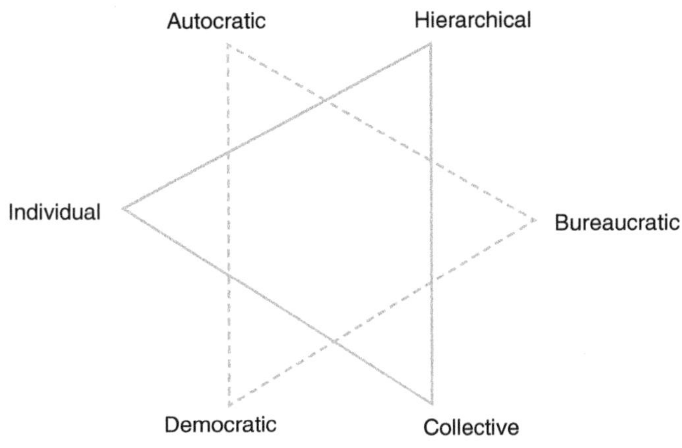

Figure 1.2 A Framework of Leadership.

to), which, in turn, give rise to three derivative styles of leadership: autocratic, bureaucratic and democratic that exist in the tension between our dimensions of leadership (Figure 1.2).

Thus, an autocratic style of leadership can flex across the spectrum from absolute and direct individual sanction to leadership at the apex of a hierarchical pyramid. Bureaucratic leadership can stretch from the hierarchical pyramid to collective will and rule by committee, while democratic leadership lies on the spectrum from collective will to a supremely powerful elected leader.

It is not, therefore, a static framework. It recognises that leadership can flex across the linear spectrums described above. So, for example, those leaders who tend towards an autocratic style will have recourse to a more singular, dictatorial approach should the need arise and equally a more hierarchical style on other occasions. And this flexibility allows us to superimpose three broad vectors of leadership onto our framework, which can be labelled: Heroic Leadership, Post-Heroic Leadership and Scientific Management (Figure 1.3).

Together, these dimensions, styles and vectors portray the shifting nature of leadership as it negotiates differing contexts. And Network Leadership is the epitome of flexibility across the entire system of possibilities and is thus at the heart of our framework. Network Leaders adapt to their environment by flexing across evolving but also repeating patterns of leadership theory and practice, because they recognise that human systems are a complex combination of subsystems, where these dimensions, styles and vectors can coexist in a kaleidoscope of shifting patterns. We will discuss the emerging notion of Network Leadership in the next section, but first we will explore the framework, beginning with our

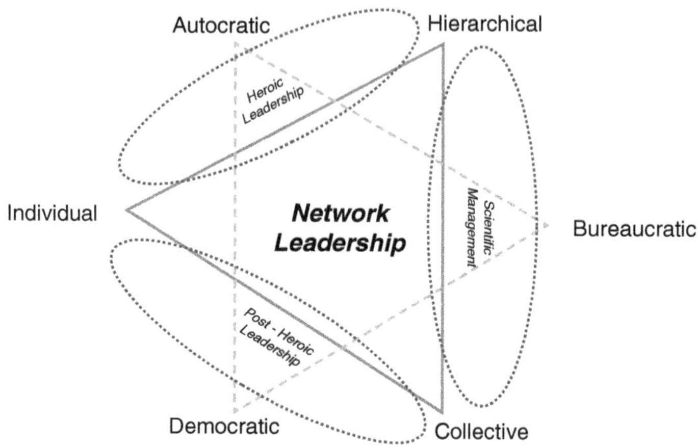

Figure 1.3 Vectors of Leadership.

three dimensions of leadership (Individual, Hierarchical, Collective), which will, in turn, enable us to draw out the associated styles (Autocratic, Democratic, Bureaucratic), the vectors of leadership (Heroic, Post-Heroic and Scientific Management) and finally their relationship to one another.

Individual Leadership

Individual Leadership describes some of the most venerable and commonly understood theories of leadership, principally Great Man Theory, Trait Theory and Behavioural Theory. The Great Man Theory of leadership was popular during the 19th century and focused on the individual qualities that distinguished leaders from followers. Great Man theories assumed that the capacity for leadership was innate and consequently great leaders were born not made – you either had it or you didn't (which was linked to a broader belief, outlined by Francis Galton in 1869, in which great talents of any sort were born, not made). Unsurprisingly, the term "Great Man" was used because, at the time, leadership was thought of primarily as a male quality and associated especially with military leadership.

Leaders were portrayed as heroic, even mythic, and destined to rise to the prominence when required, like a contemporary King Arthur returning in our time of need. The mythology behind some of the world's most famous Western leaders, such as Alexander the Great, Julius Caesar, Henry V, Napoleon and Abraham Lincoln, helped contribute to the notion that great leaders were born and not made; the right man for the job emerging almost mystically to take control of a situation and lead his people into safety or to victory.

The historian Thomas Carlyle was an early proponent of this theory of leadership, boldly claiming that "The history of the world is but the biography of great men".[1] According to Carlyle, effective leaders were those gifted with divine inspiration and possessing the right characteristics. Early explorations of leadership therefore focused on people who were already successful leaders, often including aristocratic rulers who had achieved their position through birth or divine right. The fact that people of lower social status did not achieve leadership roles only reinforced the notion that leadership was an inherent ability. The fact that people of lower status had fewer opportunities to lead was largely ignored.

Sociologist Herbert Spencer was one of the first to refute such notions of leadership, suggesting instead that the leaders were products of the society in which they lived. In *The Study of Sociology*,[2] Spencer wrote:

> You must admit that the genesis of a great man depends on the long series of complex influences which has produced the race in which he appears, and the social state into which that race has slowly grown … Before he can remake his society, his society must make him.

Yet, even today, we often describe prominent leaders (men and women) as having the right qualities or personality for the position, implying that inherent characteristics are what make these people effective leaders. We still seem smitten by the idea of charismatic, heroic leaders controlling the destiny of a company or a nation. We feel reassured by a "strong" commander at the helm: someone who commands our respect, knows where they're going and will take us with them. Equally, we are repelled by those whom we perceive as wooden, arrogant or clown-like.

The first serious research into leadership began in the 1920s. Similar to "Great Man" Theory, Trait theories attempted to identify the common characteristics of effective leaders, assuming that people inherit certain qualities and traits that make them better suited to leadership, but it also drew heavily on the broader study of personality traits, which suggested that individual personalities are composed of broad dispositions that might be genetic or environmental in origin.

A trait can be thought of as a relatively stable characteristic that causes individuals to behave in certain ways. For example, you might describe a friend as outgoing, kind and even-tempered. It has a common-sense validity to it and has therefore proved tenacious. Both authors, who attended the Royal Military Academy Sandhurst in the late 1980s, can attest to evenings bulling (polishing) boots and discussing the five or six key traits that defined a leader and then memorising the list favoured by the Academy Commandant, Montgomery, Slim or more recent British Generals. At Sandhurst, typical leadership traits usually included courage (both moral and physical), determination and integrity.

Unlike other theories of personality, such as psychoanalytic or humanistic theories, the trait approach focuses on differences between individuals: the combination and interaction of various traits forming a personality that is unique to each individual. While debate continues as to the number of traits that make up human personality, the most common criticism of the theory is that traits are often poor predictors of behaviour. While an individual may score high on assessments of a specific trait, he or she may not always behave that way and certainly not in every situation. We may be very determined to climb a mountain, but completing a critical spreadsheet leaves us cold or vice versa. Another problem is that trait theories do not address how or why individual differences in personality develop or emerge. From a leadership perspective, the critique is this: if particular traits are key features of leadership, then how do we explain people who possess those qualities but are not leaders?

Behavioural theories of leadership, which began to emerge in the 1940s, fundamentally challenged the assumption that leadership capability is innate or inherent. They focused instead on what a leader does, not what he or she is. Rooted in behaviourism, a psychological approach that concerns itself with observable stimulus-response behaviours and states, it advances the view that all behaviours are learned through interaction with the environment. Behavioural theories of leadership therefore focus on the actions of leaders not on inherited mental qualities or internal states.

Accordingly, people can learn to become leaders through instruction, observation and practice (leadership development practitioners rejoice). Behaviourists look at what leaders do by studying their behaviours in response to different situations, assessing leadership success by studying their actions and then correlating significant behaviours with success. For example, behavioural theory finds expression in situational and contingency theories of leadership, which suggest that different leadership behaviours are appropriate at different times and with different people. The best leaders, according to these theories, are those who have the adaptability to flex their behavioural style according to the contingencies or situations they encounter.

In short, leadership is dependent upon the context or situation the leader finds themselves in, and they must therefore adapt their behaviour to suit the situation, the people and the task at hand. To which most of us would no doubt reply – you don't say. It is emphatically true that there are endless contingencies in life and consequently there must be endless varieties of leadership, but behavioural theories provide little guidance as to what constitutes effective leadership in those different situations or in deciding which style of leadership is significant in enabling one group to work better than another. The conclusion, if any, appears to be that no one leadership style or set of behaviours is right for every leader under all circumstances and one particularly influential derivative of behavioural theory is Style Theory. According to Style Theory, success in any given situation depends upon a number of variables, such as the nature of the task and the skills and experience of the followers, and the leader adapts their style to suit those variables. For example, in a situation where the leader is the most knowledgeable and experienced member of a group, an autocratic or authoritarian style might be most appropriate. In other instances, where group members are skilled experts, a more democratic or participative style would perhaps be better.

Autocratic or authoritarian leadership, as the name suggests, is a "leadership style" characterized by individual control over decisions and little input from group members. Autocratic leaders typically make choices based on their own ideas and judgements and rarely accept advice from followers. In other words, autocratic leadership involves absolute authoritarian control over a group.

Autocratic leadership can be beneficial in some instances, such as when decisions need to be made quickly and consulting with a large group of people would only slow things down. Some projects require strong leadership and command in order to get things accomplished quickly and efficiently. A strong leader or commander using an autocratic style can take charge of the group, assign tasks to different members and establish solid deadlines for projects to be finished.

In situations that are particularly stressful, such as during military conflicts or crises, group members may prefer an autocratic or command style. It allows members of the group to focus on performing their specific tasks without worrying about making complex decisions. It also allows group members to become highly skilled at performing certain duties, which can be beneficial to group productivity.

What all the foregoing theories of leadership share, whether leaders are judged to be born or made, is a belief in the single heroic individual, typically male, who delivers results through the sheer power of their personal traits or abilities. It is a powerful narrative, fuelling our collective imagination, which is still fed with stories of heroes and villains, good triumphing over evil and leaders who are charismatic, powerful and influential figures, leaders who can steer organisations through stormy waters by the sheer force of their personality.

But macro social, economic and political problems have always been bigger than a single brain can cope with. And even if a single brain were sufficient, there is always the problem of succession: will the next incumbent be similarly gifted (Napoleon and Alexander both foresaw the limits of their empire and the fragmentation that would inevitably follow). There can also be a dangerous drift to vanity, with a consequent lack of objectivity, an inflated sense of their own worth and a coterie of flunkies who are reluctant to challenge their exalted leader's authority. At an extreme, heroic leaders become a single point of system failure.

The critical weakness of heroic leadership is that it doesn't sufficiently leverage the strengths of others. Research has found that autocratic leadership often results in a lack of creative solutions to problems, which can ultimately hurt the performance of the group. As the physicist Yaneer Bar-Yam has argued, a group of individuals whose collective behaviour is controlled by a single individual cannot behave in a more complex way than the individual who is exercising control.[3]

At its best, however, individual leadership can gravitate towards transformational leadership. A concept initially introduced by leadership expert and US Presidential biographer James MacGregor Burns,[4] who described it as a process in which leaders, through the strength of their vision and personality, are able to inspire followers to change expectations, perceptions and motivations, in order to work towards common goals.

Burns' original ideas were later built upon by Bernard M. Bass to develop what is today referred to as Bass' Transformational Leadership Theory.[5] According to Bass, transformational leaders garner trust, respect and admiration from their followers by doing four things:

- Providing "intellectual stimulation" by challenging the status quo, encouraging creativity and learning among their followers and exploring new ways of doing things.
- Offering "individualized consideration", support and encouragement to individual followers, in order to foster supportive relationships, the sharing of ideas and recognition of each follower's unique contributions.
- Giving "inspirational motivation" through a clear vision that they are able to articulate to followers, which, in turn, helps followers to experience the same passion and motivation to fulfil these goals.
- And finally through "idealized influence" serving as role models for their followers in everything they say and do.

In short, it is leadership conducted by a transformed and enlightened leader who seeks to transform and enlighten others.

The reality today, however, is that most organisations cannot afford to be one-man or one-woman shows. Organisations need to be far more agile, responsive and innovative than a single individual if they are to survive and prosper, characteristics that are far more likely to flourish in an environment of skilled multidisciplinary working and collaborative decision-making rather than an environment of command and control, no matter how well intentioned and articulated. Organisations still need leaders to take their teams with them, but not at the expense of their team's ideas and engagement, nor should they squash people's ability to step up and lead themselves.

Darcy Willson-Rymer echoed this observation when we interviewed him. He strongly believes that "Everyone is in a position of leadership from the person on reception to the CEO ... Every role is valuable and should have a voice". He also challenged the notion of vision being the prerogative of the "leader". "Vision", he observed:

> is not the prerogative of a single individual ... The role of the Chief Executive is not to set the vision itself, but to set the scope and scale and allow the organisation to develop its vision and enable it to deliver on that vision.[6]

Ruth Dearnley made the same point when she observed that "Leadership is not a solitary activity ... 'You can't lead alone. People have to believe they belong – they have to have skin in the game. It would fail if it was just me'".[7]

Hierarchical Leadership

The word hierarchy derives from ancient Greek, meaning "rule of a high priest" and may have first been used to describe the heavenly order of angels. The attraction of hierarchical order is that it makes the exercise of power over a group of people more efficient, centralising control and eliminating, or at least reducing, the need for time-consuming arguments about what to do, which might also degenerate into conflict, but at the same time, often restricting the worst excesses of a single leader, rather like the development of constitutional monarchy which gradually restricted the divine right of kings and queens. And bureaucracy, which tends to develop hand in glove with hierarchy, rests on two key concepts: scientific management and transactional leadership.

Scientific management has four key elements: handing power from frontline workers to managers; measuring everything you can; setting goals and targets; and linking targets to rewards. It was developed in the early 20th century by Frederick Winslow Taylor, who used targets to improve the production of pig iron in the United States. But in Britain, it had its roots in the work of the utilitarian philosopher Jeremy Bentham, who dreamed of turning government into a utility-maximising machine, an approach satirised by Charles Dickens in the character of Mr Gradgrind, who wanted to "weigh and measure every parcel of human nature".

Despite going out of favour, scientific management returned in the 1980s, driven by a combination of Thatcherism and information technology (IT), the defeat of the trade unions and the centralisation of government. The Blair government in the UK was very target-focused and identified managerialism with modernisation, and recent advances in AI algorithms have given it a further boost.

There is little doubt that management by targets can be very successful if carefully applied and metrics provide a whole raft of KPIs to evaluate organisational performance. But problems arise when they are poorly thought through. The decision to use an algorithm to decide UK A-level results in 2020 was a disaster, with individual students judged on their own performance but also the performance of their school the previous year; a system that disadvantaged bright students in larger, less wealthy schools and favoured less able students in smaller private schools.

In general, targets produce three common problems. The first is that they can produce perverse outcomes. For example, the UK's National Health Service began penalising hospital emergency departments that took too long to treat patients after an ambulance had dropped them off, which led hospitals to respond by keeping patients waiting in ambulances rather than in emergency departments. The second is that they tempt managers to manipulate the numbers. When the Metropolitan Police began linking crime reduction targets to pay and promotion, downgrading and underreporting of crime became a prevalent behaviour across the Force. Finally, an obsession with measurement diverts people from useful activity to filling in forms. We will leave you to conjure your own examples of that one.

Transactional leadership is also about performance. Much like stimulus-response in early behavioural theory, it sees leadership as a system of transactions: rewards and punishments that are contingent upon the performance of the followers. The leader views the relationship between managers and subordinates as an exchange – you give me something and I will give you something in return. When employees are successful, they are rewarded; when they fail, they are reprimanded; and in that way the organisation moves towards its goals.

Bernard M. Bass contrasted transactional leadership with his ideas, which we explored previously, on transformational leadership,[8] identifying its basic assumptions as fourfold: people perform at their best when the chain of command is definite and clear; that workers are motivated by rewards and punishments; that obeying the instructions and commands of the leader is the primary goal of the followers; and that subordinates need to be carefully monitored to ensure expectations are met.

Research has found that transactional leadership tends to be most effective in situations where problems are simple and clearly defined, but is generally considered to prevent both leaders and followers from achieving their full potential or dealing with the unexpected. It is therefore unsuited to complexity, the essence of which is its unpredictability, while the essence of bureaucracy is its quest for calculability and safety, which too often means it becomes reactive to events that it failed to predict and remain beyond its control.

In our framework, we can reflect the distinction by drawing a line down the centre of the model (Figure 1.4). On the right side is a managerial and transactional approach, encompassing hierarchy, bureaucracy, collective control and the vector of scientific management. On the left is a more transformational and leadership-oriented approach, describing a more individualistic style, whether directive or democratic.

Collective Leadership

Collective Leadership describes an approach that values awareness of group dynamics over possession of a commanding personality. And in contrast to

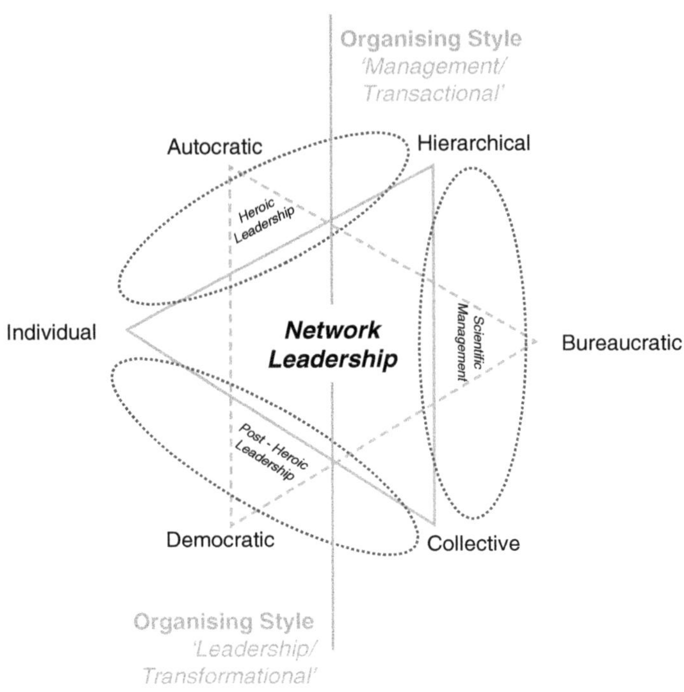

Figure 1.4 Organising Style – Leadership versus Management.

leadership that relies upon formal or positional authority, in a hierarchical chain of command, for instance, it better suits leadership in flatter structures without multiple levels of control. Unsurprisingly, its roots can be found in democratic or participative leadership.

This is an inclusive style of leadership in which members of the group are encouraged to take a more active and participative role in the decision-making. Democratic leaders encourage participation and contributions from group members and therefore, so the theory goes, help group members feel more relevant, empowered and committed to the decision-making process and the actions that flow from it.

The modern basis for the democratic leadership theory dates to a series of studies in the 1930s and 1940s when Kurt Lewin, together with his colleagues R. Lippit and R.K. White, determined three distinctive decision-making styles, which they described as existing on a spectrum from autocratic to laissez faire with the democratic style at the mid-point.[9] Lewin and his colleagues identified three core elements of democratic leadership:

1. Leaders expect subordinates to report to leaders regarding the task.
2. Leaders expect subordinates to exhibit self-confidence and the ability to get things done without constant supervision.
3. Leaders expect subordinates to involve others in the decision-making process and therefore not act alone.

Their research not only identified the three separate styles, but also compared them in terms of effectiveness. Among subordinates, the democratic leadership style stood out as the most popular method, and because group members felt more involved and committed to projects, end results were more effective. Under the more autocratic style, subordinates eventually started rebelling against authority, while laissez faire leadership led to a lack of coherence and a generally poor record of achievement against objectives. In addition, because group members are encouraged to share their thoughts, democratic leadership can lead to better ideas and more creative solutions to problems.

Consequently, democratic leadership tends to work best in situations where group members are skilled and eager to share their knowledge. It is also important to have plenty of time to allow people to contribute, develop a plan and then debate the best course of action. In situations where roles are unclear or time is of the essence, democratic leadership can lead to communication failures, uncompleted projects and missed deadlines. And in some cases, group members may not have the necessary knowledge or expertise to make quality contributions to the decision-making process. And this lack of expertise can also extend to the "leader".

Post-heroic leadership recognises this deficiency and makes it a requirement for leaders to acknowledge they do not know all the answers, and crucially, they are not required to. The post-heroic leader improves productivity and engagement by having the humility to seek answers from across the breadth and depth of the organisations and communities they inhabit. They also have the humility to recognise that in certain situations they may not be the one to lead. In this case, their role becomes one of enabling other leaders.

To take a few examples, Heifetz describes leadership as an activity that can be enacted by anyone in a system, independent of their role.[10] Bradford and Cohen describe heroic leadership leading to "over-management" and "defence of turf" rather than a concern for shared goals, teamwork and coordination. In contrast, shared, post-heroic leadership releases the potential power of everyone.[11] Drath and Paulus argue that leadership arises within communities of practice whenever people work together and make meaning of their experiences in collaborative forms of action across the dividing lines of perspective, values, beliefs and cultures,[12] while Val Sedounik describes the post-heroic leadership style as not telling people what to do, but striving "to create an environment where knowledge workers can operate autonomously and effectively".

Post-heroic leaders, she writes:

> Do not feel threatened by others who see things differently. They have a big picture view of the needs of customers and of the organisation, in the context of the external environment, and they're open to fresh perspectives on how to meet these needs. They understand that, with a trusted team around them, they can use the expertise of others to best advantage.[13]

Since its emergence, subgenres of post-heroic leadership have proliferated, including Shared Leadership, Distributed Leadership, Complexity Leadership, Intergroup Leadership and Collaborative Leadership, but they all share similar principles that contrast with heroic leadership, which are illustrated in Table 1.1.[14]

From an individual perspective, identifying yourself as a leader, no matter your formal position in an organisation, is a powerful view to have. It is a proactive stance, which gives people a feeling of agency and autonomy, a belief in their ability to craft the world around them and make necessary changes. In brief, post-heroic leadership provides an opportunity and a mind-set that encourages leaders to enable and grow other leaders, and a psychological safety net for people to step up and lead. There is a problem however: taken to an extreme, it encourages anarchy. There remains a need to balance freedom to lead with a collective and shared direction.

Table 1.1 Contrasting Principles of Heroic and Post-Heroic Leadership

Heroic Leadership	*Post-Heroic Leadership*
Position, authority	Role, behaviour
Individual	Collective
Controlling	Facilitating
Directive	Emergent
Transactional	Relational, connected
Top-Down	Bottom-Up

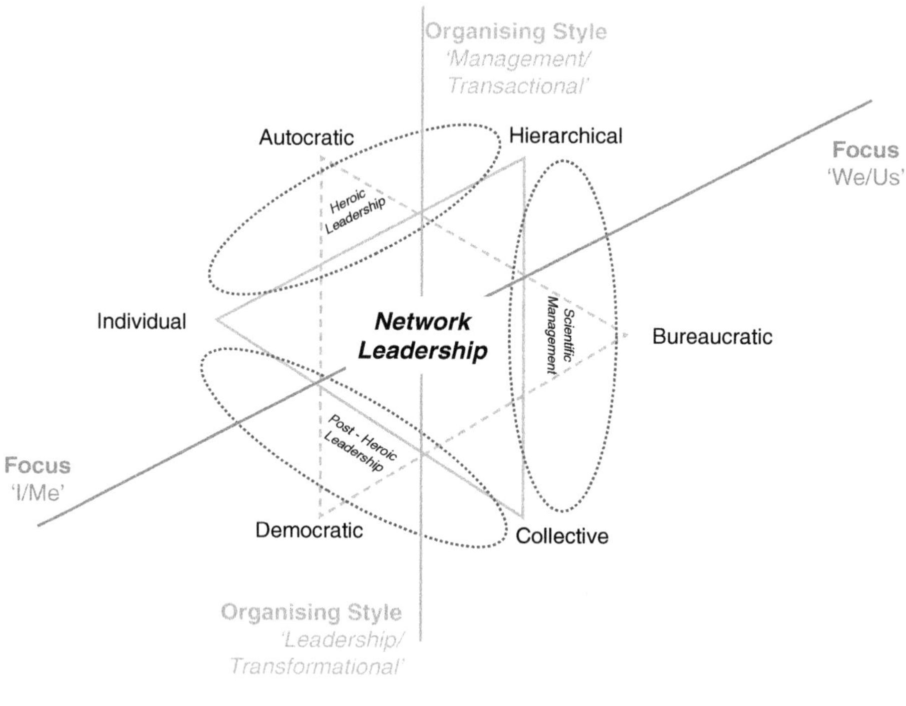

Figure 1.5 The Tension between "I/Me" and "We/Us".

It is a tension we illustrate with a line that bisects our framework, dividing what we do alone as I/Me from what we do together as We/Us (Figure 1.5). And seeks to reflect the conflict we must negotiate in pursuing our individual goals and objectives alongside or against those of the teams, organisations and societies in which we inevitably exist.

This tension is explored in *Networked Change*,[15] which seeks to identify and describe the strategies and practices that have contributed to successful advocacy campaigns in contrast to those that failed to create lasting change. The Report refers to successful campaigns as "directed network campaigns", ones which achieved *high impact*, defined as clear changes in corporate or government policy and/or widespread attitude change, and *high force amplification*, because they started with few resources yet achieved substantial victories.

Typically, such campaigns are led by a central body that framed the issues and coordinated action towards shared milestones, but gave a fair degree of freedom and agency to grassroots supporters and a diverse network of allies. They succeed, the Report concludes, because they are aligned with new sources of self-organised people power (the increasing desire of individuals to choose, customise and co-create) while avoiding the pitfalls of diminishing organisational loyalty and a decline in institutional trust. In summary, they have an executive structure that establishes strategic direction and carefully manages resources and relationships among a diverse network of support. And this, as the Report acknowledges, requires new leadership skills and technology.

The widespread disruption and immense publicity were garnered by Extinction Rebellion (XR) in 2019 when they conducted a series of non-violent actions across central London, post-dates the *Networked Change* Report, but XR cited inspiration from earlier grassroots organisations like the international progressive sociopolitical movement "Occupy". Occupy is an interesting model because it talked about being leaderless, which is counter-intuitive when viewed through the lens of a hierarchy, but from a network perspective, it simply meant there were no positional or formal leaders (Black Lives Matter is another example). There were leaders, but they emerged organically from their environment, exhibiting leadership based on energy, expertise and initiative rather than any formal appointment. However, it is widely believed that the Occupy Movement failed to achieve lasting change because they were unclear about their destination and there was no way to settle disputes, with no individual or group able to gain enough trust from all the various participants. Similarly, XR, with its devolved leadership and broad support base, has at times struggled to agree its strategy and facilitate joint action.

Another example is the Arab Spring, in which the revolutionaries were unable to build a consensus beyond the shared injustices that inspired change. The movement unseated some of the Middle East's longest standing leaders, but then fragmented into factions and interest groups, leaving behind a chaotic vacuum. The chaos was amplified by social media (ironically the very tool that had launched the revolution) through facilitating the spread of misinformation, rumours and hate speech. This polarisation allowed the Egyptian military to exploit the movement's divisions and allowed the Muslim Brotherhood to dominate the protest space. In short, while social media improved the protestors' ability to connect at a tactical level, it was no substitute for operational and strategic leadership. The fundamental Leninist insight therefore appears to hold true: nothing can be done without organisation and this takes time. And as Jayne-Anne Gadhia points out, "Movements may happen accidentally, but leaders don't, you must be determined to lead".[16]

Notes

1 Carlyle, T. (1869). *On Heroes, Hero-Worship, and the Heroic in History*. London: Chapman and Hall.
2 Herbert, S. (1896). *The Study of Sociology*. London: Appleton, p. 31.
3 Bar-Yam, Y. (2002). Complexity Rising: From Human Beings to Human Civilization, a Complexity Profile. (online) Available at https://www.researchgate.net/publication/250082400_Complexity_Rising_From_Human_Beings_to_Human_Civilization_a_Complexity_Profile (accessed 17 April 2021).
4 Burns, J.M. (1978). *Leadership*. New York: Harper and Row.
5 Bass, B.M. (1985). *Leadership and Performance*. New York: Free Press.
6 Interview with the authors 1 March 2021. See Appendix 2 Leader Biographies.
7 Interview with the authors 1 February 2021. See Appendix 2 Leader Biographies.
8 Bass, B.M. (1985) ibid.
9 Lewin, K., Lippit, R. and White, R.K. (1939). Patterns of Aggressive Behaviour in Experimentally Created Social Climates. *Journal of Social Psychology*, 10, pp. 271–301.
10 Heifetz, R.A. (1994). *Leadership without Easy Answers*. Cambridge, MA: Belknap Press of Harvard University Press.
11 Bradford, D.L. and Cohen, A.R. (1998). *Power Up: Transforming Organizations through Shared Leadership*. New York: J. Wiley.
12 Drath, W.H. and Palus, C.J. (1994). *Making Common Sense: Leadership as Meaning-Making in a Community of Practice*. Greensboro, NC: Center for Creative Leadership.
13 Sedounik, V. (2015). Why Your Organisation Needs Post-Heroic Leadership. (online) Available at https://www.hrzone.com/lead/future/why-your-organisation-needs-post-heroic-leadership#:~:text=A%20post%2Dheroic%20style%20of,beneficial%20impact%20on%20employee%20engagement (accessed 17 April. 2021).
14 Reinelt, C. (2010). The Leadership Learning Community. (online) Available at http://leadershiplearning.org/blog/claire-reinelt/2010-05-18/how-network-leadership-different-organizational-leadership-and-why-un (accessed 17 April 2021).
15 Mogus, J. and Liacas, T. (2016). Networked Change. NetChange Consulting Report. (online) Available at https://netchange.co/networked-change (accessed 17 April 2021).
16 Interview with the authors 22 March 2021. See Appendix 2 Leader Biographies.

Summary

So, if complexity is beyond the wit of a single individual and hierarchy/ bureaucracy is procedurally unsuited to managing complex environments but collective leadership is unable to gain enough trust, legitimacy and authority to coalesce ideas and energy around sustainable coordinated action, what is to be done?

It is a problem that we sum up in the final iteration of our leadership framework, with a line dividing it into two contexts (Figure 1.6). The first to the right and above the line describes a context in which we are close to certainty and agreement. We have problems and many of them are complicated, but we have ways of dealing with them. In some cases we have confronted them before and have ready-made solutions and where solutions are presently lacking, we have procedures and processes to identify them. It is a context suited to the autocratic, the hierarchical and the bureaucratic.

However, to the left and below the line, the context is entirely different. Here, we are far from certainty and agreement. Buffeted by crises and beset with complex problems that defy our best efforts to understand them, let alone solve them. This is characterised by VUCA (volatility, uncertainty, complexity and ambiguity). The acronym was first coined toward the end of the 1980s, based on the leadership theories of Warren Bennis and Burt Nanus, and was subsequently taken up by the United States Army War College to describe the multilateral complexity of the world that emerged after the end of the Cold War and has subsequently been given fresh impetus by 9/11, the 2008 financial crisis and Covid-19. Each episode reminding us how unpredictable the world is and that none of us are immune (pardon the pun).

It is our belief that Network Leadership can exist and prosper in both contexts, whether agreement and certainty are near or distant because, fundamentally, it is an understanding of leadership that evolves and yet also repeats itself over time and space. It is kaleidoscopic in nature and reflects an understanding of

DOI: 10.4324/9781003092582-6

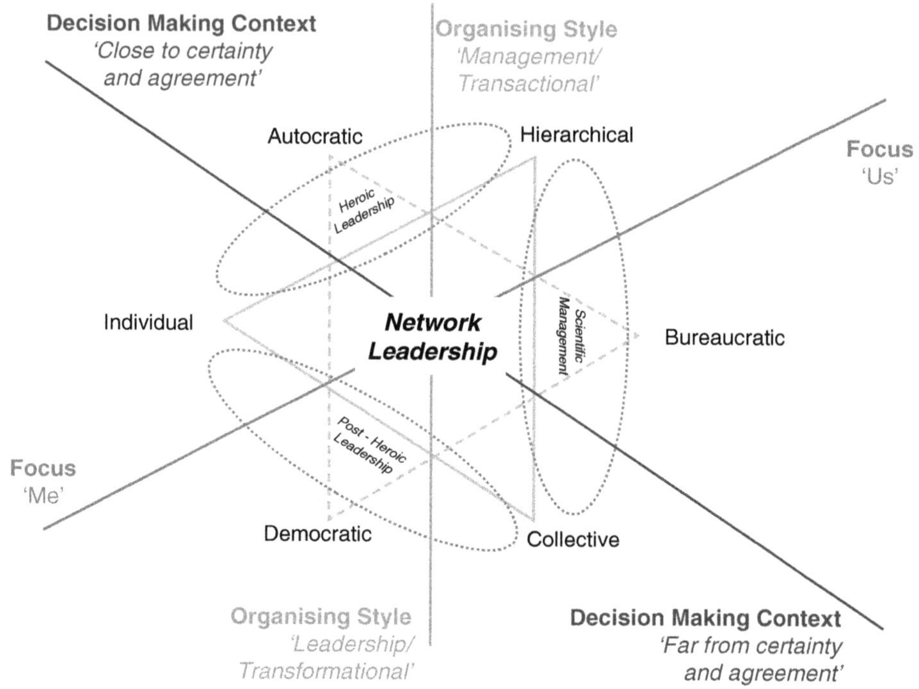

Figure 1.6 Decision-Making Context.

the constituent elements of leadership: the task, the team, the individuals and the surrounding context as they shift and change. It is an understanding that recognises there is no ideal form of leadership, there is only individual practice in context and the astute leader will adapt their approach to suit the situation, task and team, adapting their style to meet the need. Making sense of the situation for those about them, gathering the right people for the task and mobilising and energising them to drive purposeful action, and it is to a deeper examination of network leadership that we now turn. First, an overview and then a deeper dive into the four key practices as we see them. But before that, take a moment to reflect and consider our first leadership question.

Leadership Questions

Where do you currently feel most comfortable as a leader? Be honest. Considering our Framework of Leadership, where is your default leadership setting when the world is being kind to you and how does it change when you are stressed and under pressure?

To help you do this, consider the following questions:

- Do you have default organisational style – managerial/transactional or leadership/transformational?
- Is your principal focus on "I/Me" or "We/Us"?
- Do you tend to operate close to or far from certainty and agreement?
- Within each of these divides, what is your preferred leadership approach – autocratic, democratic or bureaucratic?
- Which vector of leadership appeals to you (heroic, post-heroic or scientific management), but which do you tend to operate within?

We all have our default settings, the way we do things that feels most comfortable, either because they suit our personality, the environment in which we work, or simply because we have always done it that way. So the key activity here is to consider how you might begin to flex your leadership approach: first by identifying the kaleidoscope of different contexts in which you work throughout a typical day, week or month, and then by considering how you might adapt the way you handle them.

You may find that you have it absolutely right in all situations, but most likely not. To help you explore other possibilities, watch what other people do – what works and what doesn't. The point here is to step out of your habitual and possibly narrow way of seeing the world and try new ways of getting the most out of yourself and other people to get things done.

Part II

Overview of Network Leadership

Network Leadership is not a new term, but it has yet to crystallise into a shared and widely understood concept. Currently, it is used predominantly in the public and charitable sectors, with a focus on environment, education, health and development issues. Whilst the term is less widely used in the corporate sector, its practices are in use, but unrealised, every day. The underlying practices emerge in a variety of guises, clustered around the use of networks and networking for personal, operational and strategic insight and action.

Our own perspective of Network Leadership, developed through participation and observation in all three sectors, was at first largely oblivious to the parallel and emerging theoretical perspectives in the public and third sectors. That we now find much in common with these perspectives and the small but significant body of corporate practice could therefore be described as a process of convergent evolution.

But in this case, it is ideas rather than species that have evolved similar forms and function albeit from different starting points. What follows, therefore, is an attempt to bridge the gap between these perspectives and our own experiences, to provide a measure of coherence and shared understanding as a backdrop to our own observations and ideas.

DOI: 10.4324/9781003092582-7

4
Public Sector Perspective

In *What Is Network Leadership?*,[1] Curtis Ogden, Senior Associate at the Institute for Social Change, discusses a collaborative/networked view of leadership in the context of education. Recognising that the heroic model has been found wanting, he begins with the following observation:

> Especially in this "network age" there appears to be both a growing appreciation that leadership has always been about more than the singular and highly visible heroic individual, and that going forward, leadership must be upheld as much more of a shared and multi-dimensional endeavour.

He goes on to describe leadership as being about "holding the whole". A need for groups, teams, organisations and communities to think more expansively about the state of a given complex system, such as a community, school or school district, and pay attention to what is required to support resiliency and/or change for more equitable and sustained benefit. These are situations in which the traditional top-down image of leadership often falls short.

He takes the example of "seemingly superhuman teachers and principals who are brought in to rescue failing kids and schools". The assumption underlying such a move, he argues, is that these extraordinary individuals will of their own drive and volition beat the odds and dramatically reverse the downward trajectory, just like in a great story or movie; whereas, in reality, the results are mixed at best. He is not suggesting that individuals cannot provide crucial sparks at important moments in organisations and communities:

> But holding out for heroic singular leadership ignores the systemic reality of what got us to where we are in the first place and denies the more complex and connected response that is actually required.

The alternative, he suggests, is to identify and nurture several core roles or functions under the heading of network leadership that will "collectively serve

DOI: 10.4324/9781003092582-8

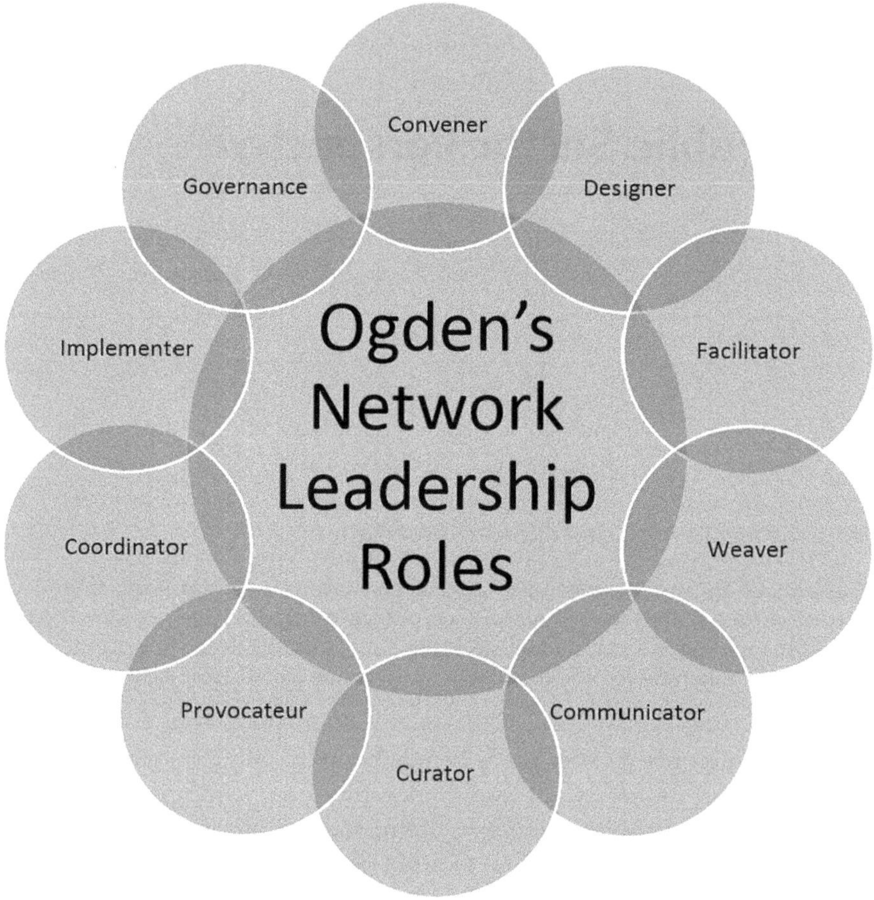

Figure 2.1 Ogden's Network Leadership Roles.

to feed the soil and nurture collaborative cultures for connections and flows to flourish", and ultimately lead to more equitable and sustainable success. Ogden describes ten such roles.

The first role he describes is that of Convener: A person or group who has "convening power" and provides the social capital and connections to pull people together and some of the resources to support a given event or ongoing initiative, whether this be money, space or technology. In practice, they are often groups of people – foundations, municipal governments, academic institutions and community-based organizations – but he also observes that a well-connected and trusted individual can be a convener. But whether individual or institutional, the role includes championing the cause, raising awareness and making the initial and ongoing invitation to come together.

The second role is that of Designer or Design Team, comprised of a diverse group of people representing different parts of the system upon which an initiative is focused. This individual or team maps out the activities that will help move a wider group of actors from disparateness to cohesion and from vision to action. Designing experiences enliven and bring out the best in a diversity of people, including the creation of space for difficult conversations, building trust and equitable access.

The third role is the Facilitator: A person or team who oversee the process of network development and the activation of individual events as part of that ongoing process. Facilitators hold the space for difficult and productive conversations, listen to the wishes and wisdom of those who are convened, help to build alignment and agreement, support self-organized activity and balance structured discussion with openness for emergent possibilities while deftly addressing power dynamics and creating space for diverse and equitable participation.

Fourth is the Weaver. A network weaver is aware of the networks around them and explicitly works to make them healthier. They do this by helping people identify their interests and challenges, connecting people where there is potential for mutual benefit and serving as a catalyst for self-organizing groups. Weaving supports the creation of internal group coherence as well as connecting to adjacent groups and networks, with a mind towards creating value for individual participants and the broader collective.

Fifth is the Communicator, which Ogden acknowledges can be a nuanced and complex role in social networks and not necessarily the same as organisational communications. Fundamentally, it is about helping to create and fill a variety of channels (one-to-one, one-to-many, many-to-many) so that people can stay connected, share freely and learn in a timely and effective manner.

Sixth is the Curator. In many cases, Ogden believes it is helpful to have a role or roles committed to content curation: soliciting, aggregating, distilling, highlighting and organising the abundance of information and other resources. The aim is to keep people engaged in seeking and sharing critical information.

Seventh, there needs to be a Provocateur or Thought Leader. Provocateurs ask the otherwise unasked questions. They challenge a group or initiative when it is reaching agreement too easily or getting too comfortable and safe with its work and thinking. Provocateurs and thought leaders are often found at the periphery of networks, spanning the boundaries.

Eighth is Coordinator. Network coordination often comes down in large part to creating and maintaining a support infrastructure, scheduling common meeting times and ensuring that people have access to relevant resources. Especially in complex action-oriented networks, this is a crucial function, without which things can quickly unravel.

Ninth is the Implementer. What exactly constitutes "implementation" can vary from network to network. It might be about putting into action a shared "strategic plan" of some kind through formalized work groups, but it can also be individuals experimenting with and honing promising ideas or trying out new things as they emerge through learning and conversation. In Ogden's view, this element of self-organisation is where the network magic happens.

Finally, there is Governance, which ironically is the function that many people want to turn to first in multi, self-organising and collaborative networks. In this case it is more about the process of governance rather than a role and it asks the governance questions: How will we make decisions? How will we develop policy or make strategic choices? How will we get things done? All valid questions, but if the default is a traditional governing board structure or a steering committee, it can limit network potential. Ogden himself holds to a network principle of subsidiarity, where matters ought to be handled by the smallest, closest to the ground or least centralized "competent authority".

In summary, Ogden's perspective provides a useful understanding of what needs to happen in a network, its component parts if you will, for it to achieve its goals. And while a single individual could conceivably perform all these roles, it illustrates that Network Leadership is in most circumstances a necessarily collaborative effort. What it leaves unaddressed are the key principles and processes around which a network might organise and function. For this, we need to turn to the example of social entrepreneurs.

Note

1 Ogden, C. (2018). *What Is Network Leadership* in Next Generation Learning Challenges. (online) Available at https://www.nextgenlearning.org/articles/what-is-network-leadership (accessed 17 April 2021).

5
Third Sector Perspective

The Stanford Social Innovation Review (SSIR) uses the term Network Leaders and "Network Entrepreneurs" to describe those who "actively catalyse networks … for systems-level social impact in environmental conservation, education, economic development, and beyond". And it explores the concept through the work of seven case studies of network entrepreneurs.[1]

The seven case studies are combined and analysed in a separate paper entitled "Five Steps to Building an Effective Impact Network"[2] by David Ehrlichman, David Sawyer and Jane Wei-Skillern, which identifies four network principles: "trust, not control; humility, not brand; node, not hub; and mission, not organization", alongside five fundamental processes of "Impact Networks": clarify purpose; convene the right people; cultivate trust; coordinate actions; and collaborate generously. They describe the five fundamental processes as follows.

At a practical level, clarifying a network's purpose or its reason for being requires sense-making: mapping the system, examining the problem from diverse perspectives, finding shared values and recognizing external forces. It also requires an understanding of the local context, including the history of the place or system, related efforts, political and power dynamics and hardwired assumptions. But there also needs to be a recognition that clarifying the purpose is an ongoing endeavour. It must be clear enough initially to identify the right partners and encourage them to meet, but as these individuals and groups convene, the network should be open to refining its purpose. Fundamentally, by clarifying purpose and context, each network member becomes keenly aware that they are just one among many participants working across the system.

It follows then that "convening right people" means not just gathering those who collectively represent all parts of the system, but those who can get things done and are willing to cross boundaries and work with people who may have very different perspectives and priorities. This includes everyone impacted by

DOI: 10.4324/9781003092582-9

the issue, even people you may not normally wish to work with or may even compete with. As the authors observe, "Real progress on complex or 'wicked' problems requires uncommon coordination and collaboration across divides". We will return to the notion of wicked problems later.

The third process they identify is "cultivating trust". Sustained, authentic relationships are the foundation of all successful collaborative efforts, and the authors argue persuasively that cultivating trust intentionally rather than passively provides the basis for a culture in which network participants embrace the network principle of trust, not control. When a network runs on trust, its potential for scaling impact drastically increases. Trust for impact, above all else, is the critical ingredient needed for successful collaboration, no matter the type of structure or the level of resources.

Cultivating trust doesn't mean that people must like each other or agree, but it does mean they have to be willing to engage in authentic and sometimes unpleasant conversations about the things that divide and challenge them. They describe it as creating "trust for impact": a specific type of trust that enables diverse actors to hold the tension through difficult conversations and find common ground and work together, despite organisational differences and personal disagreements. As they conclude:

> Especially in volatile, emerging contexts, trust for impact must be rooted not just in shared purpose, but also in shared values and a shared understanding of how to behave and treat each other when disagreements inevitably arise.

The fourth process they describe is to coordinating actions. By identifying and coordinating work that is already happening, participants can leverage organisational resources, collaborate around common goals and avoid duplication of effort:

> Network entrepreneurs don't insist that all participants across a network agree on any single issue or project. Wicked problems are constantly evolving and no single action or organization can solve them. Instead of looking for a silver bullet, it's critical to address the problem from many angles with a smart, coordinated effort.

And because emergent collaborative solutions are so dynamic, the most effective networks assign and coordinate roles as well. Like Ogden, they identify several network roles that may include a "core team" to handle certain governance decisions, a facilitator to design and lead gatherings and a network manager to serve the network's emergent needs.

Finally, network entrepreneurs "collaborate generously". A generous collaborator does not count transactions, giving only as much as they get in return. Instead, they assume positive intent, communicate frequently and consistently look for opportunities to work with others in support of shared goals, not personal gain. Generous collaboration results directly from practicing the network principles of "humility, not brand" and "mission, not organisation". And network members are most likely to embrace a mind-set of generous collaboration when they have developed a clear shared purpose, trust for impact and just enough structure to focus on their work.

In addition, the authors recognise that building a resilient and sustainable network requires "dedicated effort and a long time-horizon". And while the steps do not necessarily happen in order, they must be constantly reaffirmed as the network forms and evolves, remaining adaptive to changing circumstances. Participants may change jobs, organisations may shift priorities, external forces will shift and problems evolve, so impact networks must constantly reaffirm their shared purpose, convene the right people and cultivate trust.

Furthermore, given the complexity and time-intensive nature of building a successful impact network, they point to instances where roles are divided between multiple people. For instance, a respected individual or organization might take an initial leadership role in clarifying purpose and convening the right people based on their existing web of relationships and ability to pull together an initial meeting. But the network might then bring in a more experienced network entrepreneur to facilitate further gatherings, cultivate trust and serve the network's emergent needs.

It is noteworthy that their focus on clarifying purpose, convening the right people, cultivating trust, coordinating action and collaborating generously is similar to that of Anne-Marie Slaughter, who set us off in search of a playbook for network leadership. In the *Chessboard and the Web*,[3] she describes network leaders combining the skills of clarification, curation, connection, cultivation and catalysis.

In Slaughter's view, leadership begins with the clarification of goals when someone steps forward and makes suggestions about how to fix or achieve something. But it continues through repeatedly refining what those goals mean in practice through facilitated discussion and working through disagreements. Next, curation refers to the careful selection of whom to connect to whom: people, institutions and resources, while good connectors are synergy spotters, cross-fertilising and spreading knowledge and connections to help the network grow towards a common purpose. Additionally, a great connector continually checks in with the members of the network, which is cultivation.

Cultivation refers to the growing and nurturing talent, trust building and deepening relationships through repeated interactions, delegation and empowerment, troubleshooting and conflict resolution, the setting and enforcement of boundaries, sharing knowledge, gathering resources and holding stakeholders to account. All of which requires the final element, catalysis, the spark to sustain and rekindle activity in a network, which requires uncommon abilities of persuasion and, she points out, is often enhanced by being open to persuasion yourself. In short, it is important to role model dialogue and demonstrate that you too are prepared to change.

If Ogden's view explains the individual organs of the network, then the social entrepreneur perspective illustrates the importance of the connective tissue and the energy required to drive the network around a shared purpose, shared ideas and resources and shared ways of operating together. In this sense, it begins to address the question raised regarding social movements in the last chapter of the previous section, namely: how to strike a balance between direction and freedom.

In attempting to answer this question, a useful framework is offered by Marshall Ganz and Liz McKenna, who explore social movement leadership through five interdependent practices of relationship building, narrative, strategy, structure and action.[4]

They argue that relationship building is key to any leadership endeavour, but in social movements this goes beyond mobilising individuals to join through transactions of resources and interest. Instead, it encourages commitment to future engagement through the experience of shared values, which, in turn, builds collective capacity. In network terms, it depends on strong (homogeneous) relational ties, which facilitate efficiency (doing things right) through trust, motivation and commitment, and weak (heterogeneous) ties, which ensure effectiveness (doing the right things) by broadening access to knowledge, skills and learning. In short, it leverages the power of strong ties, but mitigates the dangers of tightly bonded teams with weak ties, which facilitate connection with other teams, thereby allowing the circulation of challenge, new ideas and the avoidance of groupthink, a key topic to which we will return.

Next is narrative, which is a powerful way to access, express and cultivate the emotional resources embedded in shared values: resources that are necessary to confront challenges with courage, resilience and agency. Narrative not only articulates pathways from the world as it is to the world as it should be, but also sparks the motivation to act on it. A good story, well told, can slip past the defences of the rational mind, pluck at our hearts and stir our emotions. Human societies they point out have flourished without the wheel, but none has existed without stories. We are storytelling animals; to be human is to tell stories. The ability to learn from vicarious experience through storytelling is thought to have provided an evolutionary advantage to our ancestors in terms of survival, the spread of innovation and the development of culture.

However, while narrative engages the emotional brain, we need strategy to engage the rational brain, drawing upon our cognitive resources for analysis, problem solving and adaptation. Strategy is the practice of turning the resources you have into the power you need to get what you want. Given the highly uncertain environments in which social movements operate successful strategising is an ongoing adaptive practice, something movement leaders do rather than something they have neatly labelled in a single document or file. Additionally, because social movements often challenge organisations and institutions with abundant traditional resources like wealth, status, expertise and political power, their leaders must find ways to compensate through greater resourcefulness and agile responsiveness. This requires an integrated analysis of the big picture aligned with highly particular knowledge of the specific context. This, in turn, requires strategic capacity and knowledge of the bigger picture to be widely distributed rather than concentrated in a strategy team that is removed from the rank-and-file implementation. High motivation (strong ties), access to diverse sources of salient knowledge (weak ties) and a commitment to learning facilitate this leadership practice.

In terms of structure, there is a balance to be struck between the absence of structure, where groups may act incoherently and sometimes at cross-purposes, and an extremely hierarchical structure that centralises all strategizing in the hands of a few individuals, leading to incapacity to respond with agility to threats and opportunities. The ideal is coordinated operations with decentralised control, a balance between efficiency, alignment and adaptability. This requires a shared understanding of the environment and our place within it, alongside a shared sense of purpose – what we are trying to achieve and why – which, in turn, requires leaders to create an ecosystem within the organisation and its environment that develops lateral as well as vertical ties to ensure shared understanding and purpose. Such systemic understanding and purpose then allow effective adaptation to emerging threats and opportunities by individuals and teams closest to the problem.

Finally, to transform individual resources into collective power, relationships, stories, strategy and structure must all be mobilised towards a common goal and deployed through diverse actions. For protests to turn into powerful movements, tactical actions must be strategic, focused and well executed. Since most movements rely on people-based voluntary resources, learning how to secure sustained commitment of these resources while asking participants to take sometimes very costly tactical action (i.e. risking arrest or worse) is a key leadership challenge. Ineffective, disorganised and poorly executed actions undermine the sustained motivation necessary to keep the movement going forward. But how do we turn these principles into practical activity? Well, the corporate sector offers some examples.

Notes

1 The Stanford Social Innovation Review. (2015). The New Network Leader. (online) Available at https://ssir.org/network_entrepreneurs# (accessed 17 April 2021).

2 Ehrlichman, D., Sawyer, D. and Wei-Skillern, J. (2015). Five Steps to Building an Effective Impact Network. (online) Available at https://ssir.org/network_entrepreneurs/entry/five_steps_to_building_an_effective_impact_network# (accessed 17 April 2021).

3 Slaughter, A. (2017). *The Chessboard and the Web: Strategies of Connection in a Networked World.* New Haven, CT and London: Yale University Press.

4 Ganz, M. and McKenna, L. (2018). Bringing Leadership Back in. In Snow, D., Sarah A., Soule, N., Kriesi, H. and McCammon, H., ed., *The Wiley Blackwell Companion to Social Movements*. London: Wiley-Blackwell, pp. 185–202.

6
Corporate Sector Perspective

The corporate perspective is less explicit in its use of term "Network Leadership", but there are two pertinent examples. In the 5 Dynamics of Network Leadership,[1] Doug Macnamara describes Network Leadership in terms of a strategic questioning perspective and refers to it as "systems-thinking leadership taken to the next level". Leadership that goes beyond "traditional inward looking and autocratic management, which encourages leaders to engage, empower, facilitate, and bring connectedness to an otherwise unwieldy mass of disparate elements". Taken together, the "5 Dynamics" provide a useful frame of reference for understanding the systems in which we operate (the subject of Part Three) as well as illuminating some of the key strategic and operational questions that a network approach can usefully pose for organisations.

The first dynamic is external focus, asking questions about the industry sector and overall marketplace dynamics. The second concerns innovation, seeking to take advantage of the organisation's employee experience and expertise. The third is knowledge dynamic, linking together a variety of stakeholders, including suppliers, partners, clients/end-users, even competitors, to address organisational learning. The fourth is a community or public accountability dynamic, which recognises that people are increasingly coming to expect more from executives and government leaders. The final dynamic recognises that there will always be constraints on organisational growth: environmental, financial and market driven.

Macnamara's 5 Dynamics will no doubt be familiar, in one guise or another, to anyone conversant with strategic analysis. The insight, however, is in visualising the different elements as dynamic and evolving networks, revealing organisations to be less like complicated machines with discrete boundaries and interfaces, but rather as complex organisms with permeable membranes.

Conversely, the Centre for Creative Leadership (CCL) approaches network leadership from an individual perspective. In *Leadership Networking: Connect,*

DOI: 10.4324/9781003092582-10

Collaborate, Create,[2] Curt Grayson describes leadership networking as building relationships and making alliances in the service of others and in the service of your organisation's work and goals. The booklet is designed to show leaders how best to enhance their networks and become effective at leadership through networking. In an article on the CCL website,[3] Grayson identifies six rules for effective leadership networking: be sincere, share resources, use power thoughtfully, communicate skilfully, be a savvy negotiator and learn to manage conflict.

All good points. Who could doubt the value of sincerity, reciprocity, the wise use of power and the advantages of skilful communication, conflict resolution and "savvy" negotiating skills? They are all good heroic leader attributes, but it tells us less about the networks themselves and how they might be used and deployed for action. For that, we turn to a selection of three articles that do not specifically mention network leadership, but nevertheless put networks at the heart of their theory and practise.

Kotter's 'Dual Operating System'

The first is Kotter's "Dual Operating System", elaborated in an article by John Kotter[4] and later developed into a book (2014). Kotter begins with the uncontroversial view that the greatest challenge business leaders face today is how to stay competitive amid constant turbulence and disruption, but further contends that in the 21st century, this will force them to evolve a fundamentally new form of organisation. He argues that the hierarchical structures and organisational processes we have used for decades to run and improve our enterprises are no longer effective in this ever faster-moving world.

His solution is a dual operating system: a traditional management-driven hierarchy working in parallel with a new strategy network, which would design and implement strategy, using an agile, network-like structure and a very different set of processes. This new system would be designed to continually assess the business, the industry and the organisation, and react with greater agility, speed and creativity than the existing hierarchical one. At the same time, freeing the traditional hierarchy to do what it is optimized to do. He makes the point that many start-ups are organized more as networks than as hierarchies and that even in mature organisations, informal networks frequently operate, albeit under the hierarchical radar.

His new strategy system builds on the eight-step method for change he developed 15 years earlier in *Leading Change,*[5] this time offering eight "accelerators". There are three main differences, however. First, the change steps he described have often been used in rigid, finite and sequential ways in effecting or responding to episodic change, whereas the accelerators he describes are concurrent and always at work. Second, the steps were to be driven by a small, powerful core group (a Guiding Coalition [GC]), whereas the accelerators pull in as many people as possible from throughout the organization to form a "volunteer army". Third, the steps were designed to function within a traditional hierarchy, whereas the accelerators require the flexibility and agility of a network.

It is important to note for our own study that one of the five key principles at the heart of the dual operating system is leadership:

> Much more leadership, not just more management. At the core of a successful hierarchy is competent management. A strategy network, by contrast, needs lots of leadership, which means it operates with different processes and language and expectations. The game is all about vision, opportunity, agility, inspired action, and celebration—not project management, budget reviews, reporting relationships, compensation, and accountability to a plan.

Interestingly, he imagines the network of the dual operating system to be like a solar system, with a GC as the sun, strategic initiatives as planets and sub-initiatives as moons or satellites:

> This structure is dynamic: initiatives and sub-initiatives coalesce and disband as needed. Although a typical hierarchy tends not to change from year to year, the network can morph with ease. In the absence of bureaucratic layers, command-and-control prohibitions, and Six Sigma processes, this type of network permits a level of individualism, creativity, and innovation that not even the least bureaucratic hierarchy can provide. Populated with employees from all across the organization and up and down its ranks, the network liberates information from silos and hierarchical layers and enables it to flow with far greater freedom and accelerated speed.

And the "Eight Accelerators" are the processes that enable the strategy network to function. The first is to create a sense of urgency around a single big opportunity, to heighten the organisation's awareness that it needs continual strategic adjustment towards opportunities. The second is to build and maintain a GC. The core of a strategy network is the GC, which is made up of volunteers from throughout the organization, selected to represent each of the hierarchy's departments and levels, with a broad range of skills and whom the leadership trusts. The third is to formulate a strategic vision and develop change initiatives designed to capitalize opportunities. The vision serves as a strategic true north for the dual operating system and critically, it is "emotionally appealing as well as strategically smart".

Fourth, it is necessary to communicate the vision and the strategy to create buy-in and attract volunteers. A vividly formulated, high-stakes vision and strategy, promulgated by a GC in ways that are both memorable and authentic, will prompt people to discuss them without the cynicism that often greets messages cascading down the hierarchy. Fifth, accelerate movement towards the vision and the opportunity by ensuring that the network removes barriers. Fundamentally, the GC and other volunteers are not a bunch of grunts carrying out orders from above. They are themselves change leaders who bring energy, commitment and enthusiasm to the task.

Sixth, celebrate visible, significant short-term wins. A strategy network's credibility won't last long without confirmation that its decisions and actions are benefiting the organisation. Seventh, never let up. Keep learning from experience and don't declare victory too soon. Organisations must continue to carry through on strategic initiatives and create new ones, to adapt to shifting business environments and thus to enhance their competitive positions. When an organisation takes its foot off the gas, cultural and political resistance will arise again like a dormant virus. And finally, it is necessary to institutionalise any strategic changes in the culture. No strategic initiative, big or small, is complete until it has been incorporated into day-to-day activities.

In summary, Kotter describes the dual operating system as "a vast, purposeful expansion in scale, scope, and power of the smaller, informal networks that accomplish tasks faster and cheaper than hierarchies can". It is a distinct type of network leadership, one that is created by the conventional hierarchy for a specific purpose. It may take advantage of existing network leaders and change champions, but fundamentally it is created and directed rather than growing organically like a social network.

Morieux's Six Rules

The second article is by Yves Morieux, who starts from the perspective that, similar to Kotter, organisations face an increasingly complex world,[6] a world in which managers find themselves spending more time writing reports and attending coordination meetings and less time managing their teams. The consequence of which is that employees are often misdirected and expend effort in vain, becoming increasingly disengaged and unproductive. Companies, he concludes, need a better way to manage complexity.

His contention is that real cooperation is not a matter of getting along well; it's about considering the constraints and goals of others in your actions and decisions. He therefore sets out an approach based on six rules. The first three focus on enabling: providing the information needed to understand where the problems are and empowering the right people to make good choices. The second three focus on impelling: motivating people to cooperate, thanks to feedback loops that expose them as directly as possible to the consequences of their actions. Together, he describes the "Six Smart Rules" as allowing companies to manage complexity not by prescribing specific behaviours, but by creating a context within which optimal behaviours will occur.

Rule 1 aims to "Improve Understanding of What Co-Workers Do". To respond to complexity intelligently, people must really understand each other's work: the goals and challenges others must meet; the resources they can draw on; and the constraints under which they operate. People can't find this kind of information in formal job descriptions; they can learn it only by observing and interacting. The manager's job therefore is to make sure that such learning takes place, because without this shared understanding, people may duplicate work, miss opportunities for collaboration and blame problems on other people's lack of intelligence, skills or collegiality rather than organisational constraints.

Rule 2 is "Reinforce the People Who Are Integrators". Conflicts between front and back offices are common. Back offices typically need to standardize processes and work, while front offices must accommodate the needs of individual customers. The same thing often happens between the corporate centre and regional offices. His solution is to empower individuals or groups to play an integrative role. In almost any unit, he argues, you will find one or two managers who already interact with multiple stakeholders (customers as well as other functions). Once you've identified them, you should reinforce their power by increasing their responsibilities and giving them a greater say on issues that matter to others.

Rule 3 focuses on "Increasing Incentives for People to Co-Operate". The people with the least power in an organization generally shoulder most of the burden of cooperation and get the least credit. When they realise this, they often withdraw from cooperation and hide in their silos. Companies that want to prevent this and increase cooperation need to give these people incentives to take the risk of moving out of isolation, trusting others, showing initiative and being transparent about performance.

Rule 4 is intended to "Increase the Need for Reciprocity". A good way to spur productive cooperation is to expand the responsibilities of integrators beyond the activities over which they have direct control. Making their goals richer and more complex, he reasons, will drive them to resolve trade-offs rather than avoid them. And in a similar vein, it may be better to take resources away. A family with five television sets doesn't have to negotiate which programme to watch because everyone can watch the show he or she wants. The result is the kind of self-sufficiency that kills family life. Removing resources could be a good way to make people more dependent on and more cooperative with one another. Eliminating internal monopolies by creating overlaps and bundling activities into cross-functional projects also increases the possibility for reciprocal action and impels cooperation.

Rule 5 "Makes Employees Feel the Shadow of the Future". The longer it takes for the consequences of a decision to take effect, the more difficult it is to hold a decision-maker accountable. For example, many of those involved at the launch of a three-year project will no longer be around when it is completed. They won't be affected by the consequences of their actions, the trade-offs they make or how well they cooperate. In other words, the shadow of the future does not reach them. People are more likely to feel the shadow of the future if you bring the future closer by reducing the lead times on projects and work processes; increasing the frequency of output performance reviews; or assigning managers to downstream work. Perhaps moving some engineers to the after-sales team where they would experience first-hand the effects of their design.

Finally, Rule 6 "Put the Blame on the Unco-Operative". Some activities involve such a long time lag between cause and effect that, between research and development, for instance, it's impossible to set up direct feedback loops that expose people to the consequences of their actions. There are also situations where jobs are so remote that it's difficult to have a direct feedback loop that makes the people who perform them feel interdependent with others. In those cases, managers must close the feedback loop themselves by explicitly introducing a penalty for any people or units that fail to cooperate on solving a problem – even if the problem does not occur in their area – and increase the payoff for all when units cooperate in a beneficial way.

Ibarra and Hunter's Leadership Transition

The final article is from 2007,[7] in which Herminia Ibarra, then Charles Handy Professor of Organizational Behaviour at London Business School, and Mark Lee Hunter, an adjunct professor at INSEAD, argued for the importance of networks in making a successful transition from functional manager to business leader, one that they described as requiring a "leap from a lifetime of functional contributions and hands-on control to the ambiguous process of building and working through networks".

They spent two years following a cohort of 30 managers making this transition, an inflection point in their careers that challenged them to rethink of both themselves and their roles. In the process, they found that networking, creating a fabric of personal contacts who will provide support, feedback, insight, resources and information, was simultaneously one of the most self-evidently important and one of "the most dreaded developmental challenges that aspiring leaders must address".

They described the typical manager as rising through the ranks through strong command of their technical discipline and hard graft. However, when challenged with moving beyond their functional specialty and addressing strategic issues faced by the business, most did not grasp that this required relational and not simply technical acumen. Instead, they often regarded exchanges and interactions with a diverse array of current and potential stakeholders as a distraction from their actual work rather than a fundamental aspect of their new leadership role. Some were positively resistant, seeing networking as "insincere or manipulative".

Observing this cohort of leaders, Ibarra and Hunter identified three distinct but interdependent forms of networking: operational, personal and strategic, each of which played a vital role in their leadership transition. The first helped them manage their current internal responsibilities, the second boosted their personal development and the third opened their eyes to new business directions and the stakeholders they would need to enlist. What was quickly apparent, however, was that even those managers who believed themselves accomplished networkers were often only operating at an operational or personal level, ignoring the value of networks for strategic purposes.

They described the purpose of operational networking as ensuring coordination and cooperation among people who must know and trust one another in order to accomplish their immediate tasks. While recognising it is not always easy, they believed it to be relatively straightforward, because the task provides a clear focus for collaboration and action. However, even though operational networking came most naturally to the managers studied, nearly everyone had important blind spots regarding the people and groups they depended on to make things happen. One of the key problems with an exclusive reliance on operational networks was:

> That they are usually geared toward meeting objectives as assigned, not toward asking the strategic question, "What should we be doing?" By the same token, managers do not exercise as much personal choice in assembling operational relationships as they do in weaving personal and strategic networks, because to a large extent the right relationships are prescribed by the job and organizational structure. Thus, most operational networking occurs within an organization, and ties are determined in large part by routine, short-term demands.

In short, the typical manager was more concerned with sustaining cooperation within their existing network rather than building relationships to face non-routine or unforeseen challenges. But as a manager moves into a leadership role, his or her network must reorient itself externally and towards the future.

The second form of networking was personal, described as a means by which managers could gain new perspectives and advance their careers through membership of professional associations, alumni groups, clubs and personal interest communities. Yet, among the managers surveyed, many questioned why they should spend precious time on activities so indirectly related to the work at hand. They could not see the value of such activity when they were struggling to find time to achieve urgent operational tasks.

What they failed to appreciate was that such contacts could provide important referrals, information and even developmental support such as coaching and mentoring. Critically:

> What makes a personal network powerful is its referral potential. According to the famous six degrees of separation principle [*to which we will return in the next section of the book*], our personal contacts are valuable to the extent that they help us reach, in as few connections as possible, the far-off person who has the information we need.

Ibarra and Hunter conclude that for people who have rarely looked outside their organisations, personal networking is an important first step, one that fosters a deeper understanding of themselves and the environments in which they operate. Ultimately, however, it will not help a manager through the leadership transition unless they learn how to bring those connections to bear on organisational strategy.

"Strategic Networking", they argue, is key to the transition from functional manager to business leader. The development of lateral and vertical relationships with other functional and business unit managers, all of whom will be outside their immediate control, becomes critical to achieving personal and organisational goals. Operating beside players with diverse affiliations, backgrounds, objectives and incentives requires a manager to formulate business rather than functional objectives and to work through the coalitions and networks needed to sell ideas and compete for resources.

Based on their research, they argue that what differentiates a leader from a manager is:

> The ability to figure out where to go and to enlist the people and groups necessary to get there. Recruiting stakeholders, lining up allies and sympathizers, diagnosing the political landscape, and brokering conversations

> among unconnected parties are all part of a leader's job. As they step up to the leadership transition, some managers accept their growing dependence on others and seek to transform it into mutual influence. Others dismiss such work as "political" and, as a result, undermine their ability to advance their goals.

Ibarra and Hunter determine that the key to a good strategic network is the ability to marshal information, support and resources from one sector of a network to achieve results in another. Strategic networkers, they believe, use indirect influence, convincing one person in the network to get someone else who is not in the network to take a needed action. Moreover, strategic networkers don't just influence their relational environment; they shape it in their own image.

A good place to start is leveraging each domain of networking into the others, for example, by seeking out personal contacts who can be objective, strategic counsellors. But the key for many managers is to change their attitude towards the "legitimacy and necessity of networking". When aspiring leaders do not believe that networking is important, they will not allocate enough time and effort to see it pay off. First and foremost, therefore, manager's need to re-evaluate how they use their time:

> Participating in formal and informal meetings with people in other units takes time away from functional responsibilities and internal team affairs. Between the obvious payoff of a task accomplished and the ambiguous, often delayed rewards of networking, naive managers repeatedly choose the former. The less they practice networking, the less efficient at it they become, and the vicious cycle continues.

In contrast:

> Effective business leaders spend a lot of time every day gathering the information they need to meet their goals, relying on informal discussions with a lot of people who are not necessarily in charge of an issue or task. They network in order to obtain information continually, not just at formal meetings.

Another important point they make is to develop relationships ahead of need: do not wait until you need something to develop a relationship. The best networkers do exactly the opposite; they take every opportunity to give to and receive from their network, whether they need help or not. Equally, good networkers take the initiative to connect two people who would benefit from meeting each other. And ultimately, they stick with it. Building a leadership network, they conclude, is a skill that requires practice, but even more than that, it requires will.

The EO Programme

The development of high aspirations and relationship networks are explicit in the authors' leadership and development programmes. For over a decade, Mike, and latterly James, ran a leadership development programme for functional managers in Total, at the French oil major's Aberdeen offices, Total Exploration and Production in the UK (TEPUK). It was for the managers who had been identified as candidates for general management roles. EO is Latin and means "to drive forward or to advance", which perfectly described the purpose of the programme, both for them and the business.

The programme included participants from the UK, France and Norway and was based on an understanding of the needs of the business, then and in the future, through feedback from members of the TEPUK Excom and research with staff and managers about what they wanted of their leaders. The result was a nine-month programme that included a core element with opportunities for feedback, personal coaching, group workshops and project work. In addition, delegates attended a 12-day programme at Cranfield University near London.

The aim of the programme was "To develop those people in whom we can trust with the future of the business". This was a high aspiration but was achieved by increasing the candidate's ability to make and take decisions, be change resilient and competent and with an ability to adapt to different cultures and environments. The objectives were that, as a result of the programme, participants should:

- Be better leaders and managers capable of representing and shaping the business.
- Grow in self-awareness and develop their behaviour and skills in their role as leaders.
- Understand their responsibility as leaders in the ownership and implementation of strategy.
- Have confidence in their decision-making and not be afraid to be accountable for the consequences.
- Raise their own visibility through interaction with senior management on the delivery of their Business Development Project.
- Add value through delivery of their Business Development Project.
- Build a strong and lasting peer network with other participants.

The programme was aimed at individuals who would benefit from a general increase in business ability and a fuller understanding about business in general, but in terms of potential participants identified as individuals who could make a substantial contribution to delivering business goals rather than simply completing their functional task list. The criteria against which they were selected and supported was as leaders who:

- Excel in their own discipline.
- Have the potential to do more.
- Have a positive attitude and always deliver.
- Are self-aware, supportive of others and adaptable.
- Exhibit initiative and are prepared to try new and different ideas.
- Communicate effectively and can form effective working relationships at different levels across the business.
- Listen and consider the wider impact of decisions and actions.
- Have courage and confidence.
- Have the willingness to develop and the time to commit to the programme.

Being eligible for the programme was only the first step; however, membership of the programme carried no guarantees about their future, but it did provide a great opportunity for them to learn new things and increase their visibility and impact within the organisational network.

We have subsequently run a series of workshops on Network Leadership for Total's Global Leadership Programme.

In summary, the three articles provide a useful illustration of the practicalities of Network Leadership. Kotter's perspective makes clear the power of a networked rather than solely hierarchical approach to ambiguity and uncertainty. He also points out that informal networks are present in all organisations, and in the right circumstances they can be created and used to get things done. The "Guiding Coalition" and "Volunteer Army" effectively make explicit the notion of networked action.

Morieux shares Kotter's belief that networks are a way for businesses to cope with ambiguity and complexity. But his solution is to facilitate greater connection by working within the existing fabric of the organisation rather than create a new system. His approach is to identify and highlight those who already connect either by nature or role, but also to bring together those who might not connect in the normal course of events, through a combination of role, process and activity sharing.

Finally, Ibarra and Hunter illustrate the individual and organisational value of managers using a networked/relational approach to navigating the transition or inflection point from functional/operational management to strategic/business leadership. Their key point is that in order to make the transition, leaders need to change what they value and how they spend their time. In essence, they must change the balance between short-term task accomplishment and longer-term relationship building.

Finally, let us turn to our own view of Network Leadership, which draws upon much of the foregoing literature, but also our own experience of leadership and management as well as our privileged observation and dialogue with leaders and managers across the corporate, public and third sectors.

Notes

1 Macnamara, D. (2018). 5 Dynamics of Network Leadership. (online) Available at https://www.cmc-global.org/content/5-dynamics-network-leadership (accessed 17 April 2021).
2 Grayson, C. and Baldwin, D. (2007). *Leadership Networking: Connect, Collaborate, Create. Center for Creative Leadership.* Greensboro, USA: Illustrated Edition.
3 Grayson, C. (2017). The Top 6 Rules of Leadership Networking. (online) Available at https://www.ccl.org/blog/top-6-rules-leadership-networking/ (accessed 17 April 2021).
4 Kotter, J.P. (2012). *Accelerate!* Brighton, MA: Harvard Business Press.
5 Kotter, J.P. (1996). *Leading Change.* Boston, MA: Harvard Business Press.
6 Morieux, Y. (2011). Smart Rules: Six Ways for People Solve Problems Without You. (online) Available at https://store.hbr.org/product/smart-rules-six-ways-to-get-people-to-solve-problems-without-you/R1109D (accessed 17 April 2021).
7 Ibarra, H. and Hunter, M.L. (2007). How Leaders Create and Use Networks. *Harvard Business Review*, 85(1): pp. 40–7.

7
Our Perspective of Network Leadership

In the preface, we defined network leadership as:

> The capability to work across social boundaries, connecting ideas with action and people with resources, in pursuit of shared goals. Leaders who, while open to possibility and opportunity, remain true to the core beliefs of alignment, synergy and restless persuasion.

It is a capacity that exists in the tension between the elements of the Leadership Framework we described in the previous chapter. And in our experience, Network Leaders facilitate network action through four key practices:

1. They understand the social system.
2. They have convening power.
3. They lead beyond their formal and positional authority.
4. They possess the power of restless persuasion.

Let us look at each in turn.

Understanding the Social System. An understanding of networks helps identify the cliques, silos and gaps in connectivity, which, when dealt with effectively, can improve productivity and responsiveness, smooth channels of communication and spur change and innovation. Network Leaders have a thorough understanding of their network and an ability to connect and energise it around a personal manifesto of what they believe and what they are trying to achieve for their organisation or community.

Convening Power. Network Leaders recognise that they don't have all the answers but that those around them might, and they draw on this web of connection to get things done. Network Leaders have something to say that is worth listening to, an attractive power based on their values, their ideas and their ability to make sense of things. But also an ability to recognise and mobilise

DOI: 10.4324/9781003092582-11

underlying movements, creating a personal manifesto that draws people to them from across organisations, businesses, communities and societies.

A leader can of course appeal to a narrow constituency and we do not have to look far for examples, whether this be politicians, warlords or religious extremists. But we are suggesting a more expansive style of leadership; one that draws together diverse groups in pursuit of shared rather than divisive goals and leaders who recognise that the only way to survive and prosper in turbulent times is to draw on a wide range of good ideas no matter the source.

Leading beyond Authority is the ability to work across boundaries, connecting ideas with action and people with resources. But unlike conventional top-down leadership, leadership in a networked world is more about enabling than directing; more about influence than control; more indirect than direct. It is leadership understood first and foremost as a social process that creates direction, alignment and commitment. It is less about formal and positional authority and more about the individual leader, their integrity and competence. It is leadership understood as something you give, not something you get through promotion to a management position.

Restless Persuasion. Network Leaders have a simple clarity and focus about what they want to achieve for their organisation or community and are driven by a personal manifesto that summarises their ambition. It is an approach that is always open to possibility and opportunity: reforming networks and ideas as projects unfold and reconfiguring in order to deliver, but remaining true to their core beliefs. And this requires an abundance of energy and resilience to keep moving forward in the face of obstacles, to feel comfortable in the chaos of networks, to live in the question and not grasp prematurely at solutions and at times it requires them to be unreasonable. To challenge the status quo, to question the way we have always done things around here. In short, to confront what others accept as reasonable but is in fact wrong.

In the first place, let us set our own perspective of Network Leadership against the other perspectives we have presented (Table 2.1). The table provides an opportunity to step back and see the metaphorical wood of Network Leadership instead of just the individual trees or perspectives. Essentially, it allows us to appreciate how the four elements of our own perspective capture and, we hope, provide a coherent structure in which to place the insights of the other perspectives, none of which on their own provide an overarching framework.

Critically, it reinforces our view of the Network Leader: someone who understands the various elements of the context in which they work and the connections between them; someone who can make sense of it for others and help them navigate through the complexity; someone able to mobilise and deploy

Table 2.1 Relationship between Our Four Key Practices of Network Leadership and Other Perspectives

Key Practices	*Public Sector Perspective*	*Social Entrepreneur Perspective*	*Slaughter's Perspective*	*Social Movement Perspective*	*Macnamara's Systems Perspective*	*CCL Individual Perspective*	*Kotter's 8 Accelerators*	*Morieux's Six Rules*	*Ibarra and Hunter's Perspective*
Understand Social Systems		Mapping the system		Integrated analysis of the big picture and the specific context	Understand the market, your business, its people, stakeholders and the wider environment			Improve understanding of what co-workers do	Personal networking
Convening Power	Convener Designer Facilitator Weaver Communicator Curator Thought leader	Clarify purpose, convene the right people, cultivate trust, collaborate generously	Clarify Curate Connect	Relationship building, narrative and storytelling		Sincerity Sharing Communicate	Create a sense of urgency, build and maintain a guiding coalition, formulate a strategic vision, communicate the vision	Reinforce the integrators, increase incentives for people to cooperate	Operational networking
Leading Beyond Authority	Coordinator Implementer Governance	Coordinate action	Cultivate Catalyse	Strategy Structure Tactical action		Thoughtful use of power Negotiate Manage conflict	Accelerate movement towards the vision	Increase the need for reciprocity, employees must feel the "shadow of the future", blame the uncooperative	Strategic Networking
Restless Persuasion		Cultivate	Catalyse				Celebrate short-term wins, don't declare victory too soon, institutionalise changes		

people for action through powerful communication, aligning storytelling for emotion with a rationale for effective action; and someone who is alive to the dynamism inherent in any system and is able to rethink and repurpose as the situation demands and yet holds true to their values and inner conviction.

Equally fascinating, however, was to see where the gaps exist in the table, namely around understanding the system and restless persuasion. Consequently, as we developed our ideas of Network Leadership, we had in our minds eye an image of two bookends, "Understanding the Social System" and "Restless Persuasion", supporting the "books" of "Convening Power" and "Leading Beyond Authority". This was simply a convenient way of visualising the supporting nature of the former to the actual leadership activity in the latter, but the metaphor is more prescient than we thought. Leadership is indeed a well-studied concept, but its supportive framework, that which nourishes it in the first place and sustains it in the long run, perhaps less so.

Under the leadership practice of "Understanding the Social System" the table shows the existing perspectives as being the creation of a map of social relationships from which it is possible to navigate. But, while this is part of the practice of Network Leaders, this is not all of it. Understanding the system is as much about intuition as intellect. We know that Network Leaders create a mental map of the social system as a way of locating the energy in the system and therefore which parts need most attention, but this makes more sense when linked with the practice of "Restless Persuasion" and the mental acuity required to keep up with an ever-shifting pattern of relationships and goals.

The table shows the limited existing research that supports our practice of "Restless Persuasion". However, when understood alongside the idea of leadership as a form of energy, it makes more sense. "Restless Persuasion" is about how leaders distribute their energy and use it to multiply its effect; their mental map, informed by intuition, identifies where to distribute that energy.

Summary

As we have repeatedly made clear, Network Leadership is neither an entirely new concept nor does it stand apart from theories of leadership that have gone before; a fact that is made abundantly clear from the multiple references in the table to the leadership practices of convening power and leading beyond authority. What the literature of leadership has perhaps paid less attention to is the importance of the key supporting elements of understanding leadership in context and the energy and resilience required to catalyse and maintain action within any social system.

With that in mind, we aim to set out in detail what we mean by Network Leadership. But first, in brief, we believe that Network Leadership sits most comfortably in the category of post-heroic leadership, which is more suited to environments characterised by volatility, uncertainty, complexity and ambiguity than leadership based on hierarchical position and authority. Unlike conventional top-down leadership, leadership in a networked world is more about enabling than directing; more about influence than control; more indirect than direct. It is leadership understood first and foremost as a social process that creates direction, alignment and commitment. It is less about formal and positional authority and more about influence and restless persuasion.

We do not, however, dismiss the power of individual attributes: the power of one's ideas, the ability to successfully communicate them and the energy and determination to see them through. Nor the importance of command in a crisis. Nor do we dismiss the value of positional and formal authority in providing a privileged position from which to understand the system – the context, the characters and the variables at play – and the convening power to get the right people in the room.

But heroic leaders run the risk of becoming one-person shows, oblivious to the ideas of others and invulnerable to constructive criticism. Leaders need to understand their limitations, which principally means a recognition that they

DOI: 10.4324/9781003092582-12

do not have all the answers, and nor are they required to. Network Leaders recognise this, but also understand that those around them might and draw on a web of connection to get things done.

The power of a Network Leader derives from an ability to work across boundaries, connecting ideas with action and people with resources. It is based on a thorough understanding of the system in which they operate and their own network within it. It is an ability to connect and energise action around a personal manifesto of what they believe and what they are trying to achieve. And as we have already said, it is an approach that is always open to possibility and opportunity: reforming teams and ideas as projects unfold and reconfiguring in order to deliver, but remaining true to one's core beliefs.

Ignatius Loyola, founder of the Jesuit movement, captured this attribute of network leadership well in describing the ideal Jesuit as "living with one foot raised". An individual always ready to respond to emerging opportunities, because they have rid themselves of ingrained habits, prejudices, cultural preferences and other baggage that blocks rapid adaptive responses, but whose core beliefs and values are non-negotiable, providing a foundation for purposeful change as opposed to aimless drifting in pursuit of the next best thing.[1]

To borrow from Aristotle, Network Leadership is a combination of what he referred to as three basic activities of humans: theoria (thinking), poiesis (making) and *praxis* (doing): theoretical knowledge, basing actions on sound reasoning and detailed reflection; productive knowledge, making or doing something; and practical knowledge, doing and acting in a way that is consistent with human flourishing, which is a moral disposition to act truly and rightly.

To reiterate, none of the skills we describe are new. Or, if you prefer a more cynical frame of reference, as André Gide, author and winner of the Nobel Prize for Literature, observed: *Everything that needs to be said has already been said. But, since no one was listening, everything must be said again.*

Napoleon recognised the importance of making sense and providing energy when he spoke of leadership as defining reality and giving hope. But turbulent times require us to understand and act in a combination of different ways. Like a kaleidoscope, the pattern and the colours are constantly rearranged and we must continually adapt what we know and how we act, discarding what no longer fits, adjusting what still has relevance and, if need be, creating the rest as we go: living and leading with one foot raised.

And in that vein, we will now examine the four elements of Network Leadership in more detail, beginning with an Understanding of Social Systems. But before that, take a moment to reflect and consider the following leadership questions.

Table 2.2 Personal Assessment of Network Leadership

Network Leadership Practice	*Novice*	*Master*	*Coach*
Understanding the System			
Convening Power			
Leading Beyond Authority			
Restless Persuasion			

Leadership Questions

- To what extent does your current practice reflect the practices of Network Leaders?
- To what extent do you understand the social system in which you currently work?
- To what extent do you have "Convening Power"?
- To what extent do you lead beyond your formal and positional authority?
- To what extent do you possess the power of restless persuasion and energy?

Rather like our first leadership question, which asked you to place yourself in our Leadership Framework, these questions require you to make an initial evaluation of your skills, attributes and inclinations as a network leader and complete Table 2.2.

In broad strokes, a novice clearly has a lot to learn and is pretty much starting from scratch. A Master has a good understanding of their environment and can navigate their way around the system, getting what they need, mobilising people around their ideas and getting stuff done. What sets the Coach apart, and we would argue the Network Leader, is that they can do all that and they can explain how they do it. They can make the implicit explicit. They can identify what it is that some Network Leaders simply take for granted without being aware of what exactly they do to get things done. Coaches can help others do it too.

Note

1 Lowney, C. (2003). *Heroic Leadership: Best Practices from a 450-Year-Old Company that Changed the World*. Chicago: Loyola Press.

Part III

Understanding the Social System

Our view of organisations contrasts the structured, analytical, mechanistic and process-driven view with the more organic, free-flowing, obscure and muddled reality of any human social system. Furthermore, it is our contention that Network Leaders understand this frustrating and often hidden network. Critically, they turn this understanding into action and results by either adapting and developing an existing network within the system, creating their own, or building an entirely new and independent network, depending upon the situation and task at hand.

A system is a collection of organised things and the relationships between them. It is synonymous with apparatus, arrangement, machinery, organisation and structure. It is also used to denote a method (a system) for organising, planning and doing, in the sense of systematisation or being systematic. But it is also used in a derogatory fashion to describe a system or cabal, a clique of elites, the rich and powerful who together oppress the individual, which, as an aside, is not a bad description of how some people feel in their place of work and perhaps about life in general.

A Network is a system. As nouns, the difference between a system and a network is not particularly helpful. A system is described as a collection of organized things, as in a solar system, while a network is a fabric or structure of fibrous elements attached to each other at regular intervals. Both speak of connection, but as a verb we begin to see "to network" as something more organic. At an individual level, it often describes social interaction for the purpose of acquiring personal connections for advantage or advancement. Collectively, it means to interconnect a group or system. In information technology (IT), for example, to network is to connect two or more computers or other computerized devices in order to share information.

DOI: 10.4324/9781003092582-13

IT provides a further useful analogy in describing the difference between System Administrators and Network Administrators. A System Administrator manages an organisation's computers, configuring them and troubleshooting computer user problems. It tends to be local and small scale, focusing on hardware and software. A network administrator, however, manages the larger scale dynamics of how the individual computers communicate with each other and, from a security perspective, the outside world. Both roles need to understand the system and be able to troubleshoot, but if an organization needs to add

When You Stand Higher on the Mountain, You Can See Further

In 1994, Mike was part of an expedition to climb Annapurna IV in the Himalayas; their base camp was at 4,800 m, the same height as Mont Blanc, the highest mountain in Europe, with Camp One higher up the mountain at 5,800 m, almost the height of Kilimanjaro, the highest mountain in Africa. But this isn't a story about climbing.

As part of the lead team, Mike's responsibility was to work with the Sherpas to establish camps on the mountain and run out fixed lines. Having toiled up to establish Camp One under heavy load, he sat in the sunshine to catch his breath and admire the view looking south towards the valley below and Pokhara. Through the haze of high-altitude exertion, he could hear that the chatter on his radio becoming more urgent. He consciously dialled his mind in to listen and at the same time turned up the volume on his radio.

The urgent chatter was from a party below base camp in the valley trying to fight a fire that had broken out in one of the lower camps that was now threatening the whole valley that was dry from the summer heat. As he looked down from Camp One, he could see how quickly the fire was spreading and the radio chatter confirmed that the porters and the climbing team that had been dispatched to help from base camp were losing control of the situation.

It was clear that from his high vantage point, he could see what was happening on the ground in a way that those on the ground who were literally fighting fires could not and that he could direct them to greatest effect. As leaders, we should have the advantage of being able to stand higher on the mountain and to see further. To try as best we can to see the whole system and how it is likely to evolve.

more computers to its network or, indeed, build an organisation's computer network from scratch, it will look to its network administrator to plan and execute the strategy. A Network Administrator, like a Network Leader, understands the individual elements of the system and the connection to its external environment, but crucially they understand and can shape the overall network, connecting people, information and resources to get things done.

Fundamentally, Network Leaders recognise that hierarchical charts and organograms do not fully reflect power structures within organisations. These organisations function more effectively when their internal dynamics are treated as marketplaces, not centrally planned economies. And these organisations cannot operate independently of their environments. Jonathan Deacon likens it to cartography, where "the perspective changes as you move. It is about detecting and interpreting".[1] But they also recognise that understanding is temporal rather than purely spatial. When following a spatial metaphor, there is a territory that can be explored and understood, but from a temporal perspective, the territory is seen as being under continuous development and formation because people systems are complex systems of emergence. They do not stand still. Understanding is therefore an ongoing continuous exploration, open-ended and always incomplete. Darcy Willson-Rymer described understanding the system as being "about interpreting the discord and filtering the noise, identifying the weak signals and recognising that greater volume doesn't make things right".[2]

Notes

1 Interview with the authors, 8 March 2021. See Appendix 2 Leader Biographies.
2 Interview with the authors, 1 March 2021. See Appendix 2 Leader Biographies.

8
Actor and Social Networks

Ethan Deviney was born without a cerebellum,[1] the part of our brain that is found at the back of our head where our skull curves down to meet our neck. It is a dense knot of brain tissue, which, while comprising only about a tenth of our brain's volume, contains half of its cells. At 18 months, Ethan was referred to a development specialist, because he was not sitting or crawling like his older brothers had done. The specialist found his cognitive development to be on track as was his social and physical development and his fine motor skills. But his gross motor skills, his ability to hold his body steady or to crawl, were behind as were his language abilities. But it was not until his fourth birthday that a brain scan revealed his missing cerebellum.

The cerebellum is effectively a quality assessment centre or feedback hub. Electrical signals from the upper brain to initiate action in the body pass through the cerebellum on the way out and signals from the muscles on how the movement is progressing pass through it on the way back. This feedback loop allows us unconsciously to regulate our motor movements and the cerebellum thus coordinates movement, including posture, balance, coordination and speech, resulting in smooth and balanced muscular activity. Effectively, it allows us to operate on autopilot and that was why Ethan was having trouble with his gross motor skills.

Despite the lack of cerebellum, however, Ethan was still able to stand, walk, run and jump. He did so rather awkwardly, but he did it and he was improving all the time. In part, this was because his neural network adjusted to compensate, other parts of his brain pitched in to help, which reinforces neuroscientists evolving network-centric view of how the brain works. No longer do they talk of a specific area for language, seeing, feeling or movement. Instead, they now see the brain in terms of patterns of interaction between different brain regions that are critical for functions like learning and memory as well as language, vision and hearing. But the other key factor was the support provided by his family, who from a young age have repeatedly shown him how to walk and

DOI: 10.4324/9781003092582-14

control his body. In effect, the lack of a portion of the network within is also made up for by the support of a network of people without. Ethan and his support network are therefore a special case illustrating a broader principle: that we all rely on an external support network to be who we are and do what we do.

The idea that being a person is something distributed beyond a specific body drives the work of Helene Mialet, a French philosopher and anthropologist. Her book, *Hawking Incorporated*, examined the human and mechanical aids that supported the genius of the late Stephen Hawking.[2] Her argument, supported by further work on people with diabetes, is that human beings are distributed across networks of our inner world, our social world and man-made objects, but because such networked distribution is so fundamental to who we are it is hard to see these networks in action, except in exceptional circumstances.

Sam Haraway, at the University of California, has taken these ideas and applied them to sport. Using the case of Lance Armstrong's 1999–2005 Tour de France victories to reconfigure sport as a competition between actor-networks, involving a network of laboratories, materials, bodies, knowledge, institutions and sponsorships.[3] Putting aside his ultimate disgrace, Haraway notes that Armstrong consistently gave credit for his victories to others. For example, Armstrong rode to victory almost entirely in the slipstream of his teammates, whose role in the race was to shield him from the wind and supply him with food and water. This common race strategy allows team leaders to save energy for the decisive moments of the race, such as mountain-top finishes, which are extremely physically demanding. But he also had the support of sponsors, physicians, trainers and loved ones, who did not participate in the competition itself but were nevertheless vital to his success.

The same is true in Formula One, with Lewis Hamilton at the pinnacle of a Mercedes Team that combines the collective power of experts in aerodynamics, composites, energy storage, fuel economy, data science, physiology, nutrition, sleep and many more, all collaborating to shave fractions of a second off overall performance. Yet we tend to remember heroes, single individuals, sporting or otherwise, rather than the network of people and ideas that supported them. In truth, success is a network phenomenon, in which the notion of the single super athlete is replaced by the collective work of their network. This does not mean that we lose sight of individual excellence, but it does recognise the individual as part of a distributed network. From a leadership perspective, actor-networks challenge the idea of the single super leader, often the CEO, and compel us to rethink leadership as something embedded in and constituted through social networks. It reinforces the notion of post-heroic or shared leadership, highlighting that a key component of better leadership performance is understanding and utilising our leader network to greatest effect.

The best single word we have heard to describe this notion is Ubuntu, an African term that is difficult to translate but essentially means "humanity to others". Significantly, it is captured in the expression "I am because we are" and describes the essence of being human. In other words, a person is a person through other persons. We are made for togetherness, to live in a delicate network of interdependence. We need other human beings in order to be human ourselves. We would not know how to walk, talk, think or behave as a human without learning from other human beings. In short, we know ourselves in the context of others.

As human beings then, we are distributed across networks, actor-networks and social networks, which also inextricably combine our inner world, or consciousness, with our external social world. Alva Noë, Professor of Philosophy at the University of California at Berkeley, describes consciousness as something we do, enact or perform in dynamic relation to the world around us. Consciousness, in other words, happens within a context.[4] In effect, we are as much a part of our networks as our networks are part of us.

We are all embedded in social networks, whether knowingly or not, and real, everyday social networks (natural networks) are not typically composed from the top down. Instead, they evolve organically from the natural inclination of humans to develop social relations and ultimately societies. They are superorganisms, which link the study of individuals with that of groups, where the whole is greater than the sum of the parts. A network, like a group, is a collection of people, but it includes something more: a specific set of connections between the people in the group. And it is these ties and patterns of connection that enable us to influence other people and for them to influence us.

It is helpful that networks are now widely recognised as a universal structure. The brain is a network of cells, which are themselves a network of molecules. Societies are networks of people. Food webs and ecosystems are networks of species. Networks pervade human technology, from the internet to power grids and transportation systems. Immersive art reflects a transition from the appreciation of an object to an experience of connection and interaction. And networks are challenging the way we organise ourselves, with top-down hierarchies being replaced by flatter and other more informal network structures of social collaboration.

Some might argue that this is a paradigm shift in the way we see and order ourselves, but this is how human beings have always implicitly understood and ordered themselves. *In the Square and the Tower*,[5] Niall Ferguson suggests that the secret of our success as a species has always resided in the collective brain of our communities. Humans learn socially through teaching and sharing, and perhaps our species should be known as "Homo dictyous" ("network man"), because our brains seem to have been built for networks.

Anne-Marie Slaughter advances similar arguments in *The Chessboard and the Web*, describing humans as Homo sociologicus (humans as social beings) as opposed to Homo economicus (humans as rational agents).[6] She points out that our early ancestors were collaborative foragers, who became interdependent on each other for food, shelter and warmth. All that has happened since, beginning with the invention of written language, is that new technologies have facilitated our innate, ancient urge to network, and today's technologies have us more connected and immersed in data than ever. As Matt Ridley observed over 20 years ago:

> Human beings have social instincts. They come into the world equipped with predispositions to learn how to cooperate, to discriminate the trustworthy from the treacherous, to commit themselves to be trustworthy, to earn good reputations, to exchange goods and information, and to divide labour.[7]

Economic history is all about connections. Sometimes, as with the pandemic, those connections can have adverse consequences. But global connections also meant that best practices for treating the disease could be quickly transmitted around the world. Viruses aside, the more people with whom we can connect, the better. Either we will find someone whose expertise is helpful or we will find someone who can offer a good or service that we desire but cannot provide for ourselves.[8]

There is, however, a darker side to our nature and our networks. There is a tendency for human societies to fragment into competing groups and with minds "all too ready to adopt prejudices and pursue genocidal feuds".[9] The great insight of Goebbels', Hitler's Minister of Propaganda, was that people believe what they want to believe. It gives them an excuse not to think or bother themselves with inconvenient truths. Networks can also reinforce inequality. Social networks hold to the "Matthew Principle" that the rich get richer while the poor get poorer. The rich benefit from preferential attachment to other rich people and their children to better education and better opportunities, creating a widening gap between those who have and those who have not. Similarly, the more famous artists on Spotify get bigger audiences, and during lockdown, the more famous churches attracted larger congregations.[10]

In summary, the social and actor networks in which we all exist allow us to do things together that a single person or a disconnected collection of individuals could not. However, because of their organic, tribal and evolving nature, they require continual care and preservation to ensure they remain positive, healthy and productive, and that, in turn, requires morally responsible leaders who understand them and can nurture them towards positive and inclusive ends. That understanding begins with an appreciation that networks are based on two fundamental principles, connection and contagion, and five rules: we shape our networks; our networks shape us; our friends affect us; our friend's friends' friends also influence us; and networks are dynamic.

Connection and Contagion

Connection refers to the shape, structure or anatomy of a network, the arrangement of its nodes (people or groups) and ties (connections between them). Contagion, however, refers to the networks function or physiology: what, if anything, flows through and across the connections. All systems have flows, movements of things, people and ideas. Understand the flows and you are on your way to understanding the system.

In a social system, there are two types of flow or contagion. The first are germs, viruses, gossip and information, where once infected additional contact is redundant. The second are norms and behaviours, which often require reinforcement through multiple social contacts. When it comes to the spread of ideas and memes,[11] it is important to understand that it is just as much about the structure of the network as it is about the content of the idea. A virile network will spread the good, the bad and the just plain ugly. It doesn't care.

To take a recent example, consider the social nature of financial markets. In an article in February 2021, discussing the media stories around GameStop and WallStreetBets, the *Economist* pointed to the increasingly social nature of investing and the questions it posed for financial economics.[12]

While acknowledging the impact of behavioural economics in shifting the paradigm away from rational man (*homo economicus*), they suggested that we should now be moving "beyond behavioural finance to 'social finance'". In part, this shift recognises that the social transmission of information (connection) has important effects on markets. Financial professionals, the article observed, would not be surprised to learn that social transmission of information is important. The "need to be close to the buzz of informal market chatter is one reason why financial-sector activity tends to be concentrated in hubs like London and New York". However, it went on to say that social connections are more than just "conduits for shop talk", they are also a channel for contagion. One financier's decision to make a particular investment may trigger others to follow their lead. And as increasing numbers invest, so the pressure increases to follow suit or miss out. The article specifically cited research by academics at Duke University, who referred to "investment contagion" during America's housing boom, most of which can be explained using the rules of social networks.

The Covid-19 Network

As the *Economist* reported back in May 2020, just as we emerging from the first lockdown, greater mobility raised the risk of a second wave of Covid-19 contagion. And that was a worry for countries where policies were set locally: outbreaks could begin in areas with lax controls and spread elsewhere. And, in theory, the risk would mirror the level of interconnectedness between regions, the amount of travel to and from each region. Lombardy was probably hit hardest by Covid-19 because it was the best networked part of Italy, and data compiled in Germany, Italy and America by Teralytics, a Swiss technology firm, supported this hypothesis.

Each time a mobile phone left one location and arrived in another for an hour or more, Teralytics logged the journey. In the week before lockdowns began, the firm recorded 5.7 billion trips. Travel fell by 40% once they were implemented. The *Economist* took this data and built two statistical models to test how interconnectedness affects vulnerability to Covid-19 and therefore predicts local infection rates just before lockdowns. The first model relied solely on each area's population density and income. The second added two measures related to propensity for travel: the number of journeys and the areas "network centrality", how many places it tends to exchange visitors with.

The more elaborate model provided 30% more explanatory power and concluded that interconnectedness matters a lot. In all three countries, better-networked areas had more infections, less networked ones had fewer. Their advice was that governments should treat travel hubs with caution. Well-networked Frankfurt was probably at greater risk than comparatively disconnected Hanover and should therefore reopen relatively slowly. Milan in Italy and Houston in America were advised to be cautious too.[13]

Rule One of Social Networks Is that We Shape Our Network

We make and remake our social networks all the time depending upon homophily and propinquity. Homophily, colloquially known as "birds of a feather flock together", is our conscious and unconscious tendency to associate with people who resemble us, either physically, emotionally or cognitively (we think the same things and often in the same way – people like us). The downside of homophily is that it tends towards polarisation, particularly when mediated by social media algorithms. The algorithms that drive Google, Facebook, YouTube, Spotify, etc. mean that much of what we read, watch and listen to is based upon what we already read, watch and listen to.

In the social sphere, people's views can become more extreme as similar views, biases and prejudices are shared in a social echo chamber that excludes alternative views – a process that can be exploited for political gain. Brexit can be described as a victory for network science because it allowed the campaign team to run different versions of ads, test them, drop the less effective and reinforce the most effective in a constant iterative process. And this, in turn, was a dress rehearsal for the US presidential election of 2016.[14] Such tribalism, the negative side of communities, has always been with us, but technology has allowed it to proliferate.

In *The Second Sleep*, a fictional account of post-apocalyptic Britain by Robert Harris, the main character looks down on a medieval-like village and speculates how different it might have been in the 2020s:

> Perhaps not so different. He could imagine the same suspicion of outsiders and eagerness to gossip, the same prejudices, superstitions and rumours. Of course, the inhabitants would not have been isolated then. They would have been able to communicate more easily, and across vast distances, using the strange devices with the symbol of the bitten apple. But would they have had anything wiser to say, or would their local vices merely have been spread more widely?[15]

We also choose the structure of our networks: we decide how many people we are connected to; we influence how densely interconnected our friends and family are; and we control how central we are to these social networks. Centrality is an important but often neglected measure of an individual's importance in a team or organisation. Centrality describes the extent to which that person is a network bridge (like travel hubs in the Covid-19 example above) between different nodes or actors. Crucial roles are played by people who are connectors, but not necessarily leaders, and individuals can be assessed in terms of their degree centrality (number of relationships), betweenness centrality (the likelihood of being a bridge between other nodes) and eigenvector centrality (proximity to popular or prestigious nodes). These are points to which we will return later.

Propinquity, however, means nearness or physical proximity, and in network terms describes our propensity to associate with people who are physically near us or who we come into frequent contact with. That is, we are more likely to form relationships with those closest to us rather than those who are more distant. Thus, groups are more likely to form among colleagues who sit together

Propinquity

Propinquity (the tendency for people to form connections with those nearest to them) was examined in one of the early social network studies, which looked at collaboration between academics in universities. One of the startling conclusions was that they tended to collaborate most closely with those whose offices were 30 feet from their own! Perhaps confirming the old adage that universities are institutions connected by nothing more than a shared central heating system!

James was able to confirm this for himself a few years ago, when he was studying social interaction within an academic team. By chance, they sat on two separate tables in an open-plan office, and social network analysis confirmed that they were more likely to communicate with, seek advice from and trust, those who sat on the same table, despite the two tables being only a few dozen feet apart.

But universities are not alone in facing this problem. The spaces created for connection in Silicon Valley headquarters by the likes of Google, Facebook, Pixar and the Crick Institute in London are a response to the same phenomena and are designed to encourage people from different parts of the organisation to collide and interact. When Steve Jobs was designing the building for Pixar, he built just one set of toilets located in the atrium. At first sight this seems inefficient but his aim was to force people out of their niches and create instead the opportunity for chance encounters.

The Francis Crick Institute, a biomedical research centre that opened in London in 2016, is a partnership between Cancer Research UK, Imperial College London, King's College London, the Medical Research Council, University College London and the Wellcome Trust, but instead of being planned by organisation, it is arranged in "interest groups", bringing together researchers from the different bodies to share insights in areas of common scientific interest and staff working in different fields. To enable this, there are interaction and collaboration facilities at the centre of each floor and the laboratories are arranged as shared neighbourhoods.

than those who work in different locations. It is summed up in the rhyming phrase: "those close by form a tie".

Ironically, another example that seating arrangements matter comes from a country that has tried to make it not matter at all. In Iceland's small parliament, all seats not occupied by ministers are allocated through the drawing of lots. A member could therefore end up sitting with allies or enemies or both. And in such circumstances, it is possible to test whether having neighbours from other parties makes a politician less beholden to his or her own party or "tribe".[16]

Alessandro Saia, an economist at the University of Lausanne, found that it does. Saia found that between 1991 and 2017, a politician who sat among others and who did not adhere to the party line was 30% more likely to rebel. Over time, Mr Saia found that parliamentary neighbours even began to use similar words in speeches. And who sits next to you, as opposed to who is in front or behind, seems to matter most, perhaps because gossip is easier if you do not have to turn round.

Rule Two of Social Networks Is That Our Network Shapes Us

This is the concept we explored through actor-networks at the beginning of the chapter, and crucially it depends upon how tightly woven your network is. If you know Alan, Alan knows Michelle and Michelle knows you, the relationship is said to be transitive. High transitivity normally indicates that people are deeply embedded within a single group, where everyone knows everyone else. Being in highly transitive groups makes you more susceptible to whatever is flowing in the network, whether it be gossip or germs.

For example, a medical study by Nicholas Christakis showed that body weight is strongly influenced by social networks of friends, to the extent that mutual best friends (those who both name each other as best friends) have a triple obesity risk. Christakis examined a densely connected network of over 12,000 people over a period from 1970 to 2003 and found that "a person's chances of being obese increased by 57% if a friend became obese, 40% if a sibling became obese and 37% if a spouse became obese".[17]

Rule Three Is That Our Friends Affect Us

As we have seen, one fundamental determinant of flow is the tendency of human beings to influence and be influenced by one another, to copy or conform to what others do. Structurally, the more paths that connect you to other people in your network the more susceptible you are to flows within it (high transitivity, as discussed above), but it is not just the number of social contacts that is important, there nature is also significant. And, as we saw in Rule 2, we tend primarily to measure ourselves against our friends. It turns out that smoking, happiness, obesity, loneliness and even terrorism spread like viruses among friends. As Scott Atran observes:

> The key difference between terrorists and most other people in the world lies not in individual pathologies, personality, education, income, or in any other demographic factor, but in small group dynamics where the relevant trait just happens to be jihad rather than obesity.[18]

This phenomenon can create niches, communities within networks that share certain ideas and behaviours, where terrorism or weight gain can become a kind of standard or norm. What is less clear is whether these ideas/behaviours exist because people of similar ideas spend time together (homophily); or because people share common exposure (conformity); or if there is a causal effect, one person causing the adoption of an idea or behaviour in another (social contagion). But the key point is that people are pre-eminently socially connected actors rather than individual performers.

The Accidental Guerrilla

In Afghanistan, part of James' required reading was *The Accidental Guerrilla: Fighting Small Wars in the Midst of a Big One* by David Kilcullen, a former officer in the Australian Army and an expert on counterinsurgency, who advised Condoleezza Rice, General David Petraeus and US Ambassador Ryan Crocker. Kilcullen's principal contention, which was linked to his experiences ten years earlier as a Company Commander in the Javanese jungle, was that War on Terror had essentially two contrasting aspects. One was the larger international coalition against Al Qaeda. The other, though largely ignored aspect, were the uprisings of local networks and fighters – smaller insurgencies that aligned themselves intentionally, or sometimes not, within the larger aspect.

These "accidental guerrillas" were the villagers Kilcullen met in Uruzgan, Afghanistan, who joined the Taliban in a 2006 offensive against an American patrol simply for the joy of fighting. "When the battle was right there in front of them, how could they not join in"? Kilcullen wrote. "This was the most exciting thing that had happened in their valley in years. It would have shamed them to stand by and wait it out, they said".

One of the larger mistakes America made in its handling of the Long War against Al Qaeda was ignoring the details of these smaller conflicts. What was needed, Kilcullen argued, were strategies that dealt both with global terrorism and conflicts at the local level. Discussing the tribal areas of Pakistan, Kilcullen showed how Al Qaeda moved in by taking over communities, establishing bonds by marrying local women, operating businesses and eventually recruiting the villagers as fighters. Kilcullen likened it to a disease spreading through the community.

Al Qaeda established its presence in a remote area of conflict, then penetrated the population the same way influenza infects a weakened immune system. Contagion then occurred when the safe haven was used to spread violence. When outside forces intervened, disrupting the safe haven, the local population aligned with Al Qaeda. The terrorists' approach was meant to be long-lasting, and it proved highly effective.

Kilcullen believed that to succeed, the West needed to refocus and remain agile, protecting the people who supported the government, in what he called "population-centric security", rather than trying to destroy the enemy. This he said demanded the continuous presence of security forces, local alliances and partnerships with community leaders to create self-defending populations. In short, the work of the international community came down to the basics of securing villages, valleys, roads and population centres – the nodes and ties of the Afghan network.

Rule Four Is That Our Friend's Friends' Friends Also Influence Us

The extent of network connections is perhaps best exemplified by research pertaining to "Small Worlds", which can be observed in the phenomena many people experience when encountering a stranger for the first time, only to discover that both share a friend or acquaintance in common. A small-world network is when any two people in a network can reach each other through a short sequence of acquaintances. The term "six degrees of separation" posits that any two people on Earth are six or fewer acquaintance links apart. A concept you may be familiar with if you have ever played the parlour game "Six Degrees of Kevin Bacon".[19]

The concept was originally suggested by the Hungarian author Frigyes Karinthy in 1929. In a short story called *Chains* his characters postulated that any two individuals could be connected through a maximum of five acquaintances. Subsequently, this caught the imagination of the public and academics. Stanley Milgram, the social psychologist, carried out a series of experiments in the mid-20th century, which showed that everyone in the United States was connected by six or seven links. Columbia University's 2008 "Small World Project" confirmed the idea, suggesting that the average number of links was six.[20]

It is worth pointing out here that these weak ties (beyond the immediate ties of our friends and family) are a rich source of new information. Acquaintances are often more important in landing a new job than our friends and family because they give access to social networks to which we don't otherwise belong. In Rebel Ideas, Matthew Syed relates an experiment led by Professor Daniel Levin of Rutgers Business School, which asked more than 200 executives to reactivate contacts that had been dormant for at least three years. The subjects asked two of these contacts for advice on an ongoing project at work and were then asked to rate the value of the advice in comparison to the advice of two people working on the project. The answer was clear: the dormant contacts offered advice of significantly higher value. And the reason for that was because they were dormant ties, who were no longer operating in the same environment, hearing the same stories or having the same experiences.[21] A valuable analogy is found in the network-centric view of our brain provided by neuroscientist Shane O'Mara:

> A useful way of imagining our brain is an enormously complicated network of cells, regions and circuits, with varying degrees of traffic between the parts of the overall network, depending upon the demands of the being made on the network. Areas that are remote from each other will tend to interact less, and areas that are close will interact more. Consider the extended network of people you call on to solve a range of problems ... you are likely to learn more from people that you don't interact with much. The brain is similar when it comes to the process of creating new ideas. We need access to far-flung remote associations between different brain areas – for this is how new and interesting, creative ideas might arise.[22]

Thus, as we move away from the strong ties of our closest social groups, there is less overlap in experience and information. We might trust socially distant people less (remember the social echo chambers that are driven by homophily), but their information and contacts are more valuable because we cannot access them ourselves as they are just beyond our immediate social horizon. We will return to the concept of strong and weak ties when we examine social network analysis in the next chapter, but for the moment it is important to understand that access to such ties, and the value they offer, depends upon the degree of network contagion.

Rule Five Is That Networks Are Dynamic

Networks are emergent phenomena. Emergence occurs when an entity is observed to have properties or behaviours which emerge only when the parts interact in a wider whole, like the murmuration of starlings in which the shapes the birds collectively form in the sky arise from the interaction of the individual birds but are beyond their individual control. They obey rules but rules that are distinct from the individual birds that form them.[23]

Emergence plays a central role in theories of complex systems. An idea is often encapsulated in the phrase the "butterfly effect", which is based on a scientific paper published by Edward Lorenz, a mathematician and meteorologist, in the 1960s entitled "Does the Flap of a Butterfly's Wings in Brazil Set Off a Tornado in Texas"? The paper was based upon his work on two identical weather simulations, which gave vastly different results because he had rounded off a number of six decimal places to three. The "butterfly effect" essentially means that things are complex, change just a few decimal places and you end up with a vastly different outcome. And the concept has since been extended from weather systems to living organisms, ecosystems and national economies, networks that have such a diverse array of interconnections that they are ultimately unpredictable.

In the human social realm, Adam Smith's famous observation regarding economic markets that man "is led by an invisible hand to promote an end which was no part of his intention"[24] is an example of emergent complexity. Markets behave as though they have a life of their own, which is neither controlled nor often even perceived by the people within them. Behavioural contagion is easy to understand in a physical linear network like a bucket brigade, where people try to put out a fire by passing buckets of water from the river to the fire, but hugely complicated in a natural social network such as an economic market. But herein lies opportunity.

Hierarchies and other linear systems are tightly coupled, in the sense that a failure in one part of the system can cascade to the rest and cause total failure. Each part of the system is dependent on the others. Think of the bucket brigade or dominoes stacked to fall one after the other; if one fails to knock over the next, then the whole system fails. Project managers call it the critical path, which contains the tasks that must be completed in order for the project to be finished on schedule. If something on the critical path changes, this change cascades to everything else on the path. Any delay to a task on the critical path will delay the entire project. Social networks however are more loosely coupled and multiple flows of informal activity within the system allow the use of different strategies and lateral connections are often created to avoid a dependency which is slowing down activity.

And the key to understanding loosely coupled systems is to look beyond simple, sequential connections and try to see the whole network at once – to understand its dynamic properties and how it changes over time. But before we examine organisational networks in more detail, it is helpful to understand the challenges that organisations face. Challenges that mirror the emergent complexity of organisations are called wicked problems.

Notes

1 The Economist. (2018). Team Ethan. The Network Within, the Network Without. December 22nd, pp. 41–26. https://www.economist.com/christmas-specials/2018/12/18/the-family-of-a-boy-without-a-cerebellum-found-out-how-to-take-its-place
2 Mialet, H. (2012). *Hawking Incorporated: Stephen Hawking and the Anthropology of the Knowing Subject*. Chicago: University of Chicago Press.
3 Techno-Sport in Action. (2016). *Lance Armstrong and the Sociology of the Techno-Athlete. Society for Social Studies of Science/European Association for the Study of Science and Technology*. Barcelona: Spain.
4 Noë, A. (2009). *Out of Our Heads: Why You Are Not Your Brain, and Other Lessons from the Biology of Consciousness*. New York: Hill & Wang.
5 Ferguson, N. (2017). *The Square and the Tower: Networks, Hierarchies and the Struggle for Global Power*. London: Allen Lane.
6 Slaughter, A. (2017). *The Chessboard and the Web: Strategies of Connection in a Networked World*. New Haven, CT and London: Yale University Press.
7 Ridley, M. (1997). *The Origins of Virtue*. London: Penguin Books, p. 249.
8 Coggan, P. (2021). *More: The 10,000 Year Rise of the World Economy*. London: Profile Books, p. 357.
9 Coggan, P. (2021) ibid, p. 250.
10 The Economist. (2021). God the Rock Star. April 23rd, p. 25.
11 The word 'meme' was coined by Richard Dawkins in his 1976 book *The Selfish Gene* as an attempt to explain the way cultural information, symbols and social ideas spread.
12 The Economist. (2021). Regression to Memes. February 27, p. 69.
13 https://www.economist.com/graphic-detail/2020/05/16/phone-data-identify-travel-hubs-at-risk-of-a-second-wave-of-infections
14 Ferguson, N. (2017) op cit.
15 Harris, R. (2019). *The Second Sleep*. London: Arrow Books, p. 188.
16 The Economist. (2019). Better Politics by Design: How We Shape Our Parliamentary Buildings and How They in Turn Shape us. July 27th, p. 52.
17 Christakis, N. (2011). *Connected: The Amazing Power of Social Networks and How They Shape Our Lives*. London: Harper Press.
18 Atran, S. (2010). *Talking to the Enemy: Faith, Brotherhood, and the (Un)Making of Terrorists*. New York: Ecco Publishers.
19 In this game, the players challenge each other to find the shortest path between an arbitrary actor and actor Kevin Bacon. The idea being that any actor can be connected to Bacon within six degrees of connection. It is interesting to note that

Rod Steiger was originally identified as the best "connected" actor, because he did lots of different movies with lots of different people, good and bad, from action to comedies, while John Wayne was much less well connected (116th) despite making 179 movies in a 60-year career because the majority of his films were Westerns. He made the same kind of movies with the same kind of people, thereby restricting his network.

20 For comparison, Twitter users are apparently 5.5 steps or less from any other tweeter and Facebook "friends" are 4.74 connections away from every other user of the social network. And LinkedIn's business model is based on the premise that we're all associated by a finite degree of connections. The name "Small Worlds" derives from the expression "It's a small world", when two people find they have friends or acquaintances in common.

21 Syed, M. (2019). *Rebel Ideas: The Power of Diverse Thinking*. London: John Murray Publishers, p. 265.

22 O'Mara, S. (2020). *In Praise of Walking: The New Science of How We Walk and Why It's Good for Us*. London: Vintage, p. 154.

23 The rules, identified through computer simulations, are follow the bird in front, keep up and don't bump. They have also been found in shoals of fish, insect swarms and animal herds.

24 Smith, A. (1776) *The Wealth of Nations*. London: W. Strahan. Book IV, Chapter II, p. 456.

9
Wicked Problems

John Kay and Mervyn King relate how in August 2004 NASA launched the probe *Messenger* towards the Mercury with the intention of entering its orbit and beginning its investigation of the planet.[1] Six and half years later, having travelled 4.9 billion miles at a speed of 84,500 mph it succeeded, entering Mercury's orbit at exactly the location NASA had anticipated. This remarkable feat of computation was possible because the underlying processes of planetary motion are almost completely understood and those processes are physical laws that remain constant over time. Critically, however, the motions of the planets are not significantly affected by human actions or at all by human beliefs about their motion. Economic and social phenomena are not like this.

While we can accurately predict the trajectory of a spacecraft over billions of miles through space, we will never reach the stage where it is possible to accurately forecast the economic outlook a year ahead, let alone six and a half years. That is because economics is a social science and not a physical one. As Philip Coggan points out, when a chemist forecasts the results of two substances reacting, the substances are unaware of the forecaster's existence. But if people knew for certain that there would be a recession next year, they would become more cautious immediately. Consumers would cut back on spending; businesses would postpone investment and new orders. The recession would be brought forward, rendering the forecast inaccurate.[2]

Kay and King liken it to the difference between a puzzle and a mystery[3]:

> A puzzle has well-defined rules and a single solution, and we know when we have reached the solution. Puzzles deliver the satisfaction of a clear-cut task and a correct answer … Mysteries offer no such clarity of definition, and no objectively correct solution: they are imbued with vagueness and indeterminacy … A mystery cannot be solved as a crossword puzzle can; it can only be framed, by identifying the critical factors and applying some sense of how these factors have interacted in the past and might interact in the

DOI: 10.4324/9781003092582-15

> present or the future. Much as we might like it, mysteries cannot be reduced to puzzles and to try and do so is to fundamentally misunderstand them.

And wicked problems fall into the category of mystery.

Wicked problems are not wicked in the sense of evil or malevolent (though it may feel that way), but wicked in the sense of being resistant to resolution. Wicked problems are difficult or impossible to solve because the problem itself is difficult to comprehend, being incomplete, contradictory and involving shifting requirements. Moreover, because of their complex interdependencies, efforts to solve one aspect of a wicked problem may reveal or create other problems.

Wicked problems were first formerly described by Horst Rittel and Melvin Webber, professors of design and urban planning at the University of California at Berkeley, in a 1973 paper, contrasting "wicked" problems with relatively "tame", soluble problems in mathematics, chess or puzzle solving.[4] In short, wicked problems are difficult to clearly define; they have multiple causes and interdependencies; they are socially complex, involving multiple stakeholders and are usually the responsibility of more than one organisation to solve; and attempts to solve them often lead to unforeseen consequences. Accordingly, solutions to such problems are often unstable and continually evolving, having no clear resolution or in fact no solution at all. There is no right or wrong answer; "solutions" can only be judged as better or worse, good enough or not good enough.

Wicked problems are often confronted in the arena of public planning and policy and in areas such as climate change, natural hazards, international drug trafficking, energy, social inequality and epidemics like Covid-19. But the concept has been extended to include a wide variety of other environments, including business strategy, terrorism and warfare. Nancy Roberts suggests that they have risen to prominence because:

> the expansion of democracy, market economies, privatization, travel and social exchanges highlight value differences and thus promote dissensus [sic] rather than consensus in the problem solving process. Perhaps the technological and information revolutions enable more people to become active participants in problem solving, and in so doing, increase the complexity of the process. Perhaps the ideological shifts in policy and management that encourage organizational decentralization, experimentation, flexibility, and innovation weaken traditional authority and control mechanisms that heretofore have kept a lid on conflicts.[5]

This would fit with Friedman's assertion that we are living in the "Age of Accelerations" in which the world continues to change, but at a faster pace than ever before.[6] Not only that, but we are also experiencing simultaneous accelerations in technology (Moore's Law), the market (globalisation) and Mother Nature (our impact on the planet), each of which acts on the others in a wicked spiral of complexity. Friedman cites Astro Teller, CEO of the Google X research unit, who believes it is the gap between the pace of technological change and human adaptability that is causing our current sociocultural angst and political upheavals and our only adequate response is to increase our society's ability to adapt.

In our own experience, wicked problems require a relentless emphasis on the problem itself. But hierarchical organisations can waste time satisfying the organisational need rather than focusing on the problem. Instead of developing a single strategy or policy to solve the issue, they create a series of individual (siloed) department programmes that are bureaucratic solutions to settle internal disputes rather than attempts to address the problem itself. Time is then devoted to reconciling, or not, the conflicted objectives between the different departments or agencies, while the actual problem only intensifies with the infusion of this added complexity.

Another typical, but wrong-headed, approach is to try and follow old rules to solve new problems. As Albert Einstein is often quoted as saying, "We can't solve problems by using the same kind of thinking we used when we created them". Too many leaders default to looking at decisions as either/or, right or wrong, good or bad, win or lose, but this binary thinking only feeds our desire for simple answers. Straightforward answers make us feel safer, especially in disruptive and tumultuous times. But wicked problems are mysteries not puzzles – there are no guarantees and no predictable timelines. While it may seem appealing in the short run, attempting to tame a wicked problem with a tried and tested solution will likely fail in the long run. The problem will simply reassert itself, perhaps in a different guise or even worse than before. As the journalist and cultural critic H.L. Mencken reputedly observed, "There is always a well-known solution to every human problem – neat, plausible, and wrong".

Common mistakes include a failure to lock down the problem definition and instead develop a description of a related problem that you can solve and declare that to be the problem; casting the problem as like a previous problem that has already been solved and ignoring or filtering out evidence that complicates the picture, declaring that there are just a few possible solutions and then focusing on selecting from among them. Effectively framing the problem in either/or terms or simply giving up and instead just following orders, doing your job and trying not to get in trouble.

So what will it take to increase the complexity of our thinking? In the first place, we have to recognise that we will not understand the problem until we have tried to develop a solution. This may sound paradoxical, but every solution that is offered exposes new aspects of the problem, requiring further adjustments. Solving wicked problems is an iterative process. And while a problem statement is important, don't expect a definitive statement of the problem. Wicked problems are ill-structured and feature an evolving set of interlocking issues and constraints. Problem and solution will evolve, which requires the flexibility of mind to adjust and the relentless determination to keep going.

Just as there is there is no definitive problem, there is also no definitive solution. Solutions are not right or wrong; they are simply better or worse, good enough or not good enough. Furthermore, the determination of solution quality is often subjective and cannot therefore be derived from following a formula; each problem is essentially unique and novel and solutions to them will always be custom designed. It is therefore a matter of creativity to devise potential solutions and a matter of judgement to determine which should be pursued and implemented. Over time, we can acquire wisdom and experience in our approach to wicked problems, but we will always be a beginner in the specifics of a new wicked problem and every solution has consequences.

This is the catch-22 of wicked problems: you can't learn about the problem without trying solutions, but every solution will have a cost and entail lasting consequences that may spawn new wicked problems. Think of them as a tangled ball of wool or string, where pulling on one thread to untie it only tightens another knot. In this sense, wicked problems are very much network problems.

Wicked Problems Are Network Problems

In the summer of 2009, shortly after he took command of the International Security Assistance Force (ISAF) and US Forces Afghanistan (USFOR-A) in Afghanistan, General Stanley McChrystal was presented with following network map as part of a PowerPoint briefing (see Figure 3.1).[7] The slide, a network map, was designed to show all the interrelationships between the key actors and problems in the Afghan theatre of operations.

McChrystal's reputed response: "When we understand that slide, we'll have won the war", we can only assume was meant in jest. We are pretty sure that the irony of trying to understand a complex, wicked problem through the medium of a single PowerPoint slide was not lost on General McChrystal.

Having been in the same headquarters in Kabul the year before, James was involved in similar efforts to understand the complexity of the conflict in

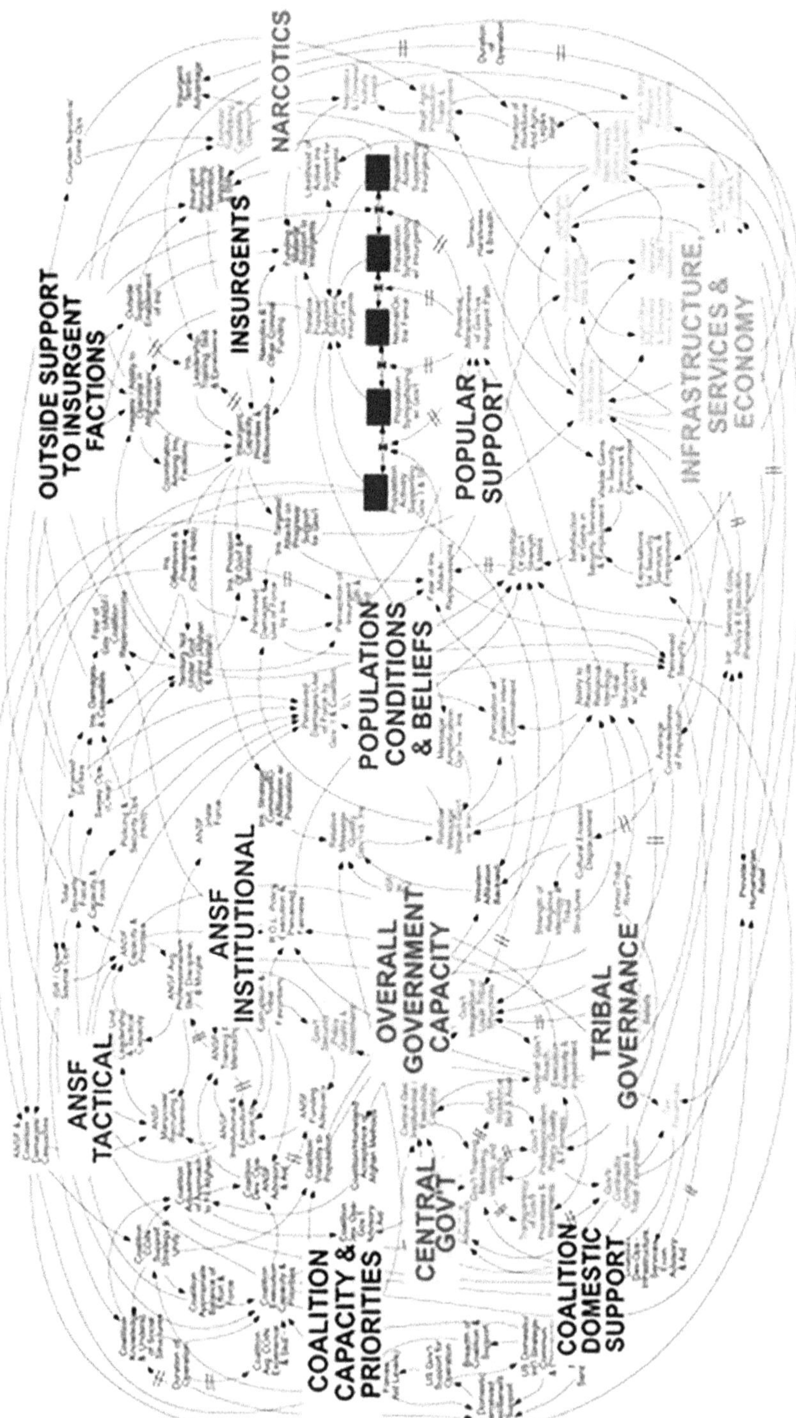

Figure 3.1 Afghanistan Stability Dynamics.

Afghanistan. Having put together similar network diagrams with his colleagues in the Influence Operations cell in ISAF Headquarters, McChrystal's slide was immediately familiar in its confusing muddle of actors and institutions, linked by supposed lines of cause and effect. Not least is the realisation that the dynamic nature of the environment renders the map obsolete almost as soon as it is complete.

The explanatory power of such network maps was admittedly limited, providing at best an overview of the main actors and the broader contextual elements with a jumble of potential relational arrows connecting them. But that does not mean they were wasted effort. Their value was at least two-fold. In the first place, they provided a valuable visual representation of the complexity James and his colleagues were trying to understand and thereby provided a degree of humility in their efforts to shape it. But more importantly, the real value of the diagram was not in its completion but in its creation. It provided them with a foundational understanding of the problem environment, if not the actual problem or its solution. To paraphrase Eisenhower, the map was nothing, but mapping was everything.

In McChrystal's case, it reinforced his already keen understanding of the power of the network approach. His experiences as commander of the US Joint Special Operations Task Force in Iraq, from September 2003 to February 2006, and then as Commander of Joint Special Operations Command Forward, from February 2006 to August 2008, had taught him that to survive and thrive in a complex and rapidly changing world hierarchical organisations like the military had to reinvent themselves as networks, breaking down silos and mastering the flexible response that comes from teamwork and collaboration at an organisational level.[8]

The enemy that the Joint Special Operations Task Force confronted in Iraq in 2003 had already mastered this operational model. While on the surface it looked like a traditional hierarchical insurgency, it in fact worked in the form of a dispersed network that proved devastatingly effective, frequently wrong-footing Western and allied forces. Its unorthodox structure allowed it to thrive in this radically different operating environment, which was faster paced, more integrated and therefore more complex than previous environments. To win, McChrystal realised, the Task Force had to change too and change in a way that was less about tactics and technology and more about structures and culture. Fundamentally, they needed to change their approach to leadership and management. McChrystal's insight was that it would take a network to defeat a network.

The key problem facing McChrystal was that the international coalition, despite all its technological advantages, did not know, let alone understand, the system in which it was operating. In a highly critical public report, published in 2007 by a right-wing think tank, Major General Michael Flynn, then deputy chief of staff for intelligence in Afghanistan, offered a bleak assessment of the intelligence community's failings:

> Eight years into the war in Afghanistan, the U.S. intelligence community is only marginally relevant to the overall strategy. Having focused the overwhelming majority of its collection efforts and analytical brainpower on insurgent groups, the vast intelligence apparatus is unable to answer fundamental questions about the environment in which U.S. and allied forces operate and the people they seek to persuade. Ignorant of local economics and landowners, hazy about who the powerbrokers are and how they might be influenced, incurious about the correlations between various development projects and the levels of cooperation among villagers, and disengaged from people in the best position to find answers—whether aid workers or Afghan soldiers—U.S. intelligence officers and analysts can do little but shrug in response to high level decision-makers seeking the knowledge, analysis, and information they need to wage a successful counterinsurgency.[9]

Intelligence, and the knowledge and understanding it hopefully provides, is a priority when dealing with any wicked or networked problem, alongside the humility to recognise that our understanding will only ever be partial and always time bound. From James' perspective in influence operations, it was only in creating network maps that he and his colleagues began to fully understand the multifaceted and emergent nature of the Afghan conflict: the actors, the breadth of connections and feedback loops with which they would have to contend as well as the depth of the relationships and evolving interdependencies. Clearly, it did not guarantee success, the conflict continues, but it did allow them to act with greater awareness and humility in an extremely complex environment.

Like most attempts to model complexity network maps suffer from being both simplistic and intricate at the same time. They are attempts to create a two-dimensional representation of a four-dimensional problem. And the challenge was further compounded by the position of James and his colleagues in the problem. It was impossible to helicopter above the problem for a neat bird's eye view, because he and his colleagues were part of the problem they were trying to solve and therefore inextricably enmeshed in its complexity. Rather like humanity's earthbound view of the cosmos, where we are unable to see our galaxy or the universe from anything but an interior perspective, they were precluded from "seeing" the problem with complete clarity and objectivity because they were stuck on the inside looking out. Furthermore, they were trying to guess how the environment might evolve and what the future might hold. It was a mystery, not a puzzle.

The problem is by no means new. As Arthur Wellesley, 1st Duke of Wellington, pointed out:

> All the business of war, and indeed all the business of life, is to endeavour to find out what you don't know by what you do; that's what I called "guessing what was at the other side of the hill".

In warfare and business, we suffer from the same problem: we walk backwards into the future. Not knowing what is ahead of us we can only rely on our biased and imperfect memories of the past to guide us. Memories that are episodic and event driven, focusing on certain points while ignoring others. We can study the past of course but, as the financial services industry constantly reminds us, past performance is not necessarily a guide to the future.

In business, strategy and planning are about using flawed, subjective knowledge to guess what's on the other side of the hill and then preparing to meet it. Strategy formulation has, therefore, to be greater than merely "destination management" in which a CEO describes an inspiring vision to which others aspire. Instead, strategy is more of a conversation between the organisation and its context, with the interlocking networks providing the intelligence to enable real-time course correction. So how might we reconfigure our organisations to meet this challenge?

Notes

1 Kay, J. and King, M. (2020). *Radical Uncertainty: Decision-Making for an Unknowable Future*. London: The Bridge Street Press, pp. 18–9.
2 Coggan, P. (2021). *More: The 10,000 Year Rise of the World Economy*. London: Profile Books, pp. 368–9.
3 Kay, J. and King, M. (2020) op cit. pp. 20–1.
4 Rittel, Horst W.J. and Webber, M.M. (1973). Dilemmas in a General Theory of Planning. *Policy Sciences*, 4(2), pp. 155–69.
5 Roberts, N. (2000). Wicked Problems and Network Approaches to Resolution. *International Public Management Review*, 1(1), p. 2.
6 Friedman, T.L. (2017). *Thank You for Being Late: An Optimist's Guide to Thriving in The Age of Accelerations*. London: Penguin Books.
7 Bumiller, E. (2010). We Have Met the Enemy and He Is PowerPoint. *The New York Times* (online) pages. Available at https://www.nytimes.com/2010/04/27/world/27powerpoint.html (accessed 17 April 2021).
8 McChrystal, S., Collins, T., Silverman, D. and Fussell, C. (2015). *Team of Teams: New Rules of Engagement for a Complex World*. London: Portfolio Penguin.
9 Krishnan, A. (2018). *Military Neuroscience and the Coming Age of Neurowarfare*. Abingdon: Routledge, pp. 77–8.

10
Organisational Networks

Networks are a fact of organisational life and flourish spontaneously in any personal or professional setting. As previously discussed, human nature, driven by mutual self-interest and a need to belong, leads people to share ideas and work together even when no one requires them to do so. As they connect around shared interests and knowledge, they build networks that can range in size from fewer than a dozen colleagues and acquaintances to hundreds. Most large corporations have a host of informal networks, which go by the name of peer groups, communities of practice, functional councils or have no title at all.

These networks organise and reorganise organically through word of mouth, face-to-face interactions and through social media. As they widen and deepen, they can mobilise talent and knowledge across a business, and in all likelihood more information and knowledge flows through these informal social networks than through official hierarchical structures. In short, the formal structures of companies, as manifested in their organisational charts, do not explain how much of their day-to-day work actually gets done.

Personal social networks and informal connections between workers increase the value of collaboration in organisations by reducing the search and coordination costs of connecting individuals and teams who have complementary skills and knowledge alongside a shared purpose and interests. A capacity that is only likely to grow in importance as the ability to create value increasingly depends on the ideas and intangibles of knowledge workers. In this data, rich environment leaders will have to do far more to harness the power of informal networks, while at the same time managing the complexity that these ad hoc groups and communities necessarily generate.

In the first place, informal networks rely on serendipity and their effectiveness therefore varies considerably. In large companies several informal networks may form on related topics but never integrate; people with valuable knowledge or skills may not join the most appropriate network or fail to discover that

DOI: 10.4324/9781003092582-16

a network exists; and crucial members, who serve as network hubs to connect others, can hobble or even undermine the network if they become overloaded, hoard knowledge or leave the company.

Further, as organisations have been forced to reshape due to the global pandemic, networks that were formerly connected through propinquity, or proximity, have been strained as more people work from home. New workers working remotely can struggle to make sense of their new workplace without the informal network to guide them.

Adding to the complexity is that not all networks will be visible to senior management, and even when they are, it's hard for organisations to take full advantage of them because they follow different rules. Conversely, unintended barriers, corporate politics and simple neglect can keep natural networks from flourishing. At worst, informal networks can make dysfunctional organisations even more so by adding complexity, muddling roles and increasing the intensity of corporate politics. While naturally occurring bonds can contribute to team efficiency, through a shared identity, they can also inhibit communication and collaboration with other groups, because they run the risk of becoming tribal. Other teams are then seen as "them", not "us", and collaboration can be poor, non-existent, even antagonistic.

Understanding Organisational Networks

There are many analytical frameworks for understanding the context in which organisations operate: PEST, Political, Economic, Social and Technological; PESTLEI, which adds Legal, Environmental and Information; PMESII, a US military model, which includes Military, Infrastructure and Information; as well as STEEPLE, RESPECT, ASCOPE and so the list goes on. Similarly, when it comes to the organisation itself, we can describe it in terms of its goals, its ownership, the sector in which it operates, its size, its scale, its scope and activities, the process by which it transforms inputs into outputs and its governance. All good quantifiable stuff. But the danger with each of these approaches is, paradoxically, that they are too analytical.

Analysis means to break things down, to reduce things or ideas into smaller parts in order to gain a better understanding of them. While this can often work for things that are complicated, it doesn't work as well for social networks which are complex. Things that are complicated may have multiple parts, but those parts are joined and operate based on cause and effect. The working of a jet engine, for example, might be confusing, but ultimately it can be broken down into a series of clear deterministic relationships, which mean you can predict what will happen if any part of the device is damaged or altered. In short, complicated problems are puzzles, they may require great effort but ultimately they yield to prediction.

Complexity, however, is by its very nature unpredictable and, despite advances in tracking and measuring using artificial intelligence, remains fundamentally incompatible with analytical and reductionist models. A leader will not truly understand the business in which they work by studying production, sales and customer service as separate entities any more than a biologist will understand an ecosystem by studying its constituent species in isolation. The danger is that we assume we can.

We operate under the assumption that the system in which we work will transform our day-to-day tasks into larger, longer-term gains and, consequently, our short-term work is valuable to the organisation. But to what extent is that simply a leap of faith? How much do we actually know about the end-to-end operations of the organisations in which we work: the informal communication channels, the handoffs and deals between departments and teams as well as the friction of political walls, structural gaps and personal animosities? If you were to look more closely, would you see a complicated, but deliberate, strategy of cause and effect or a complex patchwork of workarounds, political truces, informal agreements and shadow systems?

Ruthanne Huising, a professor at Emlyon Business School in France, conducted research to try and find out.[1] She analysed the activities of six project teams in five organisations. The teams were made up of 52 people in total (48 of whom participated in the study) and were tasked with projects like redesigning a major product process, customer service or claims procedure. Four of these organizations were Fortune 500 companies in natural resources, high technology, durable products and consumer goods sectors. The fifth was a midsize regional insurance company.

Her key finding, which accords well with our own experience, is that despite being experienced managers, seeing the "bigger picture" of their organisations was a revelation to all her subjects. As she relates:

> They had never seen the pieces—the jobs, technologies, tools, and routines—connected in one place, and they realized that their prior view was narrow and fractured. A team member acknowledged, "I only thought of things in the context of my span of control."

This lack of perspective, Huising writes, is common for three reasons. First, as we do our jobs and build our careers, we pay limited attention to how the organisations we work in are designed and operated as a system. Instead, we typically focus on our day-to-day work, interacting primarily with the people needed to get that work done. Second, organisations do not willingly lend themselves to being analysed. This is particularly true in large, complex organizations where the division of labour, functional boundaries and centralised authority generate partial and myopic views. Third, what we know about the systems in which we work is very different from what we know about working within these systems. We may be skilled at executing our role, but we often do so without being aware of how the organisation (just like the networks in which we exist) is shaping and being shaped by what we do.

Consequently, change happens, if at all, on an improvised or ad hoc basis, solutions are implemented in isolation and there is seldom any overall plan or guiding hand. Many of the rules that people find onerous and bureaucratic were put in place to deal with real abuses, problems, or inconsistencies, or as a way of managing complex environments. But while each rule may have been instituted for good reason, after a while a tangle of rules develop that make no sense in aggregate. The danger is that the company becomes overwhelmed by well-intended rules that reduce overall efficiency and effectiveness.

The study highlights just how infrequently we recognise how poorly designed and managed many of our organisations really are; we simply do not understand the system. Ironically, however, this may be a good thing. Not acknowledging the dysfunction of existing routines may in fact protect us from seeing how much of our work is wasted effort. In conclusion, Huising writes:

> Knowledge of the systems we work in can be a source of power, yes. But when you realize you can't affect the big changes your organization needs, it can also be a source of alienation.

This is a point to which we will return when we consider the requirement in Network Leaders for restless persuasion. But first we need to consider another very familiar problem for organisations, which also emerges from a lack of broader organisational perspective – the crippling tendency to operate in stovepipes or silos.

The Silo Effect

Silos are used on farms to prevent different grains from mixing; in organisations, silos are a euphemism for the limited interaction and flow of information that can occur between teams and departments. The silo effect can be found in the silent acquiescence of service heads in meetings; the lack of shared understanding across business units; messy and incomplete hand-offs between departments; competitive pay and incentives that set individuals and teams against each other; planning meetings where key players from other departments are missing; and in a host of other instances where competing priorities, cross-functional rivalry and simple ignorance overwhelm and outweigh collaboration.

In Creativity Inc. Ed Catmull describes silos in the following manner[2]:

> In animation we have many constituencies: story, art, budget, technology, finance, production, marketing, and consumer products. The people within each constituency have priorities that are important – and often opposing. The writer and director want to tell the most affecting story possible; the production designer wants the film to look beautiful; the technical directors want flawless effects; finance wants to keep the budgets within limits; marketing wants a hook that is easily sold to potential viewers; the consumer products people want appealing characters to turn into plush toys and to plaster on lunchboxes and T-shirts; the production managers try to keep everyone happy – and to keep the whole thing from spiralling out of control. And so on. Each group is focused on its own needs, which means that no one has a clear view of how their decisions impact other groups; each group is under pressure to perform well, which means achieving stated goals … Each group is trying to do the right thing, but they're pulling in different directions.

Catmull concludes with the observation:

> If any one of those groups 'wins', we lose … In a healthy culture they all understand that achieving balance is the central goal of the company.

While most leaders and managers recognise the importance of breaking down silos and instead building strong connections to help people work across departmental boundaries, they often struggle to make it happen because vertical (hierarchical) relationships in organisations, the people you report to and those who report to you, usually take precedence over the horizontal (lateral) relationships with colleagues in other departments. And this causes two principal problems.

The first is that these horizontal relationships often create most value for customers. The integrated, seamless solutions that most customers want require the tricky, horizontal collaborations with which most organisations struggle. The second is that many of the greatest innovation and business development opportunities happen at the edges, at the interfaces between teams, functions and departments, the places where different ideas and ways of doing things collide.

One way to overcome these issues is to try and break down silos by redesigning the organisational structure, but wholesale organisational redesign, depending upon the scale of ambition, can be costly, confusing and slow. And while every new structure solves some problems, it usually creates others. Matrix organizational structures, for example, in which people report to two or more bosses (often operational and functional reporting lines), can be infuriatingly hard to navigate without strong leadership and accountability.[3] There are of course examples of new organisational forms, from flatarchies to holocracies, but these tend to work in smaller organisations and start-ups. Larger organisations struggle to realise such radical restructuring unless they have grown in this way from the start, such as Zappos and WG Gore.

Instead, we are suggesting a more nuanced and realistic understanding of organisations, one that recognises and accommodates their inherent complexity as human systems, as social networks, rather than simply complicated machines.

As Krackhardt and Hanson observe:

> Many executives invest considerable resources in restructuring their companies, drawing and redrawing organizational charts only to be disappointed by the results. That's because much of the real work of companies happens despite the formal organization. Often what needs attention is the informal organization, the networks of relationships that employees form across functions and divisions to accomplish tasks fast. These informal networks can cut through formal reporting procedures to jump start stalled initiatives and meet extraordinary deadlines. But informal networks can just as easily sabotage companies' best laid plans by blocking communication and fomenting opposition to change unless managers know how to identify and direct them. Learning how to map these social links can help managers harness the real power in their companies and revamp their formal organizations to let the informal ones thrive.[4]

What is required is an appreciation of the messy complexity of the informal networks that exist in all organisations and a way of visualising them, with the explicit aim of identifying the gaps in connectivity but also finding the natural human connections that will already undoubtedly exist at some interfaces and thereby gain a measure of control over how these informal networks might be encouraged to grow in future. One method that we have found particularly helpful is Social Network Analysis.

Notes

1 Huising, R. (2019). Can You Know Too Much About Your Organization? (online) *Harvard Business Review*, December 04, 2019. Available at https://hbr.org/2019/12/can-you-know-too-much-about-your-organization (accessed 17 April 2021).

2 Catmull, E. (2014). *Creativity Inc.* London: Bantam Press, pp. 137–9.
3 It is worth reading Bryan, L., Matson, E. and Weiss, L. (2007). *Harnessing the Power of Informal Employee Networks*. It describes how networks of natural professional communities operating within an organisation might be formalised to improve the efficiency and effectiveness of matrix structures. Available at https://www.mckinsey.com/business-functions/organization/our-insights/harnessing-the-power-of-informal-employee-networks.
4 Krackhardt, D. and Hanson, J.R. (1993). Informal Networks: The Company behind the Chart. *Harvard Business Review*, July–August 1993, pp. 53–61.

11

Social Network Analysis

Social Network Analysis (SNA) is a method for visualising and understanding human networks. It is designed to locate influential groups or individuals and map the connections between them, thereby helping us to quantify and understand the dynamics of social systems. Organisational Network Analysis (ONA) is the name given to SNA within businesses and institutions, where it is used to build a 2D picture of the people, groups, tasks, knowledge and resources of organisational systems. Together, SNA and ONA are part of a broader trend in the field of People Analytics, using statistical insights from employee data to better understand human resource issues such as diversity and inclusion, innovation and employee performance. In short, it is a powerful means for making visible informal patterns of collaboration and information flow.[1]

An organisational chart or organogram is a crude representation of an organisation's social network. It is a schematic diagram which aims to capture the complexity of an organisation in a logical cause and effect diagram, showing its structure in terms of the reporting relationships between individuals, departments and teams. But the truth is that organisations only look like this on paper (Figure 3.2).

In reality, they look more like this, where the nodes (individual people) are represented by coloured shapes and the ties or edges (connections) between them are represented by dark lines (Figure 3.3).

It would be an error, however, to draw a distinction between social networks and hierarchies. A hierarchy is simply a special kind of social network with restricted numbers of horizontal connections, enabling a single ruling node to maintain a high degree of control. The essence of any autocracy, a strictly enforced hierarchy, is that the nodes further down the organisational chart cannot communicate with one another, much less organise, without going through the central node. The correct distinction to make is between hierarchical networks and distributed networks.[2]

DOI: 10.4324/9781003092582-17

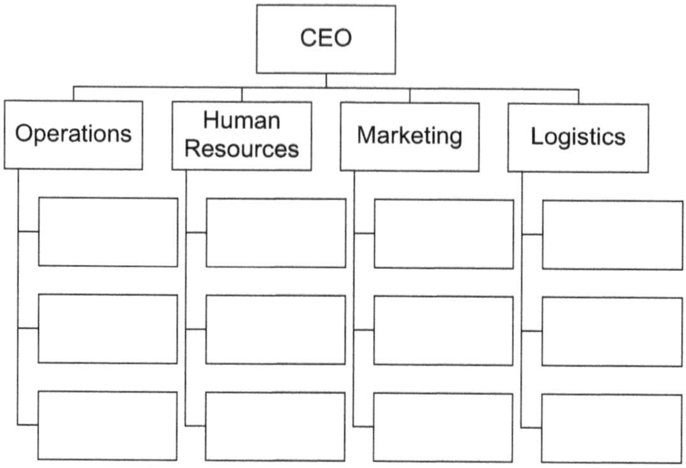

Figure 3.2 Organisational Chart.

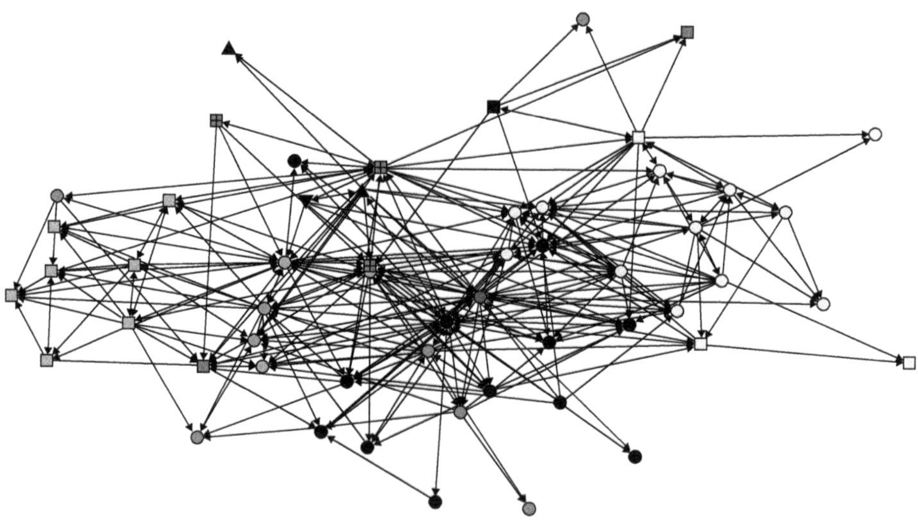

Figure 3.3 Social Network.

It would also be an error to suppose that hierarchies are alien to proper human functioning. On the contrary, we are hierarchy-seeking animals and they serve an important evolutionary purpose. According to Jon Maner, Professor of Psychology at Florida State University, "The human mind is, quite literally, designed to live within hierarchically arranged groups".[3] So attuned are we to dominance hierarchies that they emerge very quickly within groups of strangers who are given a task to complete.

As Matthew Syed explains,[4] most teams function better with a chain of command because hierarchy creates a division of labour where leaders can focus on the big picture leaving others to grapple with the detail. It also ensures that teams coordinate their actions. Without a hierarchy, team members can fall to arguing among themselves about what to do next, which can be disruptive and dangerous. Google, for example, took an early decision to get rid of all their managers and create an entirely flat structure, but it didn't work. The lack of a hierarchy created chaos. They quickly realised that Google needed managers to set direction and facilitate collaboration.

Similarly, the organisational chart or organogram is valuable in that it enables us to visualize a complete organisation. The problem is that it only shows the formal hierarchical relationships and tells us nothing about the pattern of informal human relationships, which has two principal drawbacks:

1. It can constrain thought and action, forcing us down artificial tramlines in terms of how we act and what we expect. Communication and instruction go down and responses or reports of action come back up, and it is poor form to jump the chain of command (up or down) or communicate laterally without seeking permission from above first.
2. It is manifestly incomplete, hiding gaps and blockages as well as alternative lines of connectivity. It leaves uncharted a vast terrain of connection and disconnection, which can make or break change, strangle innovation and cripple day-to-day operations.

There are times when it makes sense for a dominant leader to make decisions and for everyone else to fall into line, particularly when the requirement is for speed and coordination. But in situations of complexity, hierarchy suppresses collective intelligence, which hinges upon the expression of diverse perspectives and insights, because dissent is often perceived as a threat to the status of the leader.[5] Effective decision-making in complex situations requires the free flow of information through social networks. Groups typically need a leader; otherwise there is a risk of conflict and indecision. And yet the leader will make wise choices only if they gain access to the diverse views of the group.

Intuitively, we all know this. The term *hierarchical* is a pejorative, shorthand for a workplace that puts too much emphasis on rank and slavishly following the procedural pecking order. It is the same with *bureaucracy*, which has become a catchall term for the many ways in which organisations squander workers' potential, from needless paperwork to delusional project timelines and administrative overheads that prevent workers from doing the meaningful tasks that actually contribute to the organisation's bottom line.

Yet despite these drawbacks organisations still tend to be understood as formal hierarchies with their attendant bureaucratic procedures. We accept that because in any process involving hundreds of people a chain of command is essential. Hierarchies and structured bureaucratic environments have been designed to help large groups of people work together and excising them from organisations would be nearly impossible. Projects that involve complex technical work must be tracked and coordinated across departments, budgets must be accounted for and costs must be kept in line. Both authors have worked in highly structured, hierarchical environments that inspired high quality work and a healthy environment between colleagues. And many organisations do a good job in protecting their workers from the detrimental effects of documentation, schedules, expense accounting and budget statements. But not all. When poorly managed hierarchy and bureaucracy impede innovation and productivity.

At an individual level they cause problems when people begin to equate their own value and that of others with where they fall in the pecking order. Assigning personal worth based on rank can cause people to focus their energy on managing upward while neglecting people beneath them in the hierarchy. And this attitude causes a problem for even the best managers, because their view is obstructed by those people who are skilled at figuring out what their manager wants.

When viewed from within, a full picture of the dynamics of any group is elusive. A manager might rely on other people to alert him or her to a particular employee's lack of authenticity, but many are loath to tell tales or risk sounding envious. While we are all aware of these kinds of behaviours, most of us do not realise how they distort our own view of the world, largely because we think we see more than we actually do. It may not occur to people after they get promoted to a leadership position that people may be less candid with them. Instead, many new leaders assume wrongly that their access to information is unchanged or better than before. This may be true in terms of an organisation's operational and strategic planning, but they are unlikely to see the levels below them with as much clarity as they once did.

SNA provides an alternative lens through which to view organisational systems as well as a language to help explain and act within them, one which is dynamic, emergent, lateral and even bottom-up. In our current context, one characterised by volatility, uncertainty, complexity and ambiguity (VUCA), leaders must do more than set strategic direction, inspire others and drive execution. They also need to establish strong network performance by convening, building, aligning and enabling broad networks, both within and beyond the bounds of their teams, organisations and communities.

As Stanley McChrystal observed,[6] following his experiences in the conflicted environments of Iraq and Afghanistan, at an organisational level complexity has rendered reductionist management ineffective. While efficiency is necessary, it is no longer sufficient for successful organisations. Reductionism and top down, command and control worked in the 20th century, but is now quickly overwhelmed by the speed and hugely exaggerated impact of networks, such as terrorists, start-ups, social movements and viral trends. To which we can now add biological viruses.

McChrystal's view is that management models based on planning and predicting are no longer suited to today's challenges. Instead, organisations must be resilient and adaptive to changing circumstances. To survive and thrive, they must be networked, not rigidly hierarchical. The goal is to shift from efficiency to sustained organisational adaptability, which requires dramatic changes in mental and organisational models and approaches as well as sustained efforts on the part of leadership to create the environment for such change.

In the business world, some of the most notable examples of this approach are companies like Alphabet, Amazon, Alibaba, Airbnb, eBay, Facebook and Netflix. These are platform companies with network-based business models, who have proved themselves to be exponentially better at creating value than companies organised around products and services. Companies like Facebook, Twitter and LinkedIn applied this principle by focusing relentlessly on improving the user experience while giving away their advertising-free product. This was a radical concept at the time, but made sense because the real potential occurs after critical mass.

In the early 1990s, George Glider postulated a theory that changed how we think about networks from telephones to the Internet and social networks. He called his theory Metcalfe's Law, named after the founder of Ethernet. Metcalfe's law states that the value of a telecommunications network is proportional to the square of the number of connected users of the system and was originally presented in terms of compatible communicating devices such as telephones rather than users. The law was often illustrated using the example of fax machines: a single fax machine is useless, but the value of every fax machine increases as the total number of fax machines in the network increases, because the total number of people with whom each user may send and receive documents increases. Likewise, in social networks, the greater number of people the more valuable the network becomes.

In the parlance of SNA, the value of a network increases as its relative density increases, that is, the percentage of people in your network who are connected against the number that could be. By increasing density, new things spread more quickly through it and we dramatically increase the rate at which participants learn from each other and deepen their relationships.

However, while the likes of Amazon and Alibaba are internet-enabled platforms, platforms and networks are not solely digital. They are a business and mental model that can be developed in many ways and in many different environments, within businesses as well as beyond. The medieval marketplace was a platform business model. A place provided for the exchange of goods and services. The London coffee shops of the 17th- and 18th-century Enlightenment were places of conversation, social movement and commerce. They formed the basis of the London Stock Exchange and Lloyds of London, to name just a few. The overlapping networks of ideas and people are key to understanding platforms and the network approach.

However, the traditional way of thinking about value creation is linear and incremental. A process turns inputs into outputs and the value is in the products and services themselves. The new way of thinking about value creation is networked and exponential. In the language of networks, the value of the platform provider is not necessarily in creating the nodes (services, things, data and people) but in fostering value through the creation and nurturing of connections between the nodes.

It is our contention that the Fourth Industrial Age, which enabled network organisations, also requires them. It enabled them because of the continuing evolution of the internet and the tools that are continually being developed for coordination and collaboration. It requires them because knowledge must be utilised regardless of where it is found in an organisation, and it cannot be assumed only to be located where the organisation chart says it should be. The question then is: how do we find it?

Social Capital

Whether you work in manufacturing, service provision or the knowledge economy, it is relatively straightforward to measure and track the quantitative data of economic capital, relating to inputs, outputs and return on investment (ROI). It is less easy, however, to track the equally important contribution of social capital, the quality of our interpersonal working relationships toward the achievement of positive outcomes.

Social capital was popularised at the turn of this century by Robert Putnam. In his book, *Bowling Alone*,[7] he argued that America was undergoing a long steady decline in "social capital", by which he meant the strength of civic and community connections from labour-union membership and cross-party political collaboration to community involvement and marriage rates. In business terms, social capital is believed to enhance the performance of companies through lowering transaction costs and increasing productivity, through the exchange of ideas, information and improved ways of working, in other words an effective and efficient exchange of who has what, who needs what and who can do what.

In further work, Putnam discussed the role of networks in defining what constitutes a healthy community and introduced to the wider public the concepts of bonding and bridging social capital after the work of Mark Granovetter,[8] which we mentioned previously as strong and weak ties, respectively. Broadly speaking, bonding social capital is found within groups and bridging social capital is found between groups. Bonding social capital (strong ties) acts as the "social cement", bringing teams and communities closer together around shared norms and practices, whereas bridging social capital (weak ties) offers access to wider horizons, encouraging members to move beyond their own team or community and take advantage of new ideas and opportunities. Non-Executive Directors and consultants are a good example of weak links, because they create network links between the multiple firms they serve. They create connections between otherwise disparate groups of people and, if motivated to do so, can enable the spread of innovation and ideas.

The key of course is to find a balance between strong and weak ties. While increasing the density of social connections within groups can improve solidarity, it may insulate the group from beneficial influences from outside the group. In dense clusters of strong connections, information tends to become homogenous and redundant because it is known by all. A further danger is that bonding social capital can become exclusionary and inward looking, leading community members to view the outside world with suspicion. It can also lead to pressure on group members to comply with dominant community norms, which, in turn, become further mechanisms for exclusion and the rejection of "foreign" ideas. Those within the group benefit from its protection and help, while outsiders are seen as competitors and therefore distrusted.

So while strong ties bind individuals together into groups, weak ties bind groups together into the larger society and are crucial for spreading new information and ideas. Alex Pentland, a computer scientist and Professor at the Massachusetts Institute of Technology (MIT), argues for the value of strong and weak ties in creating culture, supporting productivity and enabling creativity.[9] As Pentland observes:

> By making group members more aware of the patterns of communication within and between groups we are improving their social intelligence, which leads to greater productivity and creative output. Managers need to

> visualize patterns of internal and external communication and take steps to make sure that ideas flow within and between all of their work groups.[10]

Pentland argues that the spreading of ideas through social networks, whether by example or story, is how traditions and ultimately culture develop. "Idea Flow", as he calls it, facilitates the transfer of habits and customs from person to person and from generation to generation. And each community or culture has its own stream or flow of ideas, which can either insulate a group from outside influences or allow members to incorporate new ideas from other groups. Consequently, we can spur innovation and change by bridging the gaps in human networks and dipping our toes into other streams of ideas and behaviour.

In terms of productivity, Pentland uses the example of work he did in the Bank of America call centre. In call centres the most important measure of productivity is average call handle time (AHT). Analysis of his data revealed that the most important factors for predicting productivity were the overall amount of interaction and the level of engagement among call centre employees. Armed with this analysis it was possible to fine tune network performance. In this case by changing the structure of coffee breaks and giving breaks to whole teams at a time, not just individuals, which increased the level of informal interaction and engagement among the teams. As a result, AHT sharply decreased, demonstrating a strong link between interaction patterns and productivity. Such informal interaction allowed employees to learn the tricks of the trade, the kind of tacit knowledge that separates novices from experts; in effect, it created a community of practice. SNA allows you to visualise that interaction.

Network Mapping

A network map (Figure 3.4) is an excellent tool for making networks explicit, visually tracking them over time and monitoring strategies to create new connections.

Figure 3.4 was created by the authors using UCINet Visualisation Software,[11] in order to analyse the relationship dynamics among geographically separate teams who were working together as part of a national public sector project. The network map (alternatively known as a sociogram as opposed to an organogram) helped us to identify where the organisation was resilient and strong and where it was vulnerable and weak. It allowed the leadership to bring out the strengths in the informal network, restructure their formal organisation to complement the informal and "rewire" faulty connections to achieve their organisational goals.

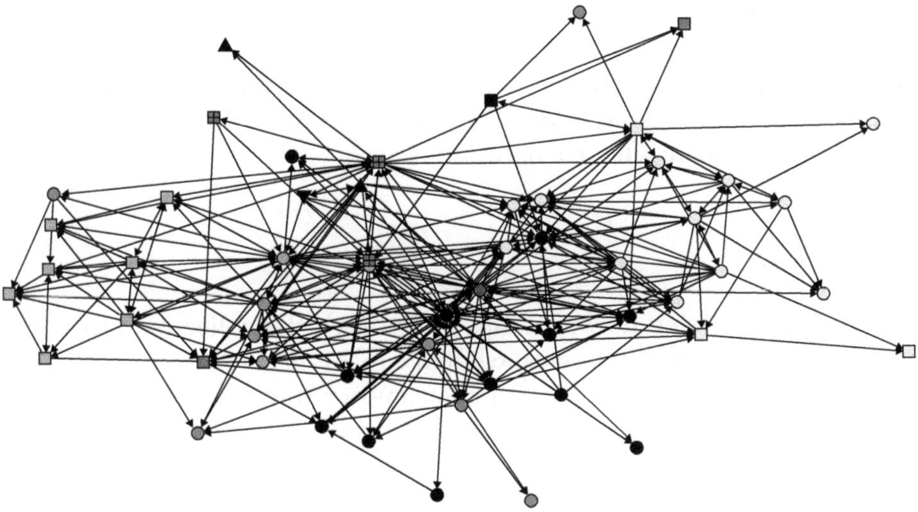

Figure 3.4 Social Network Map.

In other words, the network map helped to analyse and assess the quantity and quality of social capital, the aim being to determine how virtuous circles of positive contact could be best built and maintained over time, how insularity and distrust could be avoided and what value the positive links and relationships provided in the organisation. The results of the analysis were then used to identify environments, social structures and individual practices that were likely to generate cooperation and collaboration and those that were likely to disrupt them, such as geographical separation, departmental silos and individual animosities.

Fundamentally, SNA allows a comparison between the formal structure of an organisation, as laid down in its organisational chart or organogram, with the informal network of relationships based upon such things as family, friends, shared interests and experience (homophily) and physical location (propinquity). Equally, it can help identify the spaces or gaps that exist in networks (where knowledge and resources are not being shared) and how to bridge them. It is also helpful in identifying people's centrality to the network, the degree to which individuals connect other people and groups (the concept of centrality which we mentioned earlier), which often alerts organisations to important but under-reported individuals, those who bind the organisation together but are not recognised as part of the formal hierarchical network.

Ronald Burt coined the term "structural holes"[12] to describe the gaps between individuals or groups with complementary resources or information. When the two are connected directly or indirectly through a third individual, a bridge, the gap is filled, creating important advantages for both parties. In Burt's view, competitive advantage and building social capital is about bridging structural holes, providing access to resources, information, new ideas and new ways of working. People who act as bridges between other individuals and groups are therefore central to an effective network.

Methodology[13]

Drawing and analysing network maps begins with the collection of the raw material or data which can be gleaned from either e-mail exchanges, chats and file transfers (the *digital exhaust* of a company) or through employee surveys based on relational questions. We do the latter, which can be better focused on key problems and is more overt, removing the suspicion that "Big Brother is watching you", monitoring staff email exchanges and conversations! To get a good overall picture of the informal networks in an organisation, a good place to start is with three network questions focusing on communication, advice and trust suggested by David Krackhardt and Jeffrey Hanson,[14] although there are other dimensions that can be examined, innovation and who people get their ideas from for example.

Communication networks reveal who talks to whom about work-related matters, such as news and events, on a regular basis. Mapping communication networks can help diagnose inefficiency and low productivity, on the basis that workers are either spending too much time and energy working the rumour mill, instead of actually working, or they hardly communicate at all, leading to errors, alienation, stress and poor morale. A typical question is "Whom do you talk to every day"?

Advice networks show the prominent members in an organisation on whom others rely to solve problems and provide technical information. These networks are about solving task-related problems and obtaining technical information to perform one's duties. They show influential players in the day-to-day operations of a company and can uncover routine conflicts, recurring disagreements over how things should be done or the assumptions one should be operating by. Advice networks diagnose such disagreements by showing when there are contradictory sources of expertise, unused sources or no sources at all. A typical question is: "Whom do you go to for help or work-related advice at least once a week"?[15]

Trust networks examine the confidence people have in another person's intentions: do I trust them or is there a need to be protective or careful around them. It is often associated with the sharing of confidential or "political" information

> ### The Matrix
>
> Working in an automotive manufacturing plant, James used SNA to examine the flow of work between the engineering, production, quality and supply teams. This identified some key gaps in connection with regard to day-to-day communication, the sharing of advice, knowledge and expertise and a lack of trust. Not trust in the sense of being unreliable or deceitful, but trust in the sense of being open with colleagues; the sort of trust and understanding among colleagues that reduces transactional costs such as people double checking one another's work.
>
> The MD and his senior team decided that the solution was to change the physical layout of the offices. Breaking down the partitions between separate functional offices and creating instead an open-plan office, the layout of which mirrored the matrix structure of how the teams were meant to work, with functional teams in the horizontal rows and value (product) streams of mixed teams in the vertical. The effects were quickly felt, with gains in collaboration, productivity and problem solving.

and the provision of support for one's ideas and proposals. Mapping trust networks will often uncover the source of political conflicts and failure to achieve strategic or change objectives. You should examine trust networks when implementing a major change or experiencing a crisis. A typical question is: "Whom would you trust to keep in confidence your concerns about a work-related issue"?

Trust is perhaps the most powerful question of the three, being the bedrock of high performing teams, but it is also the most emotive, so we sometimes use the term "support" and we always emphasise that in saying you "trust" or "do not trust" a co-worker; it is not a question of whether you think they might or might not steal your wallet or your milk from the communal fridge, but a simple recognition we know and get along with some people better than others, and this affects how efficiently and effectively we work together.

Collection and Analysis

We gather the data using an online survey, with the questions followed by a list or drop-down menu of the colleagues in question (members of your team for instance) and then feed the results into the UCINET software, which creates a combined 2D visualisation and one for each question (communication, advice and trust), which can then be analysed to identify structural holes and relational strengths and weaknesses.

While there are a wide variety of structural issues that can be identified within a network, the following examples, which we have adapted from the work of Paul Leonardi and Noshir Contractor,[16] provide a useful illustration of what can be found, some of which we have already discussed.

Weak Ties (Figure 3.5). The dark grey node shows a person who communicates with people in several other networks besides their own, which makes them more likely to get novel information that may lead to new and innovative ideas. In contrast, the light grey node shows a person who communicates only with people within their network and is therefore less likely to generate ideas, even though they may be creative.

Strong Ties (Figure 3.6). The purple team members are deeply connected with one another, which is an indication that they work well together. And because

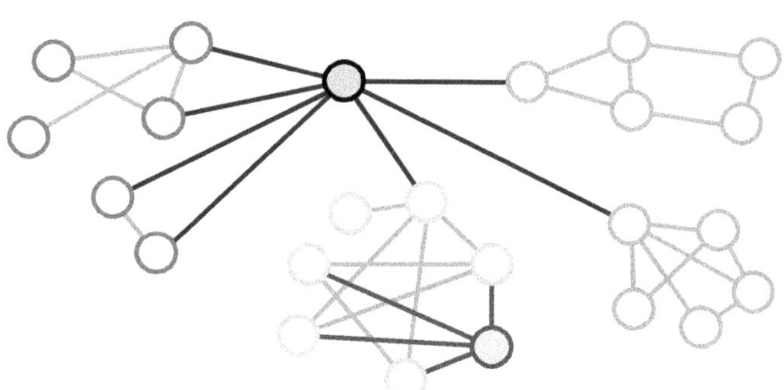

Figure 3.5 Weak Ties.

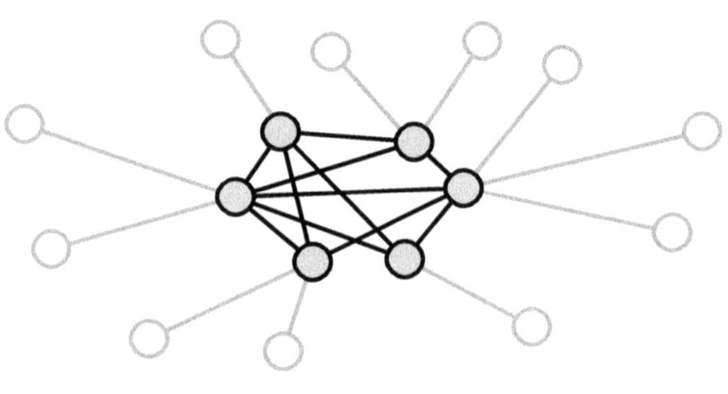

Figure 3.6 Strong Ties.

their external connections don't overlap, the team has access to a wide range of helpful external sources. The ideal arrangement is therefore a combination of "strong ties" within teams and "weak ties" between them.

Influencers (Figure 3.7). Though dark grey connects to only two people, purple is more influential than orange, because purple's connections are better connected. Light grey may spread ideas faster, but purple can spread ideas further because their connections are more connected and therefore influential.

Innovators (Figure 3.8). Dark grey team members aren't deeply interconnected, which suggests they'll have different perspectives and more productive debates. The downside is that conflict may also be higher, but if well managed this could be the grit in the oyster that makes the pearl. The members also have a wide range of external connections, which should help them gain buy-in for their innovations.

Organisational Silos (Figure 3.9). In this example, each colour indicates a different team or department. People within the departments are deeply

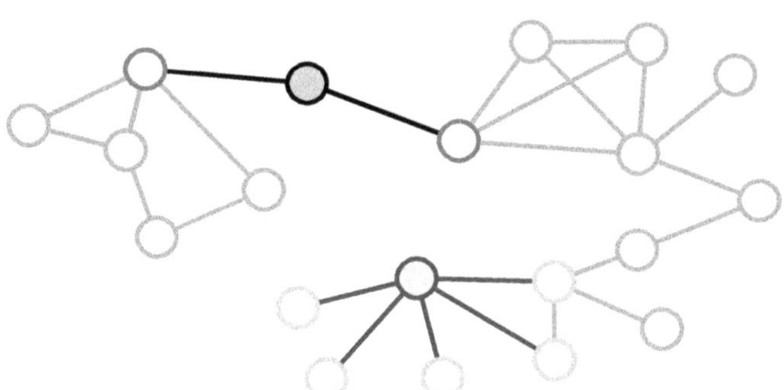

Figure 3.7 Influencers.

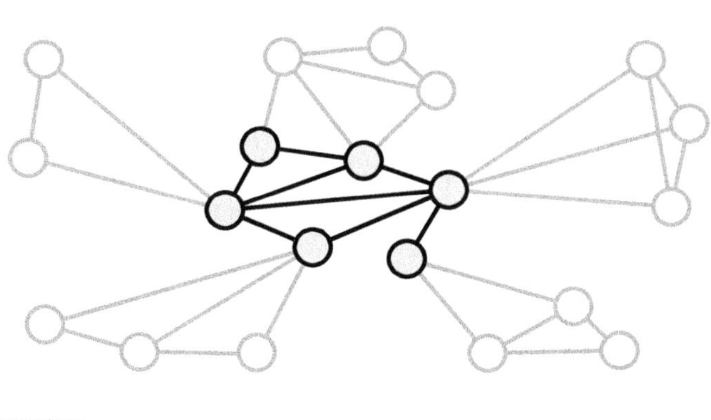

Figure 3.8 Innovators.

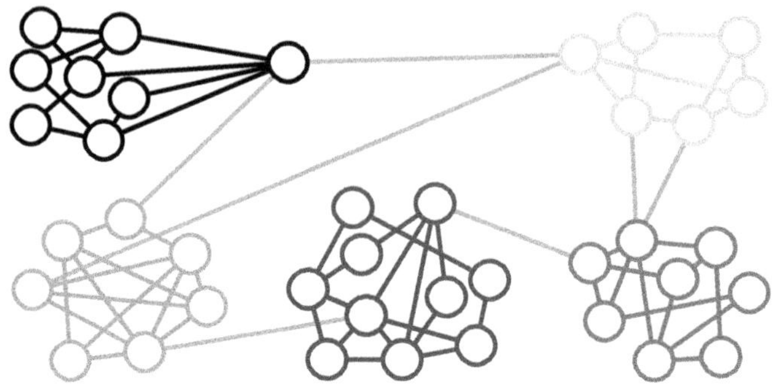

Figure 3.9 Organisational Silos.

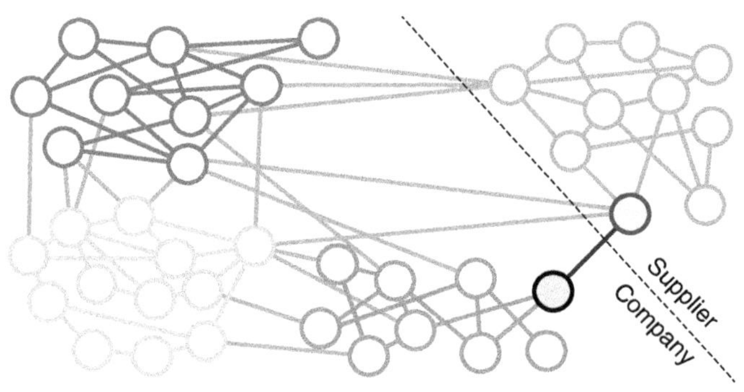

Figure 3.10 External Vulnerability.

connected, but only one or two people in any department connect with people in other departments. This is classic silo mentality. The teams may work well independently but the organisation may be crippled by poor communication and collaboration.

Vulnerability (Figure 3.10). Light grey is a critical external supplier to company departments grey, dark grey and mid grey. Six people at the company have relationships with green, but 30 other people rely on those relationships, which puts the company at risk. If blue's one connection to green leaves, the department will be cut off from the supplier. While his title may or may not reflect his importance, that employee is vital to information flow.

Managing this complexity requires leaders who can identify and direct informal networks, aligning them where possible with the formal organisational hierarchy, but always in pursuit of efficient and effective action. Not just doing things right but doing the right things. We need leaders and managers who understand the messy complexity of the human systems in which they operate.

In the words of the late Donald Schön, philosopher and professor in urban planning at the MIT, we need "reflective practitioners".[17]

Notes

1 A short history of SNA can be found at Appendix 2.
2 Ferguson, N. (2017). The False Prophecy of Hyperconnection: How to Survive the Networked Age. *Foreign Affairs*, September/October 2017, pp. 68–79.
3 Maner, J.K. (2017). Dominance and Prestige: A Tale of Two Hierarchies. (online) Available at https://journals.sagepub.com/doi/10.1177/0963721417714323 (accessed 17 April 2021).
4 Syed, M. (2019). *Rebel Ideas: The Power of Diverse Thinking*. London: John Murray.
5 Syed, M. (2019) ibid., pp. 92–3.
6 McChrystal, S., Collins, T., Silverman, D. and Fussell, C. (2015). *Team of Teams: New Rules of Engagement for a Complex World*. UK: Portfolio Penguin.
7 Putnam, R.D. (2001). *Bowling Alone: The Collapse and Revival of American Community*. New York: Simon & Schuster.
8 Granovetter, M.S. (1973). The Strength of Weak Ties. *American Journal of Sociology*, 78(6), pp. 1360–80.
9 Pentland, A. (2014). *Social Physics: How Good Ideas Spread: The Lessons from a New Science*. London: Penguin Press.
10 Pentland, A. (2014) ibid.
11 https://sites.google.com/site/ucinetsoftware/home.
12 Burt, R.S. (1995). *Structural Holes*. Cambridge, MA: Harvard University Press.
13 The British Home Office provides a "How to guide" for SNA, which is intended to help police forces undertake SNA of local gang issues. Available at https://assets.publishing.service.gov.uk/government/uploads/system/uploads/attachment_data/file/491572/socnet_howto.pdf.
14 Krackhardt, D. and Hanson, J.R. (1993). Informal Networks: The Company behind the Chart. *Harvard Business Review*, July–August 1993, pp. 53–61.
15 The use of a time qualifier, "every day" or "once a week" is designed to identify the key communication and advice networks rather than people with whom we intermittently interact.
16 Leonardi, P. and Contractor, N. (2018). Better People Analytics. (online) *Harvard Business Review*. Available at https://hbr.org/2018/11/better-people-analytics (accessed 17 April 2021).
17 Schon, D. (1983). *The Reflective Practitioner: How Professionals Think in Action*. New York: Basic Books.

12
The Reflective Practitioner

Schön described "reflective practitioners" as individuals who are able to cope with change and uncertainty by interpreting and responding to particular situations in their area of professional practice. Schön further identified two contrasting and conflicting areas of professional practice. The first was the "high ground" supported by "technical rationality", where manageable problems with a clear end could be tackled through the application of research-based theory to identify suitable means to that end. The second, and he felt more significant dimension, was the "swampy low ground" where the ends are confused and there is no clear problem to solve, what we have called wicked problems.

In the case of the swampy low ground, the professional practitioner must first "name and frame" the problem by setting boundaries and imposing coherence in order to organise and clarify the ends before he or she can consider any possible approaches or means to achieve them. The problem is that these "indeterminate zones" escape the definitions of "technical rationality" upon which much professional practice rests. Consequently, there is a gap between the prevailing conception of professional knowledge and the actual competencies or understanding required of practitioners.

Nevertheless, there are those who do very well in these "indeterminate zones", and it was a study of these individuals that informed Schön's continuing studies. Interestingly, these individuals or "outstanding practitioners" were not said to have more professional knowledge than others but more wisdom, talent, intuition or artistry. They were able to go beyond the available rules, facts, theories and operations, and in effect "remake their practice world".[1] Schön used this as his starting point to explore the relationship between practical competence and understanding, and professional knowledge.

In the first place he observed that professional artistry is only an esoteric, high-powered variant of the more familiar acts of competence that we all routinely exhibit. What he found striking was that competence did not depend upon

DOI: 10.4324/9781003092582-18

individuals being able to describe what they knew or how to do it. By way of explanation he cited our ability to recognise the faces of people we know in a crowd, in which recognition is immediate but we are not aware of any antecedent reasoning. We are not, for instance, consciously comparing the face with images of other faces held in our memory. We simply see the face of the person we know and if someone were to ask us how we did it we would be unable to tell them.

Schön called this skill "knowing-in-action", referring to a type of knowledge that we reveal in our actions, like riding a bike or driving a car. We reveal it by our ability to do it, often without thinking about it and despite being unable to explain exactly how we do it. On occasion, however, a familiar routine that we normally do without thinking produces an unexpected result. For example, the natural reaction of drivers who go into a skid when driving a car is to brake and turn away from the direction of the skid, but this is precisely the wrong thing to do and will produce the unexpected result to which Schön refers. All such experiences, Schön believed, whether pleasant or unpleasant, contain an element of surprise that we will either ignore in an effort to preserve the consistency of our usual patterns of knowing-in-action or explore in order to improve our understanding. The former is commonly known as confirmation bias, our propensity to favour information, whether true or not, which confirms our pre-existing beliefs. The alternative is that we attend to these "surprises" and evaluate them through reflection.

In this case, we either reflect during the action without interrupting it or we may reflect on our action when it is completed. In the former, our thinking serves to reshape what we are doing while we are still doing it and can make a difference to the situation in hand. For instance, we could try and correct our mistake (our natural reaction to the skid) by using trial and error with the results of each trial informing the next; Schön describes this as "reflection-in-action". Alternatively, we may later think back on what we have done (when the car has come to a standstill) to discover how our knowing-in-action may have contributed to the unexpected outcome. In this case, our reflection has no direct connection to the present action but may affect our future action. Schön described this as "reflection-on-action".

Reflecting-in-action like knowing-in-action is a process that we can deliver without being able to say what we are doing. Taken to its highest form, reflection-in-action is the skill of the outstanding practitioner, who knows instinctively the best course of action and can navigate through uncharted waters with apparent ease, the sort of artistry that we often call intuition or thinking on your feet and is a skill well worth nurturing in us all. The problem is that it often defies description, even by the practitioner, because:

> it is one thing to reflect-in-action and quite another to be able to reflect on our reflection-in-action so as to produce a good verbal description of it; and it is still another thing to be able to reflect on the resulting description[2]

Consequently, this "artistry" is a difficult concept to teach, let alone learn.

A useful German idiom for this "artistry" or instinct is fingerspitzengefühl, literally "fingertips feeling", which also describes great situational understanding and the ability to respond most appropriately. It comes from the German military and describes the ability of some commanders to maintain, with great accuracy and attention to detail, an ever-changing operational and tactical mental map of the battlefield.

Unlike a conventional map, which allows us to decide upon a suitable route for getting from one point to another, in times of war the troops, the weapons and even the terrain on a map change much more rapidly than cartographers can update them. So a commander with fingerspitzengefühl would hold such a map in their mind and adjust it by incorporating any significant information that was received. It is intended to evoke a commander who is in such intimate communication with the battlefield that it is as though he has a fingertip on each critical point. It is synonymous with the English expression of "keeping your finger on the pulse", and from a network perspective, it is about having a feel for all the moving parts in your network and how you align them to achieve your goals.

Cognitively, it is related to personal possession of multiple intelligences, notably those pertinent to visual and spatial data processing. The term suggests that in addition to any discursive processing of information that the commander may be conducting, such as mentally considering a specific plan, they are also establishing cognitive relationships between disparate pieces of information as they arrive and constantly developing their mental model of the battlefield. Though there is no physical connection between the commander and his troops other than conduits for the flow of information such as radio signals, it is as if the commander had their own sensitive presence in each spot.

Great leaders appear to do this intuitively, they reflect-in-action, knowing what to do or say almost unconsciously, based on the processing of experience and cumulative knowledge. Some would even describe it as innate, alluding to what was formerly known as "Great Man" theories of leadership or Heroic Leadership, which we discussed in Chapter 3, where leaders are born, not made. This is not something we ascribe to. For us, intuition, fingerspitzengefühl and reflection-in-action are born of experience and can therefore be quantified and their development accelerated by conscious practice and reflective thinking.

In the first place by asking the right questions of yourself and then of others, which is what Schön describes as "reflection-on-action".

Reflection-on-action is more approachable and trainable. It is the ability to stand back from an action, whether familiar or unfamiliar, and consider why you did what you did. It has a particular role to play in professional practice, which involves repetition. A professional practitioner will encounter certain types of situation many times and will therefore develop a repertoire of expectations, images and techniques. In other words, he or she learns what to look for and how to respond to what they find. As a result, they become less and less prone to surprise and confer upon their colleagues and clients the benefits of their specialisation, what may eventually be described as their artistry or intuition.

However, a high degree of specialisation can also lead to a parochial narrowness of vision, and a practitioner can be drawn into patterns of error that go uncorrected and ignore or trivialise phenomena outside their experience and expectations. In other words, they brush it aside or selectively do not attend to the signals. It is important therefore to maintain a capacity for reflection-on-action, allowing us to experience surprise, puzzlement or confusion with a view to constructing a new understanding of the situation rather than assuming it is a problem with which we are familiar. In short, it serves as a corrective to our innate subjective bias.

Typically, we imagine consciousness (our unique awareness of what happens in the world) to be something that happens inside our brains, but Alva Noë argues in a similar vein to actor network theory that it exists in dynamic relationship with our environment. For good and bad, human thought and behaviour expresses the influence of the context we inhabit:

> prejudice constrains us like a straitjacket when we are trying to understand what we are and how we work. We spend all our lives embodied, environmentally situated, with others. We are not merely recipients of external influences but are creatures built to receive influences that we ourselves enact; we are dynamically coupled with the world, not separate from it.[3]

This is crucially important when we try to understand the systems and context in which we live and work. And, just as individuals have biases and jump to conclusions because of the network of influences through which they understand the world, so do organisations. They also perceive the world, albeit collectively, through what they already know and do, but instead of personal preference or prejudice we call it culture – the way we do things around here.

While we do not dispute the need for hierarchy at times, in today's world of networking and collaboration software, big data, analytics and massive scale

The Semmelweis Reflex

Seeing the world from other people's point of view is not easy, because when we see things that challenge our mental models we tend to resist, ridicule and ignore them. This is confirmation bias, our tendency to favour information, which confirms our pre-existing beliefs. A cruel case in point is known as the Semmelweis Reflex.

The term derives from the name of a Hungarian physician, Ignaz Semmelweis, who discovered in 1847 that childbed fever mortality rates fell ten-fold when doctors disinfected their hands with a chlorine solution before moving from one patient to another.

However, despite the overwhelming empirical evidence that his procedure saved lives, his fellow doctors rejected his hand-washing suggestions, some refusing to believe that a gentleman's hands could transmit disease. In 1865, the increasingly outspoken Semmelweis, supposedly suffering from a nervous breakdown, was committed to an asylum by his colleague. He died a mere 14 days later, at the age of 47, after being beaten by his guards.

Semmelweis's practice only earned widespread acceptance years after his death, when Louis Pasteur confirmed germ theory, and Joseph Lister, acting on the French microbiologist's research, practised and operated using hygienic methods, with great success. What we always need to keep in mind, therefore, is that our mental models aren't reality; they are tools like the models weather forecasters use to predict the weather. The tool is not reality and the key is knowing the difference.

pattern recognition through artificial intelligence, we think it imprudent to continue to simply assume a static, hierarchical model of organisations for the convenience of seeing how to manage it. Now that firms' activities are so intertwined and their successes so interdependent, the old tools and techniques will no longer always work. Richard Straub puts it like this:

> To succeed in the era of platforms and partnerships, managers will need to change practice on many levels. And with the new practices of ecosystem management must come new management theory, also reoriented around a larger-scale system-level view. Both practitioners and scholars can begin by dispensing with mechanistic, industrial-age models of inputs, processes, and outputs. They will have to take a more dynamic, organic, and evolutionary view of how organizations' capacities grow and can be cultivated.[4]

In short, traditional models of hierarchical leadership and management are still necessary but no longer sufficient, and a more contemporary understanding of organisational structure is required, one which sees organisations as shared processes and individuals as deeply embedded in networks, which, in turn, allow them to harness both organisational hierarchies and social networks to get things done.

Notes

1 Schon, D.A. (1987). *Educating the Reflective Practitioner: Toward a New Design for Teaching and Learning in the Professions*. San Francisco: Jossey-Bass.
2 Schon, D. A. (1987) ibid.
3 Noë, A. (2009). *Out of Our Heads: Why You Are Not Your Brain, and Other Lessons from the Biology of Consciousness*. New York: Hill & Wang, p. 181.
4 Straub, R. (2019). What Management Needs to Become in an Era of Ecosystems. (online) *Harvard Business Review*. Available at https://hbr.org/2019/06/what-management-needs-to-become-in-an-era-of-ecosystems (accessed 17 April 2021).

Summary

The purpose of this section has been to illustrate the components, dynamics and different perspectives of the social networks within which we all inevitably work and exist. It also includes an introduction to Social Network Analysis (SNA) to help visualise some of the elements and connections within such networks. It has been done with the explicit intention of helping understand and manage social systems and to facilitate more efficient and effective action. The value of a network approach, we believe, is in allowing us to define the problem environment, if not the problem or solution, and then, map in hand, act with greater awareness and foresight.

Our approach also resonates with much of our current culture, one that is increasingly mediated through internet-enabled social networks and platform business models. Fundamentally, it builds upon our innate human desire to socialise and collaborate and helps reinforce the notion that we are all actors within networks, which we can influence to a degree but which, in turn, influence us and which, in large part, we often struggle to comprehend. Network Leadership is an approach that recognises complexity and consequently the importance of network maps and sociograms to help illuminate the reality of organisations and wicked problems.

At an individual level, this requires an approach to reflective practice that encompasses both reflection-in-action, essentially intuition or thinking on your feet, and reflection-on-action, which is an open-minded and impartial receptiveness to new ideas on the understanding that a propensity for deliberate reflection, if practised over a long enough period, will develop and refine our intuitive capabilities. In short, we must hone our capacity to reflect-on-action and approach each situation with an eye for the ever new.

DOI: 10.4324/9781003092582-19

Leadership Questions

Ram Charan, the business writer and consultant, observes that:

> You have to be able to determine what critical decisions and trade-offs must get made, and by whom, to accomplish your business goals.[1]

In other words, leaders need to know how to bring the right people together at the right frequency with the right information to make decisions. And, how do you build operating mechanisms at the critical intersections, the places where information must be exchanged, conflict surfaced and resolved and decisions must be made for specific business purposes?

The leadership question to consider, therefore, is: against my purpose, aim or objectives, what are the gaps (the missing critical intersections) in my network and how can I fill them? Consider your answer from the perspective of your current situation and the future using the prompts below.

Now

1. What is the purpose of the existing operating mechanisms?
2. How do they and their linkages combine to help deliver results?
3. Which ones should be kept, eliminated or combined?
4. Which require a total redesign and a new way to lead them?

Future

1. When you map your network, where are you strong?
2. Where is your bonding and bridging capital?
3. What are the key intersections across your network?
4. Who are the key influencers?
5. What is missing?

Note

1 Charan, R. (2008). *Know-How: The 8 Skills that Separate People Who Perform from Those Who Don't*. London: Random House.

Part IV

Convening Power

Authority is often described as the right to command and control other people, and in organisations it derives from rank and position in the hierarchy. But in Network Leadership authority is derived from the root word "authority" that means to author or write, which we use to mean having something to say that is worth listening to, which, in turn, is founded upon a personal manifesto, a declaration of your core values and beliefs, what you stand for and how you intend to live your life. It gives meaning and direction, reminding you of your priorities, motivating and inspiring you to live your purpose more fully. And, if it is worth listening to, it can also serve as a framework for others: acting as both a statement of principles and as a call to action.

This is convening power, an attractive power that is able mobilise an existing movement or create a new one, much like the World Bank's description of convening as "bringing together relevant actors to act collectively to address global or regional development challenges".[1] Significantly, Network Leaders define and fill the space in the system in which they wish to lead, instead of targeting the next place in the hierarchy from which to wield greater positional power. Positional influence can be extremely helpful but will only get you so far. When people are simply told what to do, then that is often all they will do (and incidentally only when you are looking over their shoulder). People will generally withhold their discretionary effort unless leadership is securely buttressed by faith in the leader's character and competence. In other words, they admire and respect you.

In foreign policy terms, it is described as soft power, the use of positive attraction and persuasion to achieve foreign policy objectives in place of the hard power of military and economic might:

DOI: 10.4324/9781003092582-20

> Soft power shuns the traditional foreign policy tools of carrot and stick, seeking instead to achieve influence by building networks, communicating compelling narratives, establishing international rules, and drawing on the resources that make a country naturally attractive to the world.[2]

To have something to say that is worth listening to does not require you to be a great orator, but you do need a compelling story or narrative that makes what you say comprehensible to others. It helps therefore, as Caroline Naven observes, "if you are fluent in their 'language' [*in terms of colloquial expressions and abbreviations*] ... a shared language breaks down barriers and increases commonality".[3]

In the law courts, a good narrative wins by meeting the twin criteria of credibility and coherence. It is consistent with the available evidence and the general knowledge of the judge and jurors, and it has internal coherence – it makes sense.[4] A good narrative not only articulates pathways from the world as it is to the world as it should be, but also sparks the motivation to act on it. A good story, well told, can slip past the defences of the rational mind, pluck at our hearts and stir our emotions (which is why we have used references from fiction on occasion). Human societies have flourished without the wheel, but none has existed without stories. We are storytelling animals and to be human is to tell stories. The ability to learn from vicarious experience through storytelling is thought to have provided an evolutionary advantage to our ancestors, ensuring the spread of innovative ideas and technology and the development of culture.

But the power of a story can be just that, a fabrication. The idea that our understanding of gravity sprung from a single moment of inspiration, when an apple landed on Isaac Newton's head, is powerful and unforgettable, even though it is probably untrue. In telling their stories, we believe that leaders have an obligation to act ethically, not least because it is the moral thing to do but also because it is the sensible thing to do.

A leader can of course appeal to a narrow constituency and we do not have to look far for examples, whether this be politicians, warlords or religious extremists. As Brexit and the 2016 US election illustrated, consciously or unconsciously, we tend to connect with people who are like us and share our opinions (homophily). Most of us sought confirmation from people who were more likely to vote like ourselves rather than challenging ourselves to understand those with a different view. Similar dangers lurk in organisations, and network leaders need to make a conscious effort to understand others and collaborate across organisational silos.

Network Leaders use their understanding of the social system to bring people together around a shared idea embodied in what we term their "manifesto". However, this is not created in vacuum; it is, instead, an articulation of an underlying fragmented sentiment that when brought together and given voice becomes a compelling movement.

In short, we are suggesting a more expansive style of leadership and an inclusive manifesto, one that draws together diverse groups in pursuit of shared rather than divisive goals; leaders who recognise that the only way to survive and prosper in turbulent times is to draw on a wide range of good ideas and committed people, no matter the source. Ultimately, the goal is to bring people together, to convene them, around shared endeavour, and not drive them apart, which can only ever be a zero-sum game.

Ruth Dearnley describes it as an:

> ecology, a living, moving thing. It's not a castle with a flag. We are building an ecology of wisdom … It's an intelligence led approach, collecting stories and building a rich picture and then disseminating the insights and information. It's about keeping going, about holding the space.

She concludes that "I help provide the structure and processes, the scaffolding, step in to get it back on track and lead the way looking at what is coming and ensuring we deliver today".[5]

Notes

1 World Bank (online). Available at: https://ieg.worldbankgroup.org/evaluations/-world-bank-group-global-convening (Accessed 17 April 2021).
2 Nye, J.S. (2004). *Soft Power: The Means to Success in World Politics*. New York: Hachette Publishing.
3 Interview with the authors, 29 March 2021.
4 Kay, J. and King, M. (2020). *Radical Uncertainty: Decision-Making for an Unknowable Future*. London: The Bridge Street Press, p. 212.
5 Interview with the authors, 1 February 2021.

13
Power, Influence and Behaviour

Legitimate power denotes authority to act or direct others to act. In an organisation such legitimacy is conferred by appointment, in a democracy it is by election, but informally it is conferred by the simple inclination of others to follow your lead. Max Weber, the sociologist, philosopher and social theorist, distinguished three ideal types of legitimate authority: charismatic, traditional and legal.[1] He described charismatic authority as an extraordinary and personal gift, akin to the Heroic theory of leadership. Traditional authority was based on inheritance, which is passed from one generation to the next, like a monarchical or noble line of succession, while legal-rational authority was formal or positional power that comes with a particular office.

As a manager you automatically have a measure of legal-rational authority and people expect you to use it. Traditional authority, including that which is inherited, is based on shared allegiance and can exist in any organisation where the members are united by a shared history. An example is the British military, where loyalty and therefore legitimacy is conferred on those who represent unit identity and the authority of the monarch. Charisma, however, is trickier. Like beauty it is largely in the eye of the beholder.

Charisma is essentially a degree of attractiveness or charm that can inspire devotion in others and a willingness to do what you ask without the need for coercion or extrinsic reward. Weber distinguished it from the other forms of authority because, instead of tradition or contractual obligation, charismatic rule is based on the qualities of the leader, a belief in their individual powers rather than those bestowed by birth or rank. Furthermore, in Weber's view, the actual power or capabilities of the leader are irrelevant, so long as the followers believe that such power exists. Consequently, the challenge for the charismatic leader is to generate and maintain that belief in their followers, for without it they have no mandate.[2]

DOI: 10.4324/9781003092582-21

Forty years after Weber, social psychologists John French and Bertram Raven identified several other forms of power, but the distinction between positional and personal power remained.[3] French and Raven's model included five, later six, "bases of power": coercive, reward, legitimate, referent and expert. Raven subsequently added informational power as the sixth.

In French and Raven's model, legitimate power derives from the belief that a person has the formal right to make demands and to expect others to be compliant and obedient. Reward power comes from a person's ability to compensate another for compliance or withhold it for non-compliance. Expert power is based on one's level of skill and knowledge. Referent power is the result of a person's perceived attractiveness, worthiness and right to others' respect. Coercive power comes from the belief that a person can punish others for disobedience. Informational power rests on a person's ability to control access to information that others need to accomplish something.

Positional power, therefore, includes Weber's legal or traditional authority, alongside French and Raven's power to reward, to coerce and to control access to resources and information. Personal power, however, refers to Weber's charismatic power and French and Raven's referent power, based on the followers' identification with, trust of or liking for the leader, as well as expert power, based upon the followers' perceptions of the leader's competence and aptitude. In short, personal power is a combination of competence and integrity.

There is no doubt that network leaders may benefit from the advantages of positional authority, but we would regard it as neither necessary nor sufficient. Network Leadership is, in the first instance, a combination of personal attributes based upon people's identification with you, their trust in you and their belief in your abilities, but it is trust in you that comes first. Harvard Business School professor Amy Cuddy has found that while most people, especially in a professional context, believe that competence is the most important factor generating trust. It is in fact personal integrity that counts for more. Her research suggests that warmth and honesty is the most important factor in how people evaluate you.[4] And, from an evolutionary perspective, she goes on to explain, this makes sense.

In our prehistory, it was more important to figure out if another person was going to stab you in the back and steal all your possessions than if they were competent enough to hunt or build a good fire. While competence is highly valued, it is evaluated only after trust has been established. Cuddy concludes that focusing too much on displaying your competence can actually backfire. A warm, trustworthy person who is also competent elicits admiration, but only after trust has been established does competence become a gift rather than a threat.

The weakness of positional power is that it leads to compliance but not necessarily commitment. People will do what you ask of them so long as they are legitimate requests and you can ensure compliance through your physical presence or by creating quantifiable productivity metrics which they cannot escape. The same goes for access to resources and rewards, compliance is conditional on receiving those rewards and having sufficient resources, it may well end as soon as the rewards dry up or resources run short. Commitment to positional authority is therefore transactional in nature and bounded by limits of resources and reward.

Authority derived from targets and rewards also encourages silos. Hierarchies force us to constantly look up and down, but seldom sideways. It is behaviour driven by narrow individual, team and departmental objectives which focus attention on our part of the organisation rather than the whole, an approach that the business journalist Gillian Tett describes as "eat what you kill". Individuals are rewarded so long as they meet their objectives and do not care, nor need to care, for the rest of business.[5] The same can be true within and between communities; in fact, silos are just tribes by another name, the natural human inclination to associate with those who are near us and like us and exclude those who are not. This is a classic case of "them" and "us", with the strong ties that drive efficiency working against the weak links that could provide access to other sources of information, ideas and ways of doing things that drive collaboration and ultimately greater effectiveness.

Influence

To dig a little deeper, it is helpful to describe personal power as influence, in the sense that personal power is the ability to persuade people to act other than through recourse to positional power and authority, although, as we have said, it may be an adjunct to it. As we made clear in the introduction to this section, your authority to lead comes initially from having something to say that is worth listening to. To be persuaded, people need to understand and agree with what you have to say, believe it provides an answer to the problem at hand and ideally answers an individual need of their own. With those needs satisfied they are more inclined to move with you in your intended direction.

Broadly, there are two routes to persuasion. One engages the conscious mind and deals with logic and facts and the other engages the subconscious, which is more affected by the emotional feel for a situation or person and appeals at a more intuitive level. What you may find surprising is that while the two approaches generally work in tandem, repeated studies have shown that it is the subconscious (emotional) element that is the primary driver for decision-making or being persuaded. Logic is still important, but rather as after the fact validation of a decision that has already been made intuitively. And that has not changed for at least two and half millennia.

In the 4th century BC Aristotle, the Ancient Greek philosopher and polymath, argued that to be persuaded by a speaker an audience required three types of proof: ethos, logos and pathos. Ethos referred to the speaker's reputation, their credibility or trustworthiness and their character. Logos to whether what the speaker was saying or suggesting made sense – was it logical, rational and did it make use of concrete and believable facts. And finally, pathos, the emotions felt by the audience, whether they empathised with the speaker or not.

Ethos is a fundamental starting point. As Cuddy identified, trust occurs between people when there is a firm belief in the reliability, truth and ability of someone. A positive reputation, borne of friends or trusted colleagues in common, helps conversations take on a different tone, it provides vicarious experience of your trustworthiness and makes the person to be persuaded more receptive to your suggestions.

Logos is what most of us assume drives a good argument. A sound premise followed by logical steps of cause and effect leading to a reasoned and evidence-backed conclusion. If only it were that simple. Some of our beliefs, and not just those about religion, rest on faith with little regard for logic or evidence. Others are so riddled with bias to make little sense at all. Consider, for example, confirmation bias, which we discussed in relation to reflective practice and is our propensity to favour information, whether true or not, which confirms our pre-existing beliefs. Insider Bias is another and describes our in-built distrust of strangers and the greater likelihood that we will listen to those we regard as one of "us", our in-group (with whom we share strong ties), rather than "them", a potentially hazardous member of an out-group.

But it is Pathos or empathy that is at the heart of most successful relationships. Only when we are comfortable with the person delivering the message, coloured by their reputation (ethos) and how they make us feel (pathos), do we evaluate the "logic" of what they are saying. From the leader's perspective, pathos is the ability to identify and understand other people's feelings, ideas and situation. It is the next best thing to extra sensory perception and reading their minds. Nowadays, empathetic people are often referred to as having "emotional intelligence", a phrase popularised by the work of Daniel Goleman.[6] It describes an ability to put yourself on a similar wavelength to other people, to "walk in their shoes" and consequently know what to say and how to say it.

Examples of psychological influence can be found in the work of Robert Cialdini.[7] Based on a range of social psychology experiments and extensive participant observation of compliance professionals, such as advertisers, salesmen and charity fund-raisers, Cialdini identified that the majority of tactics employed by compliance professionals fall into six broad categories, four of which apply in social networks: reciprocation, the tendency for people to return a favour; commitment and consistency, the tendency for people to repeat previous behaviour; social proof, the tendency for people to behave as they see others behaving; and likeability, that people are more easily persuaded by those whom they like.

Reciprocation is the action of responding to a gesture, action or emotion with a corresponding one. In other words, one person tries to repay in kind what another person has provided, often regardless of its perceived value or desirability. Charitable organisations rely on the principle of reciprocation to help enhance their fund-raising. Cialdini used the Disabled American Veterans organisation as an example, but the same technique will no doubt be familiar to us all. The Veterans Association used a carefully written fund-raising letter to elicit an 18% positive response rate to its appeals. However, when the group started enclosing a small gift in the envelope with the letter, the positive response rate increased significantly to 35%. The small gift they included, some personalised address labels, had minimal monetary value, but made a significant difference to the positive response rate. People reciprocated with a gift of their own.

Consistency is a human impulse to do what we have previously done and our preference for consistency can be so strong that we automatically revert to previous behaviour even when it is not necessarily the most pragmatic approach for a given situation. This desire for consistency is twofold. It is valued by society, because it is stable and reliable and for the individual it is a broadly beneficial approach to everyday life. If a behaviour works in most situations it gives us a shortcut mechanism for coping with the complexity of everyday life, providing a rule of thumb or heuristic. From a sales perspective, the compliance mechanism is known as the “foot-in-the-door technique”. Everyday examples, which again you will be familiar with, include subscriptions where a special introductory rate is offered for three months, to hook the customer, after which time the cost reverts to the full subscription rate. For most people it’s easier and less hassle to just be consistent and keep paying.

Social Proof hinges on the fact that behaviour is often seen as correct in a given situation based upon the degree that we see others performing it. It is supported by the intuitive belief that if we act in accordance with the social evidence of what we see other people doing we will likely make fewer mistakes than if we act against it. It is another behaviour shortcut that can vastly reduce the amount of time we have to spend processing information before we act and helps us avoid possible social embarrassment. Cialdini offers the example of bartenders, who seed their tip jars with dollar bills at the beginning of a night to indicate that tipping with dollar bills rather than lower denominational coins is the accepted social practice. The same is true of buskers on city streets, seeding their hat or instrument case with coins and notes to indicate that others thought their playing worthy of reward. The subtle shift in language that infers social proof can be powerful. Rewording public litter notices from "No Litter" to "Take Your Litter home; Others Do" has shown significant results.

Likeability relies on the simple premise that we more readily comply with a request made by someone we like, which Cialdini suggests derives from four things: similarity, physical attractiveness, offering praise and compliments and repeated positive contact. We described similarity when we discussed the tendency for homophily in social networks for "birds of a feather to flock together", whether it be similar opinions, way of life, culture, personality traits or social circumstances. Our natural response to physical attractiveness is often described in terms of the "halo effect", where the positive characteristic of good looks leads us to assume that attractive people will also be intelligent and competent.[8] Cialdini found evidence that people who are perceived as being attractive are better at changing other's views and securing what they request. Ever seen an attractive person advertising a particular product? Of course you have.

Compliments also help. Most people like praise, it makes us feel good. Even a relatively small compliment, such as recalling someone's name, can have a significant effect in terms of compliance with a request, ask any salesman. And repeated contact or exposure is also important, again the network effects we described as propinquity and contagion. Cialdini shows that the more times we are exposed to a given product by means of an online banner advertisement, the greater our liking for the product being advertised, and this holds true even if we have no conscious recollection of having seen the advertisement. Cialdini adds that contact is more powerful if it takes place under positive circumstances, which will enhance the liking mechanism. An observation supported by the "Contact Hypothesis", which argues that a major cause of conflict is ignorance about the "other" and can be reduced by bringing the conflicting sides together in a conducive and positive atmosphere, one where power is equally balanced and is in pursuit of a shared objective,[9] a point well worth noting if you are trying to develop weak ties between teams and departments.

So, if positional power is influence and the object of influence is to persuade people to change their behaviour and follow your lead, we now need to understand what is meant by behaviour and how it changes. The key point to note is that while ethos, pathos and logos are the building blocks of a persuasive presentation or speech and may well lead to a change in what the audience thinks or feels, it will not necessarily lead to a change in their behaviour, because there is a difference between the intention to act and the act itself.

Behaviour

Human behaviour is shaped by two systems. A systematic process using reason and logic and a more common rule of thumb or heuristic approach based upon intuition and emotion.[10] The downside of the latter is that it can lead us to disregard contradictory information, favour our in-group, form false judgements and over- or underestimate our own abilities. However, it is worth pausing to consider how important this type of thinking is. It is vital because it allows us to deal with huge amounts of information and act, for the most part successfully, in a complex world.

Psychologists have identified a variety of ways in which humans depart from rationality, describing these deviations as biases or signs of human failure. However, many of the characteristics of human reasoning which are described as biases are in fact adaptive and have been beneficial to human success. As John Kay and Mervyn King observe:

> Coping with uncertainty in all its dimensions has been an important part of human evolution. Over thousands of years of radical uncertainty humans have learnt many coping strategies and developed a capacity to make decisions in the face of imperfect knowledge of worlds they encounter for the first time and may never encounter again. To cope with the world as it is, we have developed thought processes to deal with problems that are ill defined, ambiguous and radically uncertain. Human minds approach problems in ways that are markedly different from those of computers. In particular, whereas computers are efficient in solving well-defined puzzles, human excel at finding ways to cope with open-ended mysteries.[11]

The idea that our intelligence is defective has been reinforced by the rise of computers, but the observation that we are inferior to them in solving certain kinds of routine mathematical puzzles fails to recognise that few real-world problems, wicked problems, have the character of mathematical puzzles. The assertion that our cognition is defective by virtue of systematic biases is implausible in the light of the evolutionary origins of that cognitive ability. If it were adaptive to be like computers, then we would have evolved to be more like computers than we are.[12] Humans have evolved to cope with complex problems and consequently our brains are not like computers but are adaptive mechanisms for making connections and seeing patterns. Good human decisions are often a leap of imagination rather than the result of linear reasoning.

Computers can perform calculations far more accurately and more quickly than humans and the success of an artificial intelligence (AI) programme in defeating the reigning champion of Go has led some to believe that eventually all mysteries will become soluble puzzles. But AI's success was possible because, although immensely complex, Go is defined by its rules. The success of AI is based on its ability to train itself very quickly by engaging in more games than a human could in a lifetime. Problems faced by humans in the real world are altogether different and our responses are the product of evolutionary reasoning and behaviour.

To help understand behaviour, we use a model adapted from the Theory of Reasoned Action (TRA)[13] and the Theory of Planned Behaviour (TPB).[14] The TRA is a cognitive theory concerning the decision to engage in a particular behaviour, which was designed to help understand the motivation behind risky or unhealthy addictive behaviours, such as alcoholism and gambling, and how to change them. The TPB was a later refinement of the TRA. According to both theories, an individual's decision to engage in a behaviour can be directly predicted by their intention to engage in that behaviour, which, in turn, is a function of their personal attitude towards the behaviour (how desirable or valuable it seems) and social norms (what they think the attitudes of significant others are and what other people are actually doing). To which we have added the influence of the prevailing environment, the actual ability of the individual to perform the behaviour, whether they think they can do it, their level of self-efficacy and whether they believe it to be worth their effort (Figure 4.1).

Looking at our adapted model above, we can see that an individual's decision to engage in a particular behaviour is directly related to their intention to engage, five factors permitting: the environment, whether it is permissive or not; the ability of the individual to perform the behaviour, whether they have the skills, aptitude and capacity; the personal attitude of the individual towards the behaviour, whether it is valued or not; self-efficacy, the degree to which the individual thinks they can do the behaviour and is it worth their effort; and social

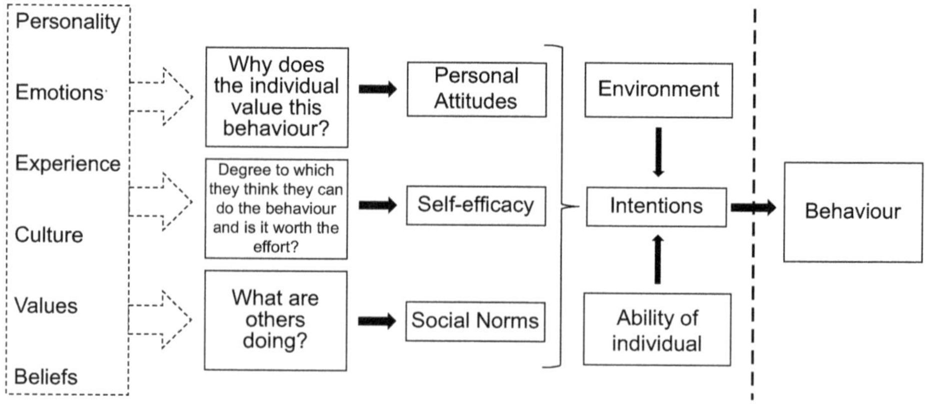

Figure 4.1 A Model of Human Behaviour.

norms, what are others doing, are they engaging in the behaviour or intending to do so (Cialdini's social proof)?

Personal attitude, self-efficacy and social norms are, in turn, a consequence of multi-faceted genetic and environmental factors acting upon each individual, including but not limited to: personality, the combination of characteristics or qualities that form an individual's distinctive character; emotions, an individual's propensity for joy, sadness, anger or fear, trust or distrust and surprise or anticipation; experience, the knowledge, skills and attitudes that individual's get from doing, seeing or feeling things; culture, the ideas, customs and social behaviour of a particular organisation or society of which the individual is a part; values, the principles or standards of behaviour that one judges to be important in life; and beliefs, what an individual accepts to be true or to exist, with or without proof.

Let's take a recent example: working from home (WFH). We had been talking about remote working, virtual teams and WFH for years before the Covid-19 crisis. It was something that a few progressive firms said and meant, but for most office-bound businesses there was only grudging approval, both from managers and fellow colleagues. WFH was normally dismissed as an opportunity to skive, the technology would be too expensive, it would be an administrative nightmare, or we couldn't survive without face-to-face collaboration and so on. And yet we did it, mainly because we had to.

From a behavioural perspective, the intention to WFH was there, but the behaviour was lacking in most cases. The first thing that happened to alter that was that the environment changed, Covid-19 happened and forced many businesses to change the way they worked. In those circumstances, organisational survival meant they had to quickly overcome the technical difficulties and make it possible to work from home. From an individual perspective, people valued this behaviour because it allowed them, where possible, to keep their job and continue working. Some people may have been sceptical of their technical ability and the ability of the technology to deliver effective collaborative working, but the rewards were huge if they could get it right. Finally, people followed the herd, and the social proof was that increasing numbers of people and businesses were making the transition. It may have been bumpy for some, but efficiency and effectiveness improved over time.

The question now becomes how or to what extent will people's behaviour stay changed in the post-lockdown world? You have the advantage over us there, as at the time of writing we simply didn't know. But the evidence suggests that it won't go back entirely to the way it was.

To summarise so far. Leadership depends upon the possession of power, but not simply the power to command because of your position or rank (although that can certainly help). Instead, it rests upon the possession of personal attributes and competence that persuades others to follow you because of who you are, what you say and what they believe you can achieve. And in the first instance that means you must get their attention, by having something to say that is worth listening to.

Notes

1 Weber, M. (1978/1922). *Economy and Society*. Roth, G. and Wittich, C. ed. Berkeley: University of California Press.
2 Weber, M. (2015/1919). Politics as Vocation. In Waters, T. and Waters, D., ed. and trans., *Weber's Rationalism and Modern Society*. New York: Palgrave Macmillan, pp. 129–98.
3 Raven, B.H. (1965). Social Influence and Power. In Steiner, I.D. and Fishbein, M. ed., *Current Studies in Social Psychology*. New York: Holt, Rinehart, Winston, pp. 371–82.
4 Cuddy, A. (2016). *Presence: Bringing Your Boldest Self to Your Biggest Challenges*. London: Orion.
5 Tett, G. (2015). *The Silo Effect*. London: Little Brown.
6 Goleman, D. (1996). *Emotional Intelligence: Why It Can Matter More Than IQ*. London: Bloomsbury Publishing.
7 Cialdini, R. B. (2007). *Influence: The Psychology of Persuasion*. New York: Harper Business.
8 The halo effect is a broader phenomenon whereby we assume that because people are good at doing A, they will be good at doing B, C and D (or the reverse, because they are bad at doing A, they will be bad at doing B, C and D). The phrase was first coined by Edward Thorndike, a psychologist who used it in a study published in 1920 to describe the way that commanding officers rated their soldiers. He found that officers usually judged their men as being either good right across the board or bad. There was little mixing of traits; few people were said to be good in one respect but bad in another.
9 Allport, G.W. (1979). *The Nature of Prejudice*. Cambridge, MA: Perseus Books.
10 Kahneman, D. (2011). *Thinking, Fast and Slow*. London: Allen Lane.
11 Kay, J. and King, M. (2020). *Radical Uncertainty: Decision-Making for an Unknowable Future*. London: The Bridge Street Press, pp. 154–5.
12 Kay, J. and King, M. (2020) ibid. pp. 400–1.
13 Ajzen, I. and Fishbein M. (1975). *Belief, Attitude, Intention and Behaviour: An Introduction to Theory and Research*. Boston, MA: Addison-Wesley.
14 Ajzen, I. (1989). *Attitudes, Personality and Behaviour*. Maidenhead: Open University Press.

14
Personal Manifesto

The word "Manifesto" comes from the Latin manifest, which means to make visible or to reveal. Party political manifestos are the most widely known, but there are far more inspiring examples. One of the most famous is *The Communist Manifesto* by Karl Marx and Friedrich Engels, but others include the Sermon on the Mount, the United States Declaration of Independence and speeches such as Churchill's "Blood, Toil, Tears, and Sweat" and Martin Luther King's "I Have a Dream". Because of their power to provoke change, manifestos are often embraced by revolutionaries and politicians, but they work in any setting and you don't have to be Karl Marx to write a manifesto.[1]

A personal manifesto is a statement of your ideals and principles; most dictionaries define it as a public declaration of intent. Your intent is what you are setting out to achieve. It is your aim or purpose. It may be a goal, a vision, a mission, an outcome, a plan or a design. A declaration is an announcement or proclamation that tells people about this intent, what you will do or create for the future, from the extremely mundane (I'm going to bed, I'm going to have a coffee or I'm going to call the boss) to the exceptional, such as the examples listed above. In linguistic terms a declaration is the opposite of a description. When we describe things, we merely define how it appears to us. Declarations are not descriptive; they are creative and describe future action. Finally, public, which is the opposite of private, and (no surprise) means going public with it. Making your declaration available to others rather than keeping it to yourself.

Simply put, a manifesto outlines what you want to achieve and it is shared publicly.

It is both a statement of ideals and principles but also a bold, even rebellious, call to action. It creates the future, a future you desire, and it does this by causing people to evaluate the gap between those principles and the current reality, it challenges assumptions, fosters commitment and provokes change.

DOI: 10.4324/9781003092582-22

Ed Catmull has an interesting take on this in describing reactions to his friend, the late Steve Jobs, and the reality distortion that people often accused him off or applauded him for.[2] Some people, Catmull writes, after listening to Steve, would feel they had reached a new level of insight, only to find they couldn't reconstruct the steps in his reasoning, and the insight would then evaporate leaving them bemused, feeling as though they had been led down the garden path, hence reality distortion. It labelled him as either a fantasist, unable to accept the rules of the world, or as a visionary. But for Catmull, there is a different meaning of reality distortion, which stems from his belief that:

> our decisions and actions have consequences and that those consequences shape our future. Our actions shape our reality. Our intentions matter. Most people believe that their actions have consequences but don't think through the implications of that belief. But Steve did. He believed, as I do, that it is precisely by acting on our intentions and staying true to our values that we change the world.

The difficulty of course is that proclaiming your manifesto can look dangerously like self-promotion – egotistical, arrogant and selfish (Steve Jobs is, arguably, a good example) – and we are not suggesting that you nail your manifesto to the front door of your organisation (glass doors aside) like some latter-day Martin Luther evangelising for religious reformation. But if you honestly believe that you have something to say that is worth listening to, then it cannot and should not stay hidden. By promoting themselves for the right reasons, using well-chosen words, backed by congruent action, Network Leaders can cut through the plethora of information that continually bombards us. In the hands of a network leader, self-promotion isn't just a tool to advance one's own career, but an opportunity for everyone to make their skills and ideas more visible across organisations, enhancing collaboration and therefore driving productivity.

Convening a gathering of people and getting them to listen is of course easier for those who already hold position or rank. It also helps if your ethos precedes you. A reputation for competence and integrity will also likely get you heard. But there are other influential strategies that will get you noticed, strategies that require no formal or positional authority and will build your reputation. The first is to craft your personal manifesto into a compelling story.

Leading with Stories

Reality, as we have discussed, is socially constructed. It is formulated from our shared mental models and allows effective leaders to establish a common tie or bond with their followers by helping them make sense of the world. Human beings have a need to make sense of things and give their lives meaning. Meaning clarifies the way things are and the way they ought to be. And one of the best ways to do this is by telling simple, but effective stories. Stories that support or confound our current mental models, but ultimately provide a clear guide to the way ahead.

We are storytelling animals. So while facts inform and logical argument persuades, it is stories that inspire and move people to action. Stories appeal to the individual by providing better self-understanding; to the group by providing better collective understanding; and both provide values and meaning as the basis for action. Good stories reduce the complex to the simple and allow people to reach a point of realisation much quicker, which is often the point of fables, fairy tales and parables. They go beyond describing facts and assumptions and instead provide a plot, a moral and a point of view. As the poet and novelist Ben Okri observed:

> Stories are the secret reservoir of values: change the stories that individuals or nations live by and tell themselves and you change the individuals and nations.[3]

Our sense of identity changes when we change the story we tell ourselves about ourselves. Organisations, groups and communities change when the stories between people change. Our view and experience of the world change as we question the prevailing meta-narratives and imagine new possibilities. And a leader is someone who significantly affects the thoughts, feelings and behaviours of a significant number of individuals. Leaders set out to alter the minds of their audiences, and as humans we like clear, simple statements and explanations.[4]

For Howard Gardner, developmental psychologist and Research Professor of Cognition and Education at the Harvard Graduate School of Education, stories are key to leadership. In *Leading Minds: An Anatomy of Leadership*,[5] he set out to create a cognitive framework for all that had been learned about leadership and brought it to life with the mini biographies of 11 20th-century leaders, beginning with Margaret Mead and ending with Mahatma Gandhi. In his view:

> The ultimate impact of the leader depends most significantly on the particular story that he or she relates or embodies and the receptions to that story on the part of audiences (or collaborators or followers) … what links the eleven individuals … is the fact that they arrived at a story that worked for them and, ultimately for others as well. They told stories about themselves and their groups, about where they were coming from and where they were headed, about what was to be feared, struggled against, and dreamed about.

Gardner's insights are reinforced by Social Identity Theory (SIT), which suggests that we place people in categories that are either favourable, because they support our own identity, or unfavourable, because they are deemed to be different from us. Once categorized we constitute differences within the in-group (us) as smaller than those between the in-group and the out-group (them). This produces negative stereotypes of those in the out-group and positive prototypes of those who emulate the social identity of our in-group.

Prototypes exemplify what members have in common and what makes them different. And those who most closely resemble the prototype are likely to have the most influence and therefore be leaders, and they will remain as leaders so long as the conditions don't change because different conditions require different prototypes. Winston Churchill was seen as a dangerous maverick in the 1930s, but the classic prototype of the stoic British bulldog during the Second World War. In the immediate post-war period a more congenial and inclusive leader was required.

For Gardner, effective leadership is about accentuating the prototype, to be more like us; seeking out and removing in-group deviants; demonizing the out-group; and standing up for the in-group. And this is often what people mean by charisma. It is not a characteristic for all time but is born of a particular context and circumstance. Charisma exists not in an individual, but in an interaction between the individual, their audience and the situation – no connection, no charisma. Hitler's hatred of the Jews, his belief that all Germany's problems stemmed from them, and his vision of how to lead Germany out of misery struck a chord with his audience, it was what many Germans at that time wanted to hear.

Conducting influence operations in Afghanistan, trying to convince people to support the international community's efforts, James was advised to think of it like making a movie. In the first place, you decide what movie to make. What effect do you want to have on the audience, the emotions you wish to elicit? Then you decide how to achieve this effect, what themes, messages or channels of communication will be most effective. Then, you produce the movie using all assets at your disposal – ideas, experiences, stories you have read or heard before, always bearing in mind your audience and the effect you want to achieve. Finally, you measure and evaluate the effect – how did you do at the box office – and use the information to adjust your story.[6]

In organisational terms, Tichy and Cohen describe it as the leader's story.[7] In their view, the best way to create leaders at all levels is to have leaders develop leaders, passing on their own experience through compelling stories and their "Teachable Point of View" (TPOV), which is the leader's opinion on what it takes to succeed in the business and what it takes to lead people. Leaders, therefore, need to develop organisation-oriented stories that explain their learning experiences and beliefs; describe their vision of the future; and how to get there in order to make the case for change. The stories can be personal or professional, born of experience or heard from others, but in constructing them leaders should consider five critical aspects:

1. Idea: the vision, mission and purpose of the organisation.
2. Values: a shared understanding of how to act in pursuit of the idea.
3. Edge: leadership is about making tough yes/no decisions. Don't waffle, don't wobble and learn to make decisions with imperfect data.
4. Energy: leaders are motivated and they motivate others.
5. Emotion: leaders have vision, passion and authenticity (as well as empathy and sincerity).

Beware, however, that stories are, by their very nature, set within certain boundaries: temporal, spatial, cultural and organisational. The stories or mental models, upheld by each culture, define a landscape of behaviour and thinking as "normal" or "common sense". And we need only think of some of humanities' biggest stories to know how bound they are to time and place. The Ptolemaic "earth-centric" view of the universe was challenged and then overturned during the Enlightenment and replaced by the "heliocentric" view. In turn, ideas of growth and continual progress, born of the Enlightenment, are now challenged by those who believe there must be a limit to progress and the capacity of the earth to sustain us. More recently, the story of careers for life has been confronted by portfolio work and the gig economy, just as the impossibilities of large scale working from home has been challenged by the realities of Covid-19. In short, people will more easily adapt their behaviour if it accords with their view of the world. If they don't then it doesn't matter how rational and persuasive the argument. People choose between stories and we do it all the time.

Stories are a specific instance designed to illustrate a more general principle. They have the advantage of being more easily understood, because they are based upon reality and tend to be presented in everyday language that makes them immediately intelligible. They are also able to catch the unique features of a situation that hold the key to its understanding and therefore provide insights into similar situations and cases. However, they are not easily open to cross-checking, leaving the storyteller open to accusations of being selective, biased, personal and subjective, which, in turn, raise questions of validity and reliability. And they may not be generalizable to other situations. However, while accepting these criticisms, we take the view that relatability is more important than generalisability. An important criterion for judging the merit of a story is the extent to which the details are sufficient and appropriate for someone working in a similar situation to relate to it. In other words, the story should be relatable in a way that will enable members of similar groups to recognise problems and see ways of solving similar problems in their own context.

We will return to validity and the ethics of leadership in a moment, but for now it is enough to understand that to establish a positive relationship with those you wish to lead it is important to display competence and integrity and to tell simple, but effective stories, to align them to your personal manifesto, which is a declaration of intent made public through your words and deeds. It lives in what you say and what you do. If it is worth listening to, people will listen. If they think it is worth doing, they will follow you. But this does not make it right. People have done and still do terrible things in emulation and adulation of their leaders. Leadership has a moral component. It must be done for the benefit of others, not simply for self-aggrandisement, and it should aim to unite, not divide.

Leaders do well to remember the words of Immanuel Kant, "Always recognise that human individuals are ends, and do not use them as means to your end". And this takes us into the realms of organisational politics, ethics and trust.

Notes

1 Many businesses have also been inspired by the Agile Manifesto, which was developed by a group of rebellious software developers, who shared ideas for improving the traditional "waterfall" approach to design and development processes, in favour of processes that enabled faster response times in volatility, uncertainty, complexity and ambiguity (VUCA) environments.
2 Catmull, E. (2014). *Creativity Inc.* London: Bantam Press, pp. 310–1.
3 Okri, B. (1998). *A Way of Being Free.* London: Phoenix, p. 112.
4 Mead, G. (2014). *Telling the Story.* London: John Wiley & Sons Ltd.
5 Gardner, H. (1995). *Leading Minds: An Anatomy of Leadership.* New York: Basic Books.
6 The difficulty of course was that the international community were competing for the Afghan's attention with the Taliban, native Afghans, who were much better storytellers because they intuitively understood Afghanistan and its people. They understood the prototype.
7 Noel, M. and Tichy, N.M. (2007). *The Leadership Engine: How Winning Companies Build Leaders at Every Level.* New York: Harper Business.

15 Politics, Ethics and Trust

New employees are normally given a physical or electronic handbook or welcome pack detailing organisational procedures, processes and the hierarchy of names, contact numbers and locations with which they need to be familiar. But if the new employee asked for advice on how to succeed in the business, there would probably be no mention of this handbook. Instead, if information were forthcoming at all, it would focus on what they must do, what they must not do and what they can get away with; a verbal map of the organisation's social jungle, the relationships and the alliances, who was trustworthy and who had power. In short, organisational politics. But politics in organisations is often a dirty word.

Politics conjures images of self-serving individuals, closed doors and backroom deals. Nor does it appear on the curricula of most MBA programmes. Nevertheless, it is the rock on which countless careers founder. Like it or not, politics is integral to any human group. As Winston Churchill observed, "When you mix people and power you get politics". You may have no interest in organisational politics, but be under no illusion; it has an interest in you. It is simply naïve to think you can bury your head in the sand and avoid organisational politics. Ibarra and Hunter argue that political understanding is what differentiates leaders as they make the transition from functional to general management:

> The ability to figure out where to go and to enlist the people and groups necessary to get there. Recruiting stakeholders, lining up allies and sympathizers, diagnosing the political landscape, and brokering conversations among unconnected parties are all part of a leader's job. As they step up to the leadership transition, some managers accept their growing dependence on others and seek to transform it into mutual influence. Others dismiss such work as "political" and, as a result, undermine their ability to advance their goals.[1]

DOI: 10.4324/9781003092582-23

It may also be naïve to believe that you don't already do politics. So, let's be clear. Politics is the process of mediating between alternative goals and desires and the subsequent allocation of scarce resources to those competing objectives. It's how stuff gets done in human groups. People, whoever and wherever they are, have a predisposition to pursue their goals and desires based upon their views, values and beliefs, which, in turn, lead them to act in certain ways. Interests, for example, can be task interests, the work one must do; career interests, those beyond the job, which introduce private preferences and aspirations; and extramural interests, which shape attitudes to job, career, family, etc. Conflict arises whenever views, values and interests collide, and power – positional and personal – is the means through which conflicts are ultimately resolved.

Choices between values, views and interests must be made and such choices can only occur in one place: the political arena. It is there that their relative importance can be decided by the relative power brought to bear on their behalf. It is only in the political arena that the distribution of power can decide matters that the distribution of fact and insight cannot. A leader must therefore be able to analyse values, views and interests; understand conflicts; and negotiate power relations in order to reconcile divergent interests and achieve their objectives with them or despite of them. And the adept leader will go one step further, using conflict as an energising force to challenge groupthink and prevent complacency.

An understanding of politics, like that of social networks, explodes the myth of organisational rationality and recognises the constructive role that conflict and relationships can play. It helps us understand how to mitigate and/or harness private views, values and interests. The danger is that it may give a Machiavellian interpretation to our actions. Influencing the behaviour of others can sound manipulative, breeding mistrust and decreasing the scope for cooperation and collaboration, thereby losing sight of politics as a constructive force, which, to be honest, is a bit unfair on Machiavelli.

Machiavelli

Niccolò di Bernardo dei Machiavelli was an Italian diplomat, philosopher and writer, best known for his book *The Prince* written in 1513. Despite his reputation for cunning and duplicity, he had a lot of sensible things to say about leadership and, we believe, would intuitively understand network leadership. He was one of the first writers to consider a world where the natural order might not be set down by God, but by unchanging human nature. He was also one of the first to consider power and how it should be used and retained in a functional rather than a utopian way. Yet, in Britain, he has always been a symbol of villainy, representing calculating evil in the plays of both Marlowe and Shakespeare.

In fact, what Machiavelli wanted was to advise a ruler how to acquire and then hang onto a princedom, and he thought the best source of information for this was twofold: shrewd observation of contemporary reality and wisdom from the past, principally gleaned from the great minds of antiquity. He was particularly fascinated by the Roman Republic and its historians, which was the subject of his less well-known book *The Discourses on the First Ten Books of Titus Livy*.

Machiavelli counselled leaders to seize the moment. A great leader must have the courage and instincts to grasp opportunities when they appear. He recognised that great leaders do sometimes benefit from good fortune, but it is by their own merit that they recognise and exploit these opportunities. He advised them to master both the big picture and the detail. A leader, he argued, must be able to set out a grand vision but at the same time master the detail for execution. Strong leaders engage with others knowing what they want the outcome to be and have a sense of direction. But he also warned that a prince, especially a new prince, "should have a flexible disposition, varying as fortune and circumstances dictate".[2]

Fundamentally, he took a dim view of human nature. He did not think that the rules of personal morality could be applied to governing a country, because men in general are not good. He believed that the end justified the means, and the end was a stable government, because only then can laws be respected and life enjoyed. Leaders, he believed, were repeatedly faced with a choice between the lesser of two evils, and what interested him was not what was right or wrong, but what worked. As he observed in The Prince: "In the actions of all men, and especially of princes, where there is no court of appeal, one judges by results".[3]

Here, however, we diverge from Machiavelli. In our opinion, the ends do not justify the means. An act is not moral and virtuous just because it achieves a moral and virtuous objective. Aims, objectives and the tactics to achieve them can and should change, but a leader's methods should always be morally virtuous.

Ethics and Morality

For some, ethics is synonymous with morality. So, for example, the aim of ethics education would be to develop morally upright persons through the instillation of certain key qualities or dispositions of character. Others, however, disagree and consider ethics to be somewhat distinct from general morality and should more properly be understood as relating to a given profession. In this case, the focus of ethics education would shift from character development to creating an understanding of the purpose and methods of a profession and the values which underpin it, such as in the legal, medical and military professions, all of which have codes of accepted practice. Complicating matters, however, some prefer to speak of ethos rather than ethics, the intangible tone, spirit or culture, which guides the behaviour of members in particular organisations, institutions or communities.

This is not the place to evaluate whether ethics should apply singly or collectively to individuals, professions, roles or organisations. Nor are we here to prescribe an ethical template for network leaders, with a list of virtues or values. Objectively speaking, ethics is a matter for personal interpretation when considering how one responds to events. All leaders will bring with them the ethical insights of their upbringing, their culture and their generation, and answers to moral questions are rarely clear-cut. Primarily, we do not wish to cast doubt over how to articulate and codify ethical values that are, we believe, intuitively well understood, albeit easier to identify by their absence than their presence.

In our view, leaders are moral agents, who must recognise their responsibility to act with integrity: a commitment to honesty and a willingness to do what is right, abstaining from cheating, lying or stealing. It is the practice of being honest, but it also describes a state of being, whole and undivided, of acting with consistency. A consistent and uncompromising adherence to strong moral and ethical principles and values, which in turn implies the capacity and will to think deeply about morality and ethics. To understand the issues involved in a meaningful way and then act.

Furthermore, at the heart of ethics is morale courage, the courage to do what one believes is right but hard in the face of pressure to do that which is easier but wrong. It is the ability to transcend the group, which, taken to its logical conclusion, means accepting that on occasion leaders may wish to disobey or withdraw entirely from a project or organisation. We do not wish to encourage destructive activity, our hope is for constructive politics, but if we are serious about ethics we must accept that it implies encouraging unlimited criticality in ourselves and in those we lead. After all, the purpose of moral virtue is to build trust and while the absolute ideals of integrity and morale courage may be out of reach to imperfect humanity, it is something to which we should all aspire.

Trust

Trust and the principled use of power are at the heart of leadership and central to organisational and community health, and it is key to effective actor-networks. Trust is the confidence among people that their peer's intentions are good and there is no need to be protective or careful around them. In an organisational setting, teams that trust are comfortable being vulnerable with one another in the conviction that their respective vulnerabilities will not be used against them, that is, weaknesses, skill deficiencies, interpersonal shortcomings, mistakes and requests for help. It is only when members feel truly comfortable with one another that they can focus their energy and attention on the task at hand rather than being disingenuous or destructively political with one another.

Like the familiar rhyming proverb "For Want of a Nail", absence of trust goes something like this. In the absence of trust there is a fear of honest dialogue; through fear of honest dialogue there is a lack of commitment to decisions; through lack of commitment to decisions there is avoidance of accountability; and through avoidance of accountability there is inattention to results. In short, why should I care what happens if I didn't agree in the first place (although I may not have said anything out of a lack of morale courage).

Teams without trust conceal their weaknesses and mistakes from one another, hesitate to ask for help or provide constructive feedback, hesitate to offer help outside their own area of responsibility, jump to conclusions about the intentions and aptitudes of others, fail to recognise and tap into one another's skills and experiences and find reasons to avoid spending more time together. Suffice to say, communication, advice and the sharing of ideas will be severely compromised without a foundation of trust.

In contrast, trusting teams admit weaknesses and mistakes, ask for help, accept questions and input about their areas of responsibility, give one another the benefit of the doubt, take risks in offering feedback and assistance, appreciate and tap into one another's skills and experiences, focus time and energy on tasks, not office politics, and look forward to meetings and other opportunities to work together as a team. However, building trust is not easy. It requires shared experiences over time, multiple instances of follow-through and credibility and an in-depth understanding of the unique attributes and contribution of team members. But it is possible to accelerate the process and the role of the leader is critical.

Building Trust

When it comes to the development of trust and authority, purposeful conversations are vital. Colonel Zinoviev Konstantin Provalov summed it very well:

> Authority is gained through the sum of daily conversations. One has to speak to soldiers. A soldier must know his task and understand it. Authority isn't cheap; it is hard won. Everyone wants to live – including heroes. But

> knowing that soldiers trust me, I know they will fulfil all my orders and risk their lives.

Not a household name in Europe and America we admit. He was commander of the Soviet Union's 383rd "Miners" Rifle Division at the beginning of the Second World War and was awarded the honour "Hero of the Soviet Union" in the early battles of 1941. But his belief resonates with the later work of Richard Sennett, who in his book *Together*[4] described "earned authority" as one side of a "social triangle", the other sides being trust and cooperation, which he identifies as the key ingredients in successful organisations and communities.

Sennett takes authority to be power endowed with legitimacy, with legitimacy defined as voluntary obedience. In war, this means that soldiers will follow orders to fight knowing that it may lead to their death, but this is an extreme example, and in civil society legitimacy is perhaps better framed in the sense of laws people obey because they seem right rather than simply because it's the law. In organisations, therefore, the leadership test for legitimacy and thereby authority is: will your subordinates obey you even though they might get away with disobeying you?

Like Provalov, Sennett argues that a leader earns legitimacy more through small behaviours and exchanges than any formal right or entitlement to rule. Earned authority comes from open dialogue with subordinates rather than formal position, technical competence and rigid dictation. And in our view, this means loosening the reins. It is the leader's job to initiate trust between management and employees, and that entails gaining employees' trust, but also conveying trust in them. As Ernest Hemingway observed, "The best way to find out if you can trust somebody is to trust them". And you can do this by delegating tasks to them while being aware that giving up control also means expanding your tolerance for mistakes. If mistakes happen, instead of taking swift corrective action, show staff how they can learn and grow from them.

Delegation is easier when you build trust by having conversations with your direct reports, by observing them doing their daily tasks and providing feedback. When it comes time to delegate a task, you'll better understand your employees' strengths and weaknesses and know who is ready to take on more responsibility and who needs more experience or coaching. This also helps you to determine whether a direct report is ready to be a manager. Leaders can also gauge their potential by assessing their interest in managing. Ask them what they believe management entails and what their approach would be in situations you are facing or have faced. Inquire about any experience they've had outside of work that could provide useful preparation. Have they captained a sport's team, for example, or been responsible for a group of volunteers? You can also seek out the opinions of their co-workers, who will have a unique perspective on whether the person is up to the task.

People follow leaders they trust because they are viewed as credible; a leader's credibility is like a bank account into which credibility is amassed over time through many small acts, ready to be drawn upon when the moment demands. The word credibility comes from the Latin *credibilis*, meaning "worthy to be believed". It is also the root word behind credit as a trusted loan and creed as a set of beliefs. Jim Kouzes and Barry Posner in their seminal work on credibility noted that the components of credibility included being honest, competent, forward looking and inspiring.[5] Break anyone of those components, and the credibility "bank account" goes into deficit and never recovers to its former balance.

For authority to be legitimate, people who are asked to obey must also feel they have a voice – that if they speak up, they will be heard. Most companies routinely ask customers for feedback about their products and services, but asking employees the same questions is less common. This is a missed opportunity. So, in addition to asking your customers questions like "Was your problem solved"? and "Are we easy to work with"?, ask your employees "How did you solve the problem"? and "Was it easy to access the tools and resources you needed to do it"? And if not, why?

Leaders encourage honesty through sharing their own mistakes and successes. This requires that you risk losing face in front of the team, but it will help you connect emotionally and encourage subordinates to take the same risks themselves. The leader must create an environment that doesn't punish vulnerability and mistakes but learns from them. Soliciting people's opinions also has the added benefit of making people feel like they belong and fostering a sense of belonging can help reduce stress levels, which improves physical health, emotional well-being and performance. Ask people's opinion and follow up with questions so they feel truly heard.

Building trust is essential to productivity and employee engagement but, as previously discussed, there is a flip side to this. Strong ties can also lead to a lack of new ideas, a failure to challenge poor ideas and unethical behaviour. Strong teams can become insular, distrusting the ideas of other teams, not wishing to engage with them or worse, competing rather than collaborating. And teams who enjoy a friendly and supportive atmosphere may be disinclined to criticise each other in case they rock the boat. Even strong and effective teams require leaders with the integrity and morale courage to challenge them, keep them straight and take them out of their comfort zone.

Notes

1 Ibarra, H. and Hunter, M.L. (2007) How Leaders Create and Use Networks. (online) *Harvard Business Review*. Available at: https://hbr.org/2007/01/how-leaders-create-and-use-networks (accessed 17 April 2021).
2 Machiavelli, N. (1981/1532). *The Prince*. London: Penguin, p. 101.
3 Machiavelli, N. (1981/1532) ibid.
4 Sennett, R. (2013). *Together*. London: Penguin.
5 Kouzes, J. and Posner, B. (2011). *Credibility: How Leaders Gain and Lose It, Why People Demand It*. London: Jossey-Bass.

16
Connective Power

Finally, we would like to add connection to the list of power dimensions. The ability to connect is often neglected as a measure of an individual's importance and it is not unusual for the word "networking" (the pursuit of connections) to evoke an involuntary sense of aversion (rather like organisational politics), evoking images of sycophancy, manipulation and the vacuous exchange of business cards. However, when pursued authentically, the art of connecting is one of the most valuable skills a leader can develop. Beyond your inner network, it is essential. A strong network provides social capital, which, as previously discussed, leverages the benefits of reciprocity, information flow, idea exchange and collective action.

Some organisations invest heavily in senior leadership development and almost invariably visionary leadership is seen as a crucial leadership competency. However, in our experience, the positive impact of visionary leadership is often lost when little or no effort is made by senior leaders to connect and align middle- and lower-level managers with the vision. The reality is that strategies are implemented not by CEOs and other top executives but by the many people who choose whether to take actions that support or undermine what top management wants to achieve. The mistake is to assume that managers charged with achieving the vision are themselves already aligned and motivated to change.

When middle and lower managers are aligned with the organisation's vision, things play out much as the widespread view of visionary leadership would suggest: the whole organisation is motivated to change through a shared understanding of where they are now, why they need to transform and where they are headed. However, when managers are misaligned, visionary leadership fails. Misalignment creates confusion and uncertainty about what an organisation is trying to achieve, which, in turn, leads to disengagement, friction and wasted

DOI: 10.4324/9781003092582-24

effort. At best, departments continue to focus on current operational and tactical activities, things they understand and can get on with. At worst, it disrupts the entire organisation and nothing gets done.

It is the same mistake made by some entrepreneurs, who build a product or service in isolation and wait for it to take off. Unfortunately, the "build it and they will come" strategy rarely works. The smartest entrepreneurs know that if you're building something new, you also need to build a community of people excited about your vision, because it is they who will provide the most useful feedback and help get the word out when your product or service hits the market.

The problem of disconnect is made worse in organisations because most leaders learn to lead in roles or circumstances where they have clear authority, they have a budget, clear accountability and a team of people whose job it is to support them. The downside of this common leadership model is that it often causes managers and therefore organisations to operate in silos, with each team, division or department looking upwards and downwards but seldom sideways at issues that cross the verticals of the organisation. What organisations need are people, network leaders, who have the capacity to make the sum of the parts greater than the whole. Leaders who can make and sustain connections horizontally and laterally in pursuit of shared goals.

Network Leaders recognise this potential for disconnect and consequently invest time and effort in creating strategic and operational alignment across organisations in support of the vision, in the same way that they create alignment around their own ideas and personal manifesto. For them, alignment starts even before strategy execution efforts have begun. Network Leaders develop relationships ahead of need and do not see them as one-time, fire and forget, communication but as a continual dialogue, in the belief that people will only follow your ideas and actions if they are continuously and consistently persuaded of their value. This is connective power, the ability to build relationships and bring the pieces together.

Connectors as Leaders

Crucial roles are played by people who are connectors but not necessarily leaders,[1] but in our experience all good leaders are connectors. As we discussed in Part One, identifying the traits that make a great leader is difficult. It's tricky because there are very few traits that are universal to all leaders, but in our experience what they do have in common is the ability to connect with and motivate people towards a shared vision or aim. And the best the leaders bring disparate groups of people together, not just because it is the moral thing to do but because it is also the sensible thing to do.

Leaders who are least successful target a very narrow network of people "like them" and tend to be those who believe that life and business is a zero-sum game. They see value as finite and guard their connections and knowledge because they think that value shared with others is value lost to them. Network leadership is about empowering others on the understanding that helping other people to succeed will not detract from your own success; on the contrary, it will increase your social capital and your ability to deploy it.

In short, leader-connectors enable organisations to make greater collective impact; they create value by connecting people, ideas and resources. Value that might otherwise remain hidden or underutilised. They make connections because they recognise that the knowledge, skills and experience of any organisation (what Pentland described as its *social intelligence*[2]) work synergistically and only reach its true potential when fully connected. They also recognise the importance of connecting with external stakeholders, systemically building relationships with the key players in their value chains to improve efficiencies and align with changing environments and market dynamics.

Connection can of course be imposed top-down by senior leadership. Top-down connection works from the outside in, from the formal to the informal, either mandating system change, rewiring the hierarchy, or redesigning the formal organisational structure. But it can be costly, confusing and slow. And if it works against the grain of informal human connection, the new structure may create new problems of its own. An alternative is to take a more organic approach and rely upon connection through things such as shared workspaces, pan-organisational leadership courses and cross-functional teams. This is a more natural approach to relationship building, but (by its very nature) it leaves connection to chance. It is an optimistic jumbling of the pieces, hoping they will find and connect in new and fruitful ways.

Network Leaders chart a middle course, working organically from the inside but in a more deliberate and strategic way. Like the top-down approach, they seek to identify who, how, where, when and to what end people should connect, but they do so by working with the natural flow of existing informal networks. They don't leave connections to chance, but they don't impose them either. It is a bottom-up, peer-to-peer approach that relies upon personal rather than positional authority in pursuit of genuine connection and relationships, which are therefore more likely to be sustainable.

Real relationships develop when you champion others and they sense that you have their best interests at heart. Network Leaders approach conversations and connections with a clear understanding of what they can offer and what they want to receive for themselves and for others. They always engage in a conversation with the aim of figuring out how they can offer the most value to the other person, whether that's domain expertise, relevant connections or helpful resources. In the knowledge that by authentically and generously sharing what they know others will feel obligated to reciprocate, and ultimately the pie becomes bigger for everyone. What they seek to create is a vibrant, productive network that takes advantage of both strong (productivity) and weak (innovation) links.

Crucially, it is connection with a purpose. Once connected, a Network Leader continually checks in with the members of their network to keep connections alive. Network Leaders recognise that organisations and communities are increasingly dynamic; they morph in size and shape over time and that their own network must do the same, growing and strengthening as required. But they are also strategic about choosing how, where and when to tap into this network.

Growing Your Network

Valdis Krebs and June Holley describe a vibrant network developing in four broad phases, each with its own distinct topology,[3] but with each phase creating a more adaptive and resilient network structure than the phase before: Scattered Fragments, Single Hub-and-Spoke, Multi-Hub Small-World Network and Core/Periphery, which are illustrated in Figure 4.2.

Most networks begin as *Scattered Fragments*, emergent clusters organised around homophily (common interests and goals) and propinquity (nearness). They tend to be small and often connected out of necessity or serendipity. Without active leaders, who take responsibility for building a network, spontaneous connections between groups emerge very slowly or not at all. But a network leader, who Krebs and Holley describe as a "network weaver", can accelerate

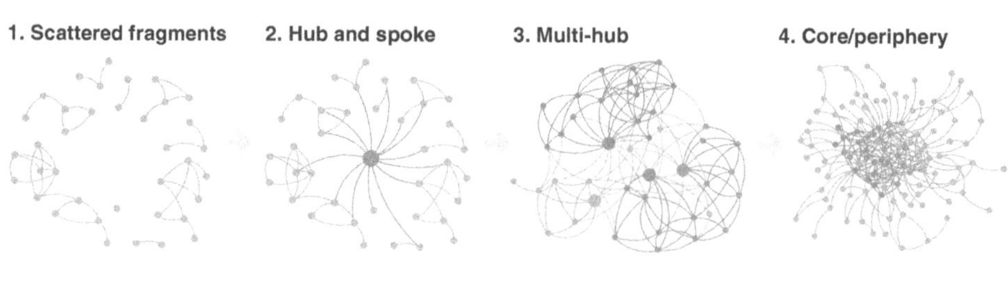

Figure 4.2 Phases of Network Growth.

the process by acting energetically to create connections between themselves and the disparate groups.

Network weavers first create a simple *Hub-and-Spoke* network, which, like a wheel, has the weaver acting as the hub or central node and the spokes being the ties from them to other nodes. The weaver can be an individual, a group or an organisation, anyone who has the vision, the energy and the social skills to connect with diverse individuals and groups, and start information and ideas flowing between them. At this point, whatever flows through the network as a whole flows through the network weaver.

In network terms it is the power of centrality, the extent to which you are central to your network and therefore exposed to what flows through it. Social Network Analysis measures centrality in three principal ways: degree centrality, the number of connections an individual has to other actors; betweenness centrality, the number of times they form a bridge between other actors, often connecting otherwise separate parts of a network; and eigenvector centrality, their proximity to powerful, popular or prestigious nodes. In effect, influence by proxy. In short, the Hub is key to the connection of people, ideas and resources.

Over time, a *Multi-Hub Small-World Network* develops. Network weavers form relationships with each of the small clusters to discover what they know and what they need, and then connect them with other clusters to facilitate mutual collaboration and exchange. An astute weaver will introduce clusters that have common goals/interests or complementary skills, experiences and resources to each other. Concurrently, the weaver also encourages others to begin weaving the network in the hope that by encouraging and supporting other network weavers the connection to the original weaver (the Hub) can weaken over time without destroying the integrity of the network. The role of the weaver then changes from being the central weaver to being a facilitator of network weaving, coordinating with and mentoring other network weavers.

As the weaver connects individuals and groups, the dynamic of weak ties is revealed, enabling information, ideas and innovation to be shared across the network. In addition, the weak ties may strengthen over time, binding previously separate groups into new larger clusters. The skill in creating such ties is to connect groups who are similar enough to build trust, but different enough to introduce new ideas and perspectives. The challenge is to counter political turf wars, where two or more departments or community organisations might split the network into competing single hub networks, ignoring the larger community and focusing on survival in their own network.

The end goal is a vibrant, sustainable network of *Core/Periphery*. This is described as a stable structure that can link to other well-developed networks.

The network core contains the organisation or community members, while the network periphery contains other stakeholders and those new to the community: bridges that connect to other diverse networks allowing access to further ideas and information not currently available in the core. Over time, the expanding periphery provides new ideas while the core solidifies, driven by increasingly strong links, which together allow efficient and effective action, implementing what is discovered and deemed useful.

From a Network Leadership perspective, the Network Leader uses their convening power to attract the scattered fragments into a hub-and-spoke arrangement, the fragments coalescing around an interest and belief in what the network leaders has to say. The Network Leader then acts to create a multi-hub network by connecting the scattered fragments to one another based upon complementary resources and needs, in order to generate collective action towards their shared goals. With this dynamic in place, the core should continue to grow and avoid stagnation by gathering new ideas from its periphery, from the edge where new ideas and ways of doing things collide. But the key to growth is the transition from hub-and-spoke to multi-hub.

Moving Beyond Hub-and-Spoke

Beyond a certain size, the hub-and-spoke arrangement is neither scalable nor sustainable. If they depend on a single indispensable hub, networks run the risk of failing to reach their potential or failing completely. If one person or organisation is responsible for all the relationships in the network, each relationship added to the network increases the amount of stress on the hub until eventually it is forced to operate at a suboptimal level or is simply overwhelmed and the network collapses. Moving to a multi-hub small-world network eliminates the danger of a single point of failure and allows the network to follow Metcalfe's Law and achieve its true potential.

Metcalfe's Law states that the effect of a network is proportional to the square of the number of those connected.[4] In other words, the potential value of a network increases exponentially as you add new nodes. The law has often been illustrated using the example of telephones or fax machines, such that a single device is useless; but its value increases with the addition of each new device to the network, because the total number of people with whom each user may send and receive messages increases. Likewise, in social networks, the greater number of users, the more valuable the service becomes.

Companies like Facebook, Twitter and LinkedIn originally applied this principle of network effects by focusing relentlessly on improving the user experience while giving away their advertising-free product, a radical concept at the time. This strategy made sense because the real potential of networks occurs after critical mass is reached. They made a bet on Metcalfe's Law, wagering that the return in the long term would far outweigh the costs in the short term. Because once a critical mass is reached, exponential growth occurs and the product increases massively in value, both to users and advertisers. With size, the act of connecting and growing the network passed increasingly from the organisational hub to its users, enabling scalability and sustainability.

Social media sites like a network leader are in pursuit of critical mass, what Malcolm Gladwell described as *The Tipping Point.*[5] The moment is when a trend, a social movement, a product or an idea spreads through social networks like wildfire, creating a craze. In effect, what platform companies and network leaders are trying to ignite is a social epidemic, where their ideas and the changes they are trying to create go viral and infect the entire social network.

Over the past year or so, we have become sadly familiar with the language and trajectory of epidemics. The spread of Covid-19 will have begun with one person, Patient Zero, who got sick and infected a handful of others, who, in turn, infected other people and so on until the virus reached a tipping point and spread with exponential speed across the globe, borne by the deadly power of human networks of connection. And, as we know, ideas, messages, behaviours and products can spread through a population in the same way that viruses spread. They gain a life and momentum of their own, profiting from the two fundamental aspects of social networks: connection and contagion.

Connection, as you will remember, refers to a network's shape or structure, its topology, the arrangement of nodes and the ties or connections between them. Contagion, however, refers to the networks function or physiology, what, if anything, flows through and across the connections. Being more central to the network makes you more susceptible to whatever is flowing through the network, whether it be gossip, a new behaviour or germs. Network position therefore is key. To increase the adoption of a particular behaviour in a network, it is necessary to identify and target the hubs in the social network. Those individuals who are well connected and central to the network – those who have social capital.

Gladwell's book focuses on the key ingredients of a social epidemic: the messenger, the message itself and the context of the message, which he labels, respectively, as the "Law of the Few" that certain types of people are especially effective at spreading an infectious idea, product or behaviour; the "Stickiness Factor" that by changing the presentation of a message, you can make it more contagious, that is, stickier, and have a more lasting impact; and the "Power of Context" in which the environment, the context in which the message or idea is delivered, can have a huge impact on whether enough people adopt and spread it for a tipping point to be achieved.

In other words, returning to our model of human behaviour, ideas and actions spread when people have the motivation to act and the system allows it. People change behaviour when they believe that the effort they invest will equal the expected performance – they believe they can do it. When they believe that the effort will equal the reward, it will be worth it. And when they can see other people acting on the same ideas and doing the same things, it's not just me, it's us. And finally, the context, the overall environment, must be conducive to the new ideas or ways of working.

Modelling these social relationships is like creating an index of social power as opposed to hierarchical and positional power. Specifically, in his description of the "Law of the Few", Gladwell referred to connectors, mavens and salespeople. Connectors are gregarious and intensely social, and they know the right people and therefore spread the message. Mavens, from the Yiddish meaning "one who accumulates", know lots of important stuff, whether this be expertise and/or innovative ideas. Salespeople have the skills to persuade us when we are unconvinced of what we are hearing. They are energetic, enthusiastic, charming and likeable.

In short, Mavens are data banks who provide the message, connectors are the socially contagious who spread it and salespeople are the ones that persuade us to believe it. And just being aware of these individuals and how to get them on board can help increase organisational "social intelligence" and consequently organisational performance. And through our work with public and third sector organisations, we have found the same to be true in communities.

Community Networks

Community network analysis is about mapping, weaving and building. Mapping to uncover inherent value in communities. Weaving to connect providers and clients, public servants, community activists and voluntary groups to facilitate the exchange of resources, skills and knowledge between those who have and those who need. And finally building, allowing organisations, whether public bodies or charities, to target their finite resources to where their impact will be greatest. Targeting gaps in provision or doing the stuff that only they can do, such as the provision of specialist knowledge, skills or resources. The aim is to uncover and create value through greater connectivity and co-creation rather than simply relying on traditional models of resource management. Done well, community network analysis offers a solution to the challenge facing many charities and most public sector services: that of being asked to do more and more with less and less.

Traditionally, some local government institutions and charitable bodies have adopted a deficit approach to community development and regeneration, meaning that they start by looking at the problems of an area, such as crime, unemployment and poor health, but are slower to ask what is right and what is valued in the locality, an approach which can be very damaging to the self-esteem of local communities.

In contrast, Asset-Based Community Development (ABCD)[6] and Community Asset Mapping[7] seek to uncover value. Community Asset Mapping is a networked approach, which, like social network analysis, aims to catalogue everything of value in a community and create a more balanced picture of what it is actually like to live there. With this picture in hand, you are then able to ask insightful questions to help connect those who have with those who need and target your own organisational resources more effectively and efficiently. Such questions might include:

- Are the right connections in place?
- Are any key connections missing?
- Who are playing leadership roles? Who is not, but should be?
- Who are the experts in process, planning and practice?
- Who are the mentors that others seek out for advice?
- Who are the innovators?
- Are ideas shared and acted upon?
- Are collaborative alliances already formed or forming between individuals, groups, departments, organisations, institutions and communities?

We will return to the power of questions as a tool of leadership when we consider the practice of Leading beyond Authority, but for the moment it is important to highlight the link here to Professor Reg Revans, specifically action learning and questioning insight. Revans, the founder of Action Learning, stated that organisational survival is based on the ability to learn at a rate equal to or greater than the rate of change. He went on to propose a learning methodology that valued questioning over being taught, or as he put it "more learning and less teaching", founded on the equation: L = P + Q (Learning = Programmed Knowledge + Questioning insight).[8]

The importance of questioning insight links to the distinction we made earlier between puzzles and problems, which was a distinction that Revans also made. He argued that puzzles have "best" solutions and can be resolved by applying knowledge with the help of experts (and, if he were alive today, he would add Artificial Intelligence [AI]). Problems, however, lack known answers and are therefore best approached through the search for fresh questions. Revans argued that for anyone stuck with a difficulty or dilemma questions could reveal new possibilities, even simple questions: What are you trying to do? What is stopping you? What can you do about this? But especially in relation to organisational problems: Who knows? Who cares? Who can?[9] Such questioning also informed Revans' broader thinking about organisational learning, which he described as depending upon "the upward communication of doubt" (1982, pp. 280–6).[10] In his discussions with managers, he would often restate this principle as "doubt ascending speeds wisdom from above", an adage that challenges the hierarchical assumptions that underpin many change models and is fundamental to community asset mapping.

Mapping

Before you can improve your network, you need to understand it. Improved connectivity, whether in organisations or communities, starts with a network map, identifying Who knows, Who cares and Who can.[11] This can be as crude as pen and paper or as sophisticated as network visualisation software used in Social Network Analysis (SNA), but the result is a picture of the elements in the network and the relationships between them. A network map shows the existing nodes and links in the network, where nodes are people, groups or organisations, and links reveal the relationships, information flows and transactions between them. Going forward, it also allows the design of strategies to create new connections and to track the spread and density of networks.

In a community context, mapping has made its way from the work of NGOs in the developing world[12] to communities in the developed world with the aim of enabling communities to map the details of their surrounding infrastructure and assets, and at the same time empower those communities to act themselves. It encourages the community to consider what it can achieve itself before seeking assistance elsewhere, putting them in a stronger position to represent themselves with charities, and local and national government.

At its heart is the assumption that communities are capable and knowledgeable about the services and resources they want and need, though they do not necessarily have equal or fair access to them. The process not only makes communities aware of what they can achieve by themselves by working together, it also helps develop skills and capacity within the community, and that knowledge also stays with the community. It can be managed, built upon and improved as the community achieves and undergoes change.

Broadly speaking, Community Asset Mapping identifies three types of Assets:

1. Individual – skills, talents, abilities, knowledge and enthusiasm.
2. Community – groups, associations, teams, activities, streets and neighbourhoods.
3. Institutional – schools, colleges, churches, mosques, amenities, cafes, shops, parks, facilities, libraries, businesses and other services.

Not only is it important to list the assets, but also to understand how they are currently being used and could be used. Asset map in hand, we are then able to uncover and share resources, helping connect those who have with those who need.

Weaving. There are two parts to network weaving: relationship building, particularly across traditional divides, so that people have access to innovation and new information; and facilitating collaborations for mutual benefit. The nature of these collaborations should be such that it creates a state of emergence, where the outcome, a vibrant organisation or a healthy community is more than the sum of the many collaborations. The local interactions benefit from the inherent emergent complexity of networks, creating a synergistic outcome that no one could have accomplished alone.

Network Leaders, therefore, have two key roles. The first is to create a conducive environment by overcoming barriers to collaboration and aligning the system towards collective action. And the second is to enable other people to act as connectors, hubs and Network Leaders, and create a sustainable and scalable Multi-Hub Small-World Network within the broader core-periphery system of other networks.

Building. There are several benefits to network weaving, not least of which is building relationships, particularly across traditional divides, so that people have access to innovation and new information as well as facilitating collaborations for mutual benefit within and between communities. In other words, moving from a hub-and-spoke to multi-hub networks. But in addition, by identifying who they can work with and through, network analysis allows institutions and organisations to focus on what they do best and target their finite resources more effectively and efficiently to where their impact will be greatest, thereby unlocking the conundrum of doing more with less.

In this sense, it is an aid to strategy, allowing organisations to look carefully at what they do and identify their core or unique offering in the broader network:

- Which of our products or services are most distinctive?
- Which of our products or services are most sustainable and provide the greatest return on investment?
- Which of our customers are most satisfied?
- Which of the activities in our value chain are the most different and effective?

This allows organisations to refocus on their distinctive resources and capabilities and realign effort towards the stuff that only they can do and the things that they do best.

Crucially, an asset-based approach builds from the bottom up. Identifying what is already there rather than assuming solutions to problems needs to be externally imposed. It adopts a collaborative mind-set and seeks win-win solutions, unifying coalitions and helping build and sustain communities. It requires public and third sector organisations to help build and repair existing networks by putting the right people in touch with each other, garnering the endorsement of credible community members and building trust by providing the support they actually need.

In short, connective power is about bringing the pieces together from across an organisation or community to make them greater than the whole. It is an ability to work across boundaries, aligning ideas with people and resources in pursuit of action. Having identified the assets in the system, network leaders are connectors and synergy spotters, accomplished at connecting those who have with those who need, cross-fertilising and spreading knowledge and making connections to help things grow towards a common purpose. It should not therefore be confused or maligned by associations with personal networking (although that is inevitably a part). Connective power is about connecting people, skills, knowledge and resources for the benefit of the whole, not for selfish ends.

Furthermore, instead of being the sole driver of an idea, you can achieve a lot more by collaborating with people who know and trust you. Organisations and communities are not built, sustained and best served by a single hub (individual, organisation or institution). To be sustainable, they depend upon multiple hubs that are themselves connected to a larger network of cores and peripheries, providing the power of both strong and weak links and creating a conducive environment for things to happen.

Caroline Naven – Leading a Preparation for Adulthood Programme

Caroline leads a new multidisciplinary programme in a large urban local authority in the UK. Her team and its many stakeholders aim to improve the lives of young people to enable a smooth transition to adulthood, by tackling both structural and personal socio-economic factors that contribute to poor outcomes for young people. Structural factors can include poverty, variable access to health and social care, poor housing, lack of employment and educational opportunities and the impact of austerity which has led to cuts in statutory provision. Personal factors can include trauma and adverse childhood experiences such as domestic abuse, bereavement, experience of the care system and substance misuse. The overarching approach is one of prevention and early intervention, but if this is not possible, then tackling problems pre-emptively before they get worse, working to put small solutions in place early on, which will reduce the need for larger and more costly solutions in later life.

Examples of initiatives include primary-level interventions by coaching and resilience and restorative justice workers in pupil referral units and direct work with young people by family support workers. Specialist employment and housing officers use a strengths-based approach to assist with employment opportunities and independent living. At secondary level, a programme of on-line activities provided an opportunity for young people to be connected to their community, thus reducing social isolation and maintaining good health and well-being.

Caroline's approach to leading the preparation for adulthood programme is founded on the principle of collaboration and co-production of initiatives with partners and communities across the whole system, which depends upon creating and maintaining relationships with the many agencies involved and, in turn, requires effective systems and structures for continuous improvement, all focused on reducing costs while improving outcomes for young people and their families/carers. All of which is founded on a strategy of map, weave, build and track.

Mapping began by identifying stakeholders to work with on the programme, which she broke down into three categories: internal, external and, most important of all, young people and their families/carers. Internal stakeholders included managers within Directorates across the Council and Children's Trust to ascertain what had already been done to map the environment and the range of current expectations. External stakeholders included a wide variety of partner organisations: statutory providers such as education and health providers; private sector organisations (primarily in relation to employment opportunities); the voluntary and community sector, such as Community Catalysts who supported the team to develop an online programme of activities during the pandemic; and finally, young people and their families/carers, which recognised the relative youth and rich ethnic diversity of the urban environment. Special emphasis was placed upon better outcomes through co-production and co-design of support and interventions with young people and their families.

The views of the Parent Carer Forum and the Rights & Participation Service as well as marginalised "easy to ignore" young people attending the Youth Offending Service were also sought. Not only did this approach take account of the diversity of views, values and culture across the education, health and social care systems, it also allowed a thorough examination of system readiness to co-design the project and what would be needed to achieve transformational change. In addition, it provided hard evidence to establish a baseline to enable measurement of impact.

With the initial mapping and analysis in place, Caroline and her team were able to start to weave and build the network. They began by weaving the programme agenda into existing fora and partnerships. They looked at existing work, noting who was involved, what the project entailed, why they were set up and when and where they took place. They also built upon the drive within local authorities for an asset-based community development approach.

She, her colleagues, partners and young people worked together to develop the way forward, identifying "natural leaders and ambassadors" to work alongside her team. With so many stakeholders, they also established a number of implementation teams, consisting of key partner agencies, which established a shared purpose and decision-making structure to develop radical ideas and pool resources. Internally, Caroline drove the changes by ensuring that each member of her staff had clear objectives and measurable performance and behavioural targets, all of which drove collective programme outcomes.

Crucially, to overcome the uncertainties of such a shared endeavour, she ensured that a co-developed clear vision engaged people, empowered people to share and contribute, encouraged creativity and innovation by being genuinely humble herself and cultivating a culture of openness to suggestions and ideas, encouraging data sharing and identifying further opportunities for impact, such as social enterprise.

She and her team are also at pains to highlight the potential cost effectiveness of the approach, which requires a thorough system of tracking and monitoring. Alongside the analysis of data, intelligence and other resources, they ensured the development of new metrics so that performance could be understood at all levels. After six months, a report was produced detailing outcomes as well as corrective action taken to keep the programme on track. Monthly reports presented to Boards, comprising of senior officers from health and social care, identify progress against outcomes and KPIs as well as highlighting necessary changes to ensure continuous improvement.

In conclusion, she observes, sustainability has always been at the heart of the programme and requires staff buy-in, strong leadership, stakeholder engagement, an evidence base and consideration of competing priorities, which, in turn, depends upon team and stakeholder alignment, autonomy for managers to promote ownership and accountability, innovation through delegation and empowerment, challenging underperformance, maintaining momentum by sharing good news stories and wins, big and small, utilising analytics from all agencies to enable the monitoring of outcomes, continually testing and developing processes and systems and finally, being forward thinking – monitoring the horizon and being ready to adapt collectively in the face of threats and opportunities.

See Appendix 2 Leader Biographies.

Notes

1 Think of Paul Revere and other members of the "Sons of Liberty", a secret group organised around opposition to British taxation in the American colonies, who regularly carried rebel communications between Boston and Philadelphia before his famous "midnight ride" and the War of the American Revolution. It is worth noting that Revere's "midnight ride", later immortalised in verse, significantly underplays the role of the other network members who also rode that night.
2 Pentland, A. (2014). *Social Physics: How Good Ideas Spread: The Lessons from a New Science*. New York: Penguin Press.
3 Krebs, V. and Holley, J. (2006). Building Smart Communities through Network Weaving. (online) Available at https://community-wealth.org/content/building-smart-communities-through-network-weaving (accessed 17 April 2021).

4 Metcalfe's Law was postulated as a theory in the early 1990s by George Glider and changed the way we think about networks, from telephones and fax machines to the internet and social networks. Gilder called it Metcalfe's Law after the founder of Ethernet.
5 Gladwell, M. (2000). *The Tipping Point: How Little Things Can Make a Big Difference*. London: Abacus.
6 See, for example, Nesta. Available at https://www.nesta.org.uk/feature/realising-value-resource-centre/asset-based-approaches-in-a-health-and-wellbeing-context/?gclid=EAIaIQobChMIp-bzvP3i6gIVhe3tCh2pkAXVEAAYASAAEgKoCPD_BwE (accessed 17 April 2021).
7 See for example, McKnight, J.L. and Kretzmann, J.P. (1990). Mapping Community Capacity. (online) Available at https://mn.gov/mnddc/parallels2/pdf/90s/90/90-MCC-McKnight_Kretzmann.pdf (accessed 17 April 2021).
8 Revans, R.W. (1982). *The Origins & Growth of Action Learning*. Bromley, UK: Charwell Bratt.
9 Revans, R.W. (1982) ibid. p. 715.
10 Revans, R.W. (1982) ibid. pp. 280–6.
11 Revans, R.W. (1982) ibid. p. 715.
12 See Water Aid. (online) Available at https://washmatters.wateraid.org/publications/community-mapping-a-tool-for-community-organising-2005-0 (accessed 17 April 2021).

Summary

Convening power begins with a recognition that leaders have something to say that is worth listening to, a personal manifesto that they articulate and demonstrate in words and actions. Having made sense of the system for themselves, they make sense of it for others. Bringing them into a shared understanding of where we are now and then sharing their personal manifesto of purpose, ethics and core beliefs, to describe where we are going and how.

Network Leaders don't profess to know all the answers but they recognise that those around them might. A Network Leader is a humble leader, drawing on their web of connections to bring people together from across organisations, businesses, communities and societies to find solutions, identify ways forward and get things done.

Network Leaders understand the dynamics of power, influence and politics, but use this understanding in a principled manner, valuing integrity and morale courage in themselves and others. It is a candour that draws people to them, driven by purposeful conversations that cultivate trust and a character that creates a desire in others to follow.

Leadership Questions

- What is your personal manifesto?
- What are you trying to achieve?
- What is the underlying movement you are tapping into?
- Who knows, Who cares and Who can?
- How can you begin to build your network and connect them?

DOI: 10.4324/9781003092582-25

Part V

Leading beyond Authority

If convening power is the ability to attract and gather people around you by having something to say that is worth listening to, then leading beyond authority is the ability to turn those ideas into action without the need for formal or positional power. It is leadership defined by personality, not role or job title, and gives you permission to operate across the organisation in pursuit of shared goals. And, as Julia Middleton observes, in this space "Nothing happens without networks".[1]

Most leaders have an inner network, their team or department, where they have formal and positional authority to lead; an outer network, the wider organisation, where their formal authority gradually diminishes; and a peripheral network, beyond the organisation, where they may have no formal authority at all. Leadership in the outer and peripheral networks requires different leadership skills, and experience from formal leadership positions will not necessarily help, it may even hinder, because out there no one need do what you say.

Many successful people learn to lead in roles where they have clear authority; they have set objectives, a budget and a team of people whose job it is to support them. The result of this leadership model, however, is that many organisations operate in silos, with each team or department looking upwards and downwards but seldom sideways at issues that cross the verticals. What organisations often need are leaders who can see across the whole organisation and make the sum of the parts greater than the whole.

This is particularly important for those making the transition from functional manager to business leader. The development of lateral and vertical relationships with other functional and business unit managers, all of whom will be outside their immediate control, becomes critical to achieving personal and

DOI: 10.4324/9781003092582-26

organisational goals. Operating beside players with diverse affiliations, backgrounds, objectives and incentives requires a manager to formulate business rather than functional objectives, and to work through the coalitions and networks needed to sell ideas and compete for resources.

Network Leaders have an intuitive understanding of the importance of context and recognise that as leaders they need to understand the complexity of human interactions. They also understand how the sum of those interactions scales up into the ebb and flow of corporate life and a daily operating rhythm. They hold in balance two key aspects: a rich understanding of organisational life as social system and their role within it, alongside a keen appreciation of how they use that understanding to make things happen.

The organisation, understood as a social system, means recognising that when people come together, they influence each other and develop mental models about how to get things done. The process of decision-making and the exercise of authority are not solely a function of hierarchy, but are instead processes of negotiation that occur at the intersections of people's ideas and energy. At a practical level, energy can be created through these interactions or lost as emotional friction allows that energy to dissipate. The network leader is attuned to that flow of energy and how to use it. While this runs the risk of being seen as nothing more than playing "organisational politics", this is a naïve interpretation. As we discussed previously, there is a reality about organisations as coalitions of competing interests.

Skilled Network Leaders have a high degree of self-awareness that enables them to reflect and interpret what is happening internally to themselves in order to develop an understanding of the wider collective dynamic. This internal process values intuition over logic and informs how they interact with others, and this insight allows a better understanding of others and especially the interplay of differing motivations and intentions. It also favours the informal over the formal and influence over power; it creates an ability to work across an organisation and the hierarchy.

Hugh Willmott, in his seminal paper "Strength Is Ignorance; Slavery Is Freedom: Managing Culture in Modern Organizations"[2] coined the term "corporate culturists" to describe the dominance of organisational culture by design and the prevalence of a defined vision, mission and values that shapes and enlists employees to sign up to the corporates definition of success and a set of behaviours compliant with an espoused set of values. Both leadership as a series of traits and organisations as a collection of winning formulae neglect the very human nature of people coming together and working collectively to achieve something.

Leading beyond authority is leadership defined by personality not by role and consequently depends upon personal rather positional power. We have already discussed aspects of personal influence in the context of convening power, in which leaders are able to gather people around them by having something to say worth listening to. What follows is a discussion of personal power in the context of turning ideas into action and results, which we believe requires us to lead from a different place and in a different way.

Notes

1 Middleton, J. (2007). *Beyond Authority: Leadership in a Changing World*. London: Palgrave Macmillan, p. 112.
2 Willmot, H. (1993). Strength Is Ignorance; Slavery Is Freedom: Managing Culture in Modern Organizations. *Journal of Management Studies*, 30(4), pp. 515–52.

17
Leading from a Different Place

Leading from a Different Place is about overcoming your assumptions by looking for the boundaries and edges of your knowledge, broadening your horizons, identifying patterns in multiple streams of information and finding time for thinking it through, reflecting on what you have learned and making sense of what you now know. It is a continual process of accumulation and iterative understanding.

When you are immersed within a paradigm, it is difficult to see beyond it. There is a conceptual centre of gravity that acts as a filter for ideas and opportunities. This deep familiarity with the status quo makes it psychologically difficult to deconstruct or disrupt it. Which is why novices, new starters and outsiders (weak ties) can be helpful. The lack of immersion in how things are done around here or experience of having seen something different provides the psychological latitude to questions, conventions and assumptions. But you don't have to step outside the walls to see things differently. What is required is a new perspective and new information that allows individuals to see something familiar in a new way. As Marcel Proust wrote, "The real voyage of discovery consists not in seeking new landscapes but in having new eyes".

As a challenger bank, Virgin Money under the leadership of Dame Jayne-Anne Gadhia[1] took on the conventions of banking by focusing on the customer and fundamentally reappraising its business model. Guided by a belief that was captured in the expression "Everyone's Better Off" or simply "EBO", this became a guiding philosophy that demanded all colleagues personally interpret it to guide their action. It was most notably captured in a diagram drawn hastily at a management treat.

Matthew Syed relates how in his 2018 letter to shareholders, Jeff Bezos talked about the importance of incremental innovation, doubling down on existing ideas and exploiting their value. Yet Bezos also recognised that if you want to innovate in more profound ways, you need to step outside the existing

DOI: 10.4324/9781003092582-27

Figure 5.1 Where the Magic Happens.

framework, which he called "wandering". It is challenging for many people because it is not efficient but it's not random either. Bezos writes that it is guided by a hunch, gut instinct, intuition and curiosity, and is an essential counterbalance to efficiency, because the outsized discoveries, the non-liner ones, require wandering.[2] And Bezos is not being fanciful in this regard.

Neuroscience suggests that "mind-wandering", drifting in and out of engagement with our environment rather than being idleness or time-wasting:

> is a necessary part of mental housekeeping, allowing us to integrate our past, present and future, interrogate our social lives, and create a large-scale personal narrative … Task focused attention and mind-wandering are two sides of the same mental coin. We focus on tasks in order to perform them, and we focus away from those tasks to gather resources to allow us to solve them when they are difficult, or simply to integrate the information that we have learned during the focus on the task. This flickering between states is what allows us to live a productive and creative life; a variety of experiments show that active mind-wandering facilitates subsequent creative problem-solving.[3]

Overcoming Assumptions

Problem solving should always include a question about assumptions. However, what you are assuming is, by its very nature, a difficult question to answer. An assumption is a thing that is accepted as true or as certain to happen. It is taken for granted. We all hold implicit assumptions, theories, heuristics (rules of thumb) about how things are done or the way things work. Typically, those assumptions hold true and provide a helpful framework. Without them, we would be unable to cope with the avalanche of information with which we are bombarded daily. We would be unable to function. Occasionally, however, these assumptions can backfire, stifling progress and limiting potential because we didn't think to question them. In Rebel Ideas, Matthew Syed quotes the actor and comedian John Cleese, "Everybody has theories. The dangerous people are those who are not aware of their own theories. That is, the theories on which they operate are largely unconscious".[4]

One method to overcome assumptions is Double-Loop Learning, a concept and process that encourages people to think more deeply about their beliefs and taken-for-granted ideas. It was created by Chris Argyris,[5] an academic and organisational trainer, and developed into an effective management learning tool in concert with Donald Schon,[6] who we discussed earlier in relation to reflective practice. Argyris conceived double-loop learning in contrast to single-loop learning. The latter is concerned with adapting and improving the efficiency of our strategies and actions in response to the observed results and consequences; it is about doing things right. Double-loop learning is about changing the objectives themselves by revaluating our underlying goals, values, beliefs and theories (doing the right things).

The most easily understood analogy is a household thermostat. Single-loop learning is about achieving a given temperature: we set the thermostat to 20 degrees and it turns up the heat whenever the temperature drops below 20 (the objective). Double-loop learning involves changing the setting on the thermostat (changing the objective of the system). In human systems, however, double-loop learning is not only about changing the objective, but involves questioning the assumptions about that objective, discovering and inventing new alternatives and identifying new ways of approaching problems.

The method used to achieve this type of deeper learning is through encouraging dialogue among the learners. It proposes that the facilitator/educator drill down into a topic to identify and bring to the surface taken-for-granted assumptions and beliefs. The intention is to help people acquire and integrate new information and develop new skills, to question and possibly discard familiar and perhaps dysfunctional ways of thinking, feeling and acting. It aims to take learners past the obvious, focusing at first on what we perceive to be true and then moving towards what may be hidden or less obvious. So here's a challenge for you.

You and a partner are given a large piece of paper (a sheet from a flipchart or a broadsheet newspaper for example) which is placed on the floor in front of you. Now, the challenge is for you both to stand on the paper but without being able to touch one another. Sounds impossible, but there is a simple solution (the answer is at the end of the chapter). When using it in workshops we have had all manner of imaginative, though incorrect, suggestions: ranging from turning back-to-back, tying each person's hands together, putting each person in a bin bag to a variety of contortionist options that would not look out of place in a game of Twister, but none of them come anywhere close. So why do most people not see the simple solution immediately?

It has been said that assumption is the mother of all cock-ups. It may not be the mother, but it is certainly a close family member in many day-to-day challenges. The problem is that our brains are very adept at recognising and creating patterns in disparate data. It is these mental models, rules of thumb or heuristics that allow us to function effectively, allowing us to rapidly sift and sort information into useful knowledge according to whether it confirms or contradicts the patterns already embedded in our minds. The danger is that we misread the signals and lock onto patterns that aren't there. Take the example of hot dogs.

Every 4th of July, about 40,000 people gather in Coney Island in the United States and more than one million tune in on ESPN, the sports cable channel, to watch men and women defy human digestive limits in a hot dog eating competition. Prior to 2001, the record was 25 hot dogs and buns in ten minutes, but in that year Takeru Kobayashi, a young man from Japan, smashed the record consuming a staggering 53 hot dogs and buns within the set time. So what enabled a young man, weighing just 112 lb, to consume nearly 8 lb of bread and sausage, more than twice the amount of anyone before him?

Mr Kobayashi's winning insight was not to assume that he must eat the hot dog and bun as you or I would. Instead, he broke the hot dogs in two, stuffed them in his mouth with one hand, while dunking the bun in water with his other hand to make it easier to swallow. Neither of which is forbidden in the rules and water is always provided. His breakthrough was to avoid the mental shortcuts of the other competitors and do something different. His insight was to go beyond what the other competitors assumed to be true and focus on what was actually there.

It turns out that much of our understanding is based upon assumption not observation and disrupting conventional thought patterns can lead to new associations and ideas. Assumption reversal, for example, takes the core notions in any statement, problem or subject and turns them on their head. For example, restaurants have a physical location, what if they didn't, and taxi companies have cars, what if they didn't? (both of which have been turned into innovative business models: "ghost restaurants" during lockdown and Uber). A more systematic approach is to stop and investigate your assumptions by asking the right questions. Rudyard Kipling, according to his short poem, kept six honest serving men – "What, Why, When, How, Where and Who" – and used them to interrogate problems and assumptions.[7]

Take his advice by writing down the problem and your thinking. Put the problem at the top of the page and write down your thoughts on the topic – what, why, when, how, where and who. When you've filled as much of a page as you can, stop, go back and find the assumptions – what are you taking for granted? An assumption is anything you don't have actual proof for, an interpretation you've made of someone else's motivations or something implied by something you wrote. Write your assumptions on a separate piece of paper and then examine them to see where they might lead (try reversing them and see what happens). Writing things down forces us to think more deeply about them; it also tends to widen our perspective beyond the obvious and taken for granted.

At the end of the first verse of his poem, Kipling also suggested that you give those questions a rest; so take his advice and have a break. If you have the leisure to mull over a problem, or even better sleep on it, do so. It seems that brilliant flashes of insight have a unique aspect to them. They almost never occur when you are focused on solving a problem, but after an intense, prolonged struggle with the problem, followed by a break – a change of scene, time away doing something else, or after a rest. Rest frees the mind from control of the conscious mind, allowing the free association of memories and ideas, which lead, in ways that are not yet fully understood, to unexpected connections and combinations.

Another way to avoid self-limiting assumptions is to get a second opinion, but paired or group solutions can be equally incomplete unless a diversity of knowledge and experience is represented. As previously discussed, homogenous groups tend to exist in an echo chamber, producing ideas that are nothing more than updated versions of existing thinking, which still leave assumptions unquestioned. To break out of a rut, we need to solicit advice from unlikely sources who may see the problem in an entirely different way. In his TEDx NASA talk, Stephen Shapiro[8] observed:

> If you're working on an aerospace challenge, and you have 100 aerospace engineers working on it, the 101st aerospace engineer is not going to make that much of a difference. But you add a biologist, or a nanotechnologist, or a musician, and maybe now you have something fundamentally different.

In a similar vein, best practice is to not over-rely on best practice, which typically emerges from our current assumptions and worldview. In complex systems, feeling your way counts for more than working by rote, and this begins with asking two key questions: what am I not seeing here and what else might be true? Most of us tend to default to what we already know because it makes us feel safe. Early in childhood, we begin to develop an internal narrative about how the world works and what we think is true. Over time, without realizing it, we come to believe that this subjective story is objectively true (we call it common sense) and most of us spend the rest of our lives sticking to it. As Einstein observed, "Common sense is the collection of prejudices acquired by age eighteen". At a personal level, this requires that we look for information at and beyond the boundaries and edges of our knowledge.

Look for Boundaries and Edges

The most exciting things happening in science, technology and business occur where networks converge, the weak links at the intersections and edges. The divisions between formerly separate industries and disciplines are breaking down and the real opportunities for growth are where they interconnect. Self-driving cars, for example, don't just need automotive engineers; they also need people who understand software, traffic engineering, the psychology of drivers and regulatory processes.

And if everything is connected and interdependent, then we are going back to the idea of the polymath: the generalist not the specialist. The most innovative developments of the future, in business, science and the arts, are likely to come from creative generalists who blend unique disciplines with broad understanding. The continued success of today's organisations, companies, communities and societies will depend on individuals capable of solving problems by thinking outside the proverbial box of their own discipline: T-shaped individuals who combine deep specialist knowledge (the down bar of the T) with a broad understanding of other domains, departments and disciplines (the crossbar).

George Murray's study of the most significant scientists[9] found that 15 of the 20 were polymaths: Newton, Galileo, Aristotle, Kepler, Descartes, Huygens, Laplace, Faraday, Pasteur, Ptolemy, Hooke, Leibniz, Euler, Darwin and Maxwell were all generalists. Darwin developed his ideas about evolution by drawing on disciplines from geology to zoology, and a contemporary example of a business polymath is Elon Musk, who has combined an understanding of physics, engineering, programming, design, manufacturing and business to create several multibillion dollar companies in completely different fields.

Yet, despite the need for polymaths, such individuals are quite rare. That's because society has traditionally promoted specialisation over generalisation. The history of human labour has been one of increasing specialisation. In the days of the hunter-gatherers, every member of the tribe would have been expected to be proficient in every task. As we progressed however, from agricultural to industrial and now post-industrial economies, workers have become increasingly specialised, based on a long-standing assumption that the more deeply you specialise, the more easily you can find well-paid employment.

There was an interlude, in the 14th to 16th centuries, when polymaths found favour, often exemplified by Leonardo da Vinci. However, we soon reverted to the specialist, not just for its economic benefits but also for the specialist's undoubted contribution to the advancement of knowledge. We need specialists to dig ever deeper into their chosen field, but we also need polymaths, because generalists offer three distinct advantages.

The first, as previously noted, is that innovation comes from the edge. The most creative breakthroughs come from atypical combinations of skills and knowledge. Brian Uzzi, a professor at the Kellogg School of Management, and his colleagues analysed more than 26 million scientific papers going back hundreds of years and found that the papers with the most impact often had teams with an atypical mix of backgrounds. In a second study, he found that the top performing studies also cited atypical combinations of other studies: 90% conventional citations from their own field and 10% from other fields.[10] What we need are people who can bridge the gaps between disciplines and departments, acting as idea translators and synergy makers.

The second is avoidance of bias. Specialisation has undoubtedly been important for the advancement of knowledge. But one of the dangers of such specialisation is that it often coincides with cognitive bias: a mental blind spot that overlooks potential solutions because of erroneous assumptions and established patterns of thought. At an organisational level, it is known as Groupthink, which is a common phenomenon in political, business and scientific spheres. To counteract this tendency, we need people who can see beyond the bias of their cherished but often isolated domain or department.

The third is that complex "wicked" problems require multidisciplinary approaches. Many of the greatest challenges currently facing individuals and society benefit from solutions that integrate multiple disciplines. Climate change, for example, will require us to transform the way we generate, store and use energy and the ways in which we manage more extremes of weather and climate. For that, we will need to integrate our meteorological understanding with our understanding of ecological systems, human psychology, the built environment as well as financial and socio-economic factors. We need people who can identify and champion the synergies between these various disciplines and challenge what Matthew Syed calls the "clone fallacy: thinking in linear way about complex, multidimensional challenges".[11]

Polymaths bring the best of what has been discovered across various fields to help them be more effective in their core specialisation. They build atypical combinations of skills and knowledge across domains, and then integrate them to create breakthrough ideas and even brand new disciplines and industries. And this isn't just an aspiration for those wishing to be pre-eminent scientists or multibillionaire business leaders. We can all benefit from becoming polymaths, from becoming more T-shaped: combining our deep specialist knowledge with a broader, strategic understanding of the business and industry in which we operate. In this sense, the polymath advantage is essentially entrepreneurial.

Not necessarily in the sense of starting their own business or launching a start-up (though they may well do this), but it is in their tendency to harness innovation and find better ways of doing things wherever they are. Most organisations, especially large corporations, are overflowing with creative ideas that never get executed. Entrepreneurship, in this sense, is the process that turns those ideas into actual innovations, and when it occurs in large corporations, we tend to refer to it as intrapreneurship or corporate innovation, which means acting like an entrepreneur, but within the ecosystem of a larger, more traditional, organisation.

Network Leaders constantly seek out information about how the system works and how it is likely to change in the shape of new projects and opportunities, organisational restructuring and reorganisation, resource allocations and budgets and long-range plans. Being "intrapreneurial" is about empowering yourself to make change happen, and empowerment, as is well attested, leads to greater employee engagement and productivity. Even a simple reframing of your role, not letting your job specification define you, can make your work more intrapreneurial and meaningful. This is particularly true if you are generally reward sensitive, meaning you are more motivated by chasing carrots than avoiding sticks. In fact, people who are typically cautious and risk (stick) averse may end up suffering if their role becomes more intrapreneurial, because in the realm of uncertainty they will have to make choices. But those who relish the opportunities of uncertainty can make things happen beyond their job role and authority.

Clearly, there is too much knowledge in the world today for one person to know everything that is known, like Da Vinci's "Renaissance Man", but it is possible to read, research and create a network of ties that allows us to learn from people in other disciplines and become sufficiently knowledgeable in more than one discipline. Anyone who is curious and loves learning can use the polymath advantage to be more successful in their life and career. And that requires that we broaden our horizons.

Broaden Your Horizons

Leading from the boundaries and the edge requires that you identify them. You can't investigate or lead at the interfaces if you don't know where they are. Yet many organisations unwittingly encourage employees to look no further than their own immediate environment, their function or business unit. Consequently, they miss out on the potential insights employees could gain if they scanned their inner, outer and peripheral networks. The focus for most organisations, and consequently their people, is on what's directly ahead, which means they lack peripheral vision. This can leave them vulnerable to rivals who detect and act on weak or ambiguous signals.

Network Leaders look for game-changing information beyond the current boundaries of their team and organisation and at the periphery of their industry. And to do this, they learn extensively, building wide external networks to help them scan the horizon. Equally, however, they are discerning. Critical thinkers question everything. They reframe problems to get to the bottom of things, in terms of root causes. They challenge assumptions, current beliefs and mind-sets (including their own) and they uncover hypocrisy, manipulation and bias in organisational decision-making. Following conventional wisdom exposes you to fewer raised eyebrows and less second-guessing, but if you swallow every management fad, every herd-like belief and new opinion at face value, you, your team and your organisation will flounder and lose competitive advantage.

Network Leaders tap into expertise outside their organisation and even outside their industry. The domains of human knowledge that span science, technology, business, geography, politics, history, the arts, the humanities and so on, and the interfaces between them, because any of them could hold innovations and new business opportunities. The tricky part is finding the ideas most relevant to your goals. Although many innovations stem from what Abraham Flexner called the "usefulness of useless knowledge",[12] most of us simply do not have the time to pursue an open-ended exploration for new ideas. But two approaches are possible.

The first is to locate knowledge domains with high potential for value creation that have already been identified. Machine learning, for example, might be the key to an organisation's future and a Network Leader might take online courses or attend industry conferences about that technology in order to bring back and share ideas about its implications, perhaps organising workshops with colleagues to discuss its potential applications. Alternatively, given the speed at which new knowledge is being created and the difficulty in determining what might be important, Network Leaders might invest time searching for promising interfaces and proposing conferences in other industries that they and their colleagues could attend, or courses on new skill sets they'd like to take or identifying domain experts their organisation could invite for workshops. But whatever they do with new data, Network Leaders are always alert to new knowledge and emerging patterns.

Identify Patterns

We have pattern-making minds. Our memory is essentially a database of patterns, things we have learned about the world through trial and error from a very early age – if I cry, someone will pick me up and cuddle me. Patterns get stored in our long-term memory waiting to be used to help us understand and respond quickly to new or uncommon situations. The more accurate the patterns you have learned, the more options you have for solving new problems. Our minds are always simulating different courses of action, but sometimes there's not enough information to ensure that a perceived pattern is accurate.

Ambiguity is unsettling and it is tempting to reach for a fast but potentially foolish solution. Without complete data our minds fill in the missing details by interpreting what we sense via the patterns we have stored in our memory (just as the brain will fill in the missing details from our field of vision caused by the blind spots in our retina), and in the absence of information to the contrary, we will jump to conclusions by relying on the existing interpretations our mind has created. But a good strategic leader holds steady, synthesising information from many sources before developing a viewpoint: seeking patterns in multiple sources of data, questioning prevailing assumptions, looking for opportunities and weak signals in a sea of data and encouraging others to do the same. Leaders need to recognise what is constant (applies all the time) and what is variable (unique to the situation).

Network Leaders do this by creating connections between ideas, places, plans and people that others fail to see. In other words, they connect the dots. They interpret what might appear to be ambiguous and incomplete and help make sense of it. Superior pattern matching is one of the primary reasons why experienced people tend to make better decisions than inexperienced people, because they have a larger mental database, and this expertise is often called intuition. Intuition, however, is a rather elusive concept.

There was a moment during the Battle of Salamanca in 1812 as the French and Anglo-Portuguese armies manoeuvred fruitlessly to achieve a more advantageous position, when Wellington, who had been eating a chicken leg while glancing restlessly at the French through his telescope, suddenly declared, "By God that will do"! Throwing his chicken leg in the air, he jumped into the saddle and cantered up the hill to get a better view, before riding off to deliver his orders. It was a moment of realisation which turned the confrontation in favour of the alliance and ultimately won the battle.[13] It was a moment of coup d'oeil (pronounced Coo Die), a glance or quick view that led to a moment of realisation or intuition. Over 100 years later, T.E. Lawrence (known to posterity as Lawrence of Arabia), wrote in *The Army Quarterly and Defence Journal* of October 1920 that:

> Nine-tenths of tactics are certain, and taught in books: but the irrational tenth is like the kingfisher flashing across the pool, and that is the test of generals. It can only be ensured by instinct, sharpened by thought practicing the stroke so often that at the crisis it is as natural as a reflex.

Intuition, also known as tacit knowledge, is when our unconscious mind synthesises what we know to produce new ideas and theories. Knowledge is key: combining theory and practice, experience and intellect, big picture and detail. Research psychologist Gary Klein's working definition of insight is "an unexpected shift in our understanding that leads to a better story". The discovery of new patterns of thinking using the patterns you already have.[14] Neurologically, insight appears to be a combination of the central executive and the daydreaming mode. Famously, it is something that happens when you are doing something else. The left brain lines up what we know about a problem, while the right brain, where the neurons are more broadly tuned and better connected, lets go of the problem. This allows the mind to go into free flow and make unexpected connections, where disparate neural networks are brought together creating a previously unrelated whole.

In his exploration of insight, Klein begins with a four-stage model developed by Graham Wallas, an early advocate for the use of psychology in politics and business, in his 1926 book *The Art of Thought* which breaks down insight into four stages: a Preparation Stage, where we investigate the problem; an Incubation Stage, where we stop thinking consciously about the problem and let our unconscious take over; an Illumination Stage, when the insight bursts forth; and a Verification Stage, when we test whether the idea is valid. Wallas also claimed that people can sometimes sense that an insight is brewing in their minds. It is a useful model, but it is not a full explanation of insight.

As we can probably all attest, some insights involve no preparation, some involve no incubation and we may have no time to validate them. Klein identifies several occurrences that spark an insight: contradictions, connections, coincidences, curiosities and desperation. A contradiction is the insight we get when we think "No way, that can't be right". He gives the example of Galileo and the Heliocentric universe alongside several overlooked contradictions. The financial crash of 2008, for example, was based on a belief that the housing market would keep growing alongside a decline in lending standards – but why would standards have to decline if people really believed the housing market would keep growing? And the Phoenix Memo, which was ignored by the CIA prior to 9/11 of Middle Eastern men booking flying lessons, but not interested in how to take off or land.

In terms of connections, coincidences and curiosities, he cites the Battle of Taranto in November 1940 and Pearl Harbour just over a year later. Taranto, where the British put half the Italian fleet out of commission, showed that battleships were vulnerable to airplanes launched from carriers and torpedoes designed not to dive too deep. The Japanese Admiral Yamamoto used it as a blueprint for Pearl Harbour. In developing his theory of evolution, Darwin wondered what drove the variation in species he had seen on his voyage in The Beagle. He knew farmers deliberately selected the best traits in their animals and crops, favouring their continuation, but how could it happen in nature. He saw his way to natural selection after reading Malthus's *An Essay on the Principle of Population*, which featured population growth and competition for resources. Alexander Fleming developed penicillin after he became curious during an experiment, when bacterium on one of his petri dishes became contaminated with a mould which destroyed the bacterium.

Desperation is where we re-examine our assumptions in order to break free, literally in the case of Aron Ralston. The fate of Aron Ralston, dramatized in the film *127 Hours*, describes his ordeal of falling into a rock crevice and being trapped for five days with his arm pinned by a boulder. He couldn't cut through the bones of the dead arm but using the boulder as leverage, he reasoned that he could snap the bones and then cut through the flesh. Less gruesomely, two Estonians, who met while working in London, realised that they faced converse but related problems. One was being paid euros by his Estonian HQ, but needed sterling to live in London, the other was being paid in sterling by his London HQ, but needed euros to pay his mortgage in Estonia, costing them both 5% of their salaries in bank charges. Their solution was to find a fair exchange rate and then transfer money between their personal accounts. They soon realized that others were in the same boat and set up "TransferWise". The inventor of the Internet of Things (IoT) began with the problem of how to keep track of a popular shade of lipstick in stores. His solution was to put a radio chip onto the lipstick and an antenna on the shelf. It is estimated that there will be over 27 billion networked devices in 2021.

Klein also discusses what prevents us from grasping an insight. From an organisational perspective, new ideas, surprises and errors play havoc with smooth operations. In their zeal to reduce uncertainty and minimize errors, organisations fall into what Klein calls predictability and perfection traps. The *Predictability Trap* is where high value is placed on predictability because a manager's job is made easier if they can predict the workflow, resources and schedules. Insights are the opposite of predictable, they are disruptive. They get in the way of completion and productivity because they reshape tasks and revise goals. Managers are therefore most receptive to new ideas that fit with existing practices and maintain predictability.

The Perfection Trap, on the one hand, is pervasive because errors are easy to define, easy to measure and easy to manage. Insights, on the other hand, are difficult to identify, elude measurement and are therefore difficult to manage. In well-ordered situations, with clear goals, standards and stable conditions, the pursuit of perfection makes sense (like judging a gymnast by their mistakes); but not when we face complex and chaotic conditions, with standards that keep evolving. A process may be internally valid, and therefore perfectible, but that does not mean it is externally valid, which is akin to Drucker's observation that a system may be efficient (doing things right) without being effective (doing the right things). Insights take us beyond efficiency and show us ways to improve the original plan and continually update effectiveness.

From an individual perspective, a key blockage occurs because of cognitive dissonance; the uncomfortable feeling we get when something contradicts our ideas, beliefs and theories that we use to make sense of events and arrive at judgements about other ideas. And the more central it is to our belief system, the harder it is to give up. Dissonance leads us to ignore, explain away or distort evidence that could lead to new insights. A second is inexperience. Experience is about how we use our knowledge to tune our attention and, as previously discussed, a prepared mind will recognise opportunities that the less experienced will miss. Another is a passive stance to new ideas. To be receptive to new ideas, we need to be active and open to unexpected possibilities; sceptical and ready to question the prevailing wisdom; open to collecting data; and curious. An active attitude leads to persistence in seeking new knowledge and overcoming obstacles. The problem is that some people become overly impatient with speculation and desire action. They see exploration of ideas as a waste of time and want closure, when what is required is that we take time to think.

Find Time to Think

Under the twin pressures of productivity and efficiency, most leaders and managers squeeze out thinking time. The temptation is to deal with what's directly in front of you because it always seems more urgent and concrete. The result is that most decisions are based more on reflex (what has worked before) than on reflection (what could work in future). Reflex would be fine if our world was static and problems simply repeated themselves, but it isn't and they often don't. In which case, doing what you've always done can be as risky, even more risky, than trying a new and unproven approach. The paradox is that while we are so often told that we should be more innovative and embrace change, our individual instincts and organisational culture are often the complete opposite.

Network Leaders are what Donald Schon described as reflective practitioners. They take time to think before making decisions and they consider the consequences of their actions. What is involved? Who is involved? What is at stake?

What is the opportunity and what are the risks? They recognise that what at first seems like an opportunity might reveal significant risk and what seemed risky at first might reveal a significant opportunity. But fundamentally, network leaders know that if they are to operate effectively beyond their authority, they need to value different things and use their time more judiciously, valuing thinking as much as acting. Most leaders we encounter have every minute of their calendars filled typically with meetings and catching up with their emails, and the relentless demand and pressure to respond rapidly undermine more complex thinking. Critical as decisiveness can be, effective solutions, like intuition, often emerge from taking time to wrestle with the most difficult issues rather than prematurely closing in on a solution and a decision.

One of the most powerful things a leader can do therefore is focus. Scheduling time to think about problems is a way of ensuring that they give complex issues the time and attention they need; time that might otherwise be consumed by more urgent but less intellectually demanding and value-adding priorities. Even if you can only manage ten minutes a day or an hour a week, it is worth taking time to reflect upon what you've learned and try to anticipate what might be coming next and not just what's approaching head on. It is important to sit back and look up. So take the time to schedule a meeting with yourself.

With regard to the challenge we set you at the start of this chapter, the flash of insight is to recognise the unstated assumption that you can't move the paper – you can. The answer is to place the paper under a door. You then stand on the paper on one side of the door and your colleague stands on the paper on the other side of the door. With the door shut, you will be unable to touch each other. We have also seen a large table manhandled into position between two people so that they couldn't touch each other, but I think you will agree that the door is the simpler and more satisfying solution.

Notes

1 See Appendix 2 – Leader Biographies.
2 Syed, M. (2019). *Rebel Ideas: The Power of Diverse Thinking*. London: John Murray, pp. 142–5.
3 O'Mara, S. (2020). *In Praise of Walking: The New Science of How We Walk and Why It's Good for Us*. London: Vintage, pp. 148–9.
4 Syed, M. (2019) ibid. p. 21.
5 Argyris, C. (1993). *Knowledge for Action: A Guides to Overcoming Barriers to Organizational Change*. San Francisco: Jossey-Bass Publishers.
6 Argyris, C. and Schon, D. (1978). *Organizational Learning: A Theory of Action Perspective*. Reading, MA: Addison-Wesley Publishing Co.

7 Kipling, R. I keep six honest serving men, published in Just So Stories (1902) following 'The Elephant's Child.'
8 https://www.youtube.com/watch?v=wo07i-Gf72A.
9 Murray, C. (2005). *Human Accomplishment: The Pursuit of Excellence in the Arts and Sciences, 800 B.C. to 1950*. London: Harper Collins.
10 Uzzi, B., Mukherjee, S., Stringer, M. and Jones, B. (2013) Atypical Combinations and Scientific Impact. (online) *Science*, 342. Available at https://www.kellogg.northwestern.edu/faculty/uzzi/htm/papers/Science-2013-Uzzi-468-72.pdf (accessed 17 April 2021).
11 Syed, M. (2019) op cit. p. 245.
12 In *The Usefulness of Useless Knowledge*, originally published in the October 1939 issue of *Harper's Magazine*, American educator Abraham Flexner explored what he described as the dangerous tendency to forgo pure curiosity in favour of pragmatism. Available at https://faculty.lsu.edu/kharms/files/flexner_1939.pdf.
13 Holmes, R. (2003). *Wellington: The Iron Duke*. London: Harper Collins, p. 166.
14 Klein, G. (2014). *Seeing What Others Don't: The Remarkable Ways We Gain Insights*. Boston, MA: Nicholas Brearley Publishing.

18 Leading in a Different Way

Leading is often characterised as providing answers. We follow because leaders have, or appear to have, the solution to our problems. Leading in a Different Way turns this assumption on its head. Leading beyond authority is about leading with insights and ideas, but it is also counter-intuitively about leading with questions rather than providing answers. It also requires a sense of managerial irreverence, an approach that questions received wisdom and the way we do things around here. And, in the first instance, that requires a capacity to live in the question.

Living in the Question

"Living in the question" can be uncomfortable for the leader and the led. Followers look to leaders to provide order and structure in the midst of uncertainty and possibly chaos. Network Leaders have a capacity to be "containers of anxiety", creating what the pioneering British psychoanalyst Donald Winnicott[1] identified as a "holding space" based on how he had observed parents who were reassuring rather than intrusive, responsive but not over-reactive and available without being demanding. As "containers of anxiety", leaders don't hide their fear nor diminish the fear of others; instead they create a feeling of safety that is a natural requirement for performance.

This is particularly important during times of stress and uncertainty when our innate human tendency is to cling to old ways of doing things, rush in with a solution to fill the void or find an answer, any answer, and move on as quickly as possible. Staying with the uncertain and the ambiguous makes us nervous. It is reassuring to come up with action items that promise to take us towards an imagined solution. The problem is that we become reactive to our environment, not proactive agents. A Network Leader pauses, able to live in the question and uncertainty, creating the space and time for joint exploration of complexity and for more promising answers to emerge.

DOI: 10.4324/9781003092582-28

It is a facilitative approach and good facilitation keeps people focused and receptive. Effective facilitation enables individuals to contain their fears and probe their discomfort, letting go of old patterns, avoiding spur-of-the-moment responses and instead co-creating the emerging future. It is a practice with which both authors are deeply familiar and is most often associated with the methods and processes used by trainers and consultants during workshops. But this is too narrow. Facilitation means to simplify or make easy, and if done well, it is a dynamic and effective tool for leaders, helping them develop new ideas and processes in an inclusive, focused and energising way. Facilitation creates a safe space, a container for exploration, enabling the emergence of new ideas and ways of doing things through collaboration and co-creation, helping to align discrete actions and entities with and towards a larger purpose.

Effective facilitation is also networked, in the sense that it is about moving the process along in the most effective and inclusive manner possible. This means tapping into the diversity of the group and holding multiple perspectives even in the face of cognitive dissonance. One of the hallmarks of effective facilitation is to stay with paradoxes, feel the dissonance and not give in to an "either/or" view. This requires creating a safe container for all the voices to emerge, to help the team, organisation or community see and sense what is surfacing and make the most of a shared exploration. Network Leaders are aware of the different capacities of individuals and understand the necessity to broaden and deepen individual's abilities to hold diverse perspectives, especially in the face of complexity. People always run the risk of being closed to new ideas or slipping into an "us" and "them" mind-set. As a facilitator, this requires questions and interventions to keep biases from taking over.

Network Leaders understand the system, but they also help the system see itself. A good facilitator is a pattern connector and sense-maker for the system. Through effective processes and holding the space, they can connect the specifics to the larger context, thus helping the system to discover the patterns at play. This shared awareness creates the conditions for fast, flexible and fluid decision-making at the point of need. This is what makes an organisation responsive, adaptable and effective. Helping organisations build shared awareness and enabling the system to sense and see itself are critical skills that can transform how an organisation perceives itself, its connection with a larger purpose and its role in society.

Leading with Insights and Ideas

Network Leaders recognise that we are all the sum of our prior experiences, be they good or bad, and they go out of their way to cultivate knowledge and experience in search of insights: bringing new thinking and frameworks into the room; challenging existing assumptions; and generating new ideas. As previously discussed, we each bring our own frames of reference to any encounter with another. These frames or mental constructs shape the way we see the world and consequently the goals we seek, the plans we make, the ways we act and what we believe to be good or bad. A Network Leader seeks to discover other people's frames and explain their own, in order that understanding is shared and enriched. The intention is not to "win" arguments, but to encourage a reflective posture in pursuit of shared understanding and collective action.

In the first place, this requires a change of approach. One that replaces "If only..." signifying a lack of control and resignation, with "If I/we..." demonstrating control and agency. This requires that if we are to lead, we speak up, step up and act; embracing responsibility even if you are faking it at first. It isn't realistic to expect people to follow you and trust your ideas if you seem unsure of yourself or unwilling to act and take responsibility for new projects, develop new initiatives or improve a system or process that already exists. And don't be afraid to mess up, so long as you "fess up". Admit your failures and describe what you learned from the experience and then try again.

Leadership requires energy and enthusiasm, and like all emotions they are contagious. Think about the leaders you are drawn to, those who have vision, passion and belief in a better tomorrow. They are going somewhere awe-inspiring and we want to be part of it. Now think about the emotions you display. Be honest with yourself. Are you a complainer, often portraying yourself as a victim of circumstances beyond your control – if only? Or perhaps you like to fly quietly under the radar waiting for someone to magically invite you to lead? Sorry, that is simply not going to happen. We are drawn to passionate people on a mission that we believe in. So give people a reason to follow you. Even if you're not in charge, you can always take responsibility for raising the energy in the group and rallying people around a shared mission. Just don't be an idiot about it, no one is drawn to people who are trying to keep the proverbial Titanic afloat, they want to be led to the lifeboats. Stay focused, remember your personal manifesto and pick your battles.

And if you are feeling short of ideas and inspiration don't wait for them to come to you. Have your finger on the pulse of what is going on in the organization, remember Fingerspitzengefühl (fingertip feel) and seek out new information. And don't forget the ideas and influence that can come from your background, experience, qualifications and career accomplishments. Do you have content knowledge and experience? Do you have access to valuable data, information and evidence? Are you a thought leader? Do you understand the processes needed to accomplish objectives? You can influence others by providing a clear logic, an explanation of the benefit and reassurance that it is the right course of action. A powerful way to increase your influence at work is to be recognised as an expert in your organisation, sector and industry. It will take effort, but you can take steps to develop business-critical expertise and know-how. Immerse yourself in your chosen topic by regularly attending industry conferences, enrolling in classes or specialised certification programmes or taking on a leadership role in a relevant professional organisation.

But that's not enough. Don't keep your knowledge under wraps. What you know and who you know is important, but the critical element is who knows what you know and is it acted upon. Are your colleagues and managers aware of your expertise? If not, don't be the best kept secret in your organisation. Find appropriate and effective ways to promote your accomplishments and maximize your expertise influence. Try writing about your subject on LinkedIn or for your company newsletter and show what you know.

And it's not just technical expertise and cognitive intelligence that counts. Social intelligence is also key. Social intelligence, emotional intelligence, empathy, call it what you will, offers insight into interpersonal issues that interfere with work and can help facilitate resolution of those issues. If you have social intelligence, people trust that you'll be able to help them work together effectively; that you'll put the right people in touch with each other; and that you'll garner the endorsements of credible people and get the support you need.

A critical start in this is to build connections and establish rapport ahead of need. You don't have to be scintillating company, a brilliant raconteur or have the looks of Aphrodite or Adonis. You just need to have good rapport with your colleagues. This won't necessarily translate directly into influence, but it does make it more likely that others will at least hear you out. And the best time to ask for help or support is not when you first meet someone. So, work on cultivating personal connections with your colleagues before you need them, allow them time to get to know you and that way they are less likely to attribute you with Machiavellian intentions or motives.

The best way to prime colleagues for backing you and your agenda is to make them feel heard. So listen before you try to persuade. The most basic and powerful way to connect to another person is to listen. Just listen. Perhaps the most important thing we ever give each other is our attention. So ask colleagues, direct reports and managers for their perspectives and advice, and when you do, give them your undivided attention, whether it be in one-on-one situations or larger meetings. Don't fidget, look out of the window or keep reaching for your phone. Instead, practice the discipline of focus. Turn your phone off and your body towards the other person, look them in the eye and listen. A big part of workplace disgruntlement is people feeling disrespected because their voices aren't being heard.

And remember, you can increase your influence on a particular issue by authentically framing it as a benefit to the people you want on your side. Speaking genuinely with people allows you to understand and consider each person's needs, perspectives and temperaments. Do your homework to find out what your stakeholders want and need to hear and you are more likely to capture their attention. For each person, make sure you're answering the question, "What's in it for me"? Hopefully, most will also want to know how your ideas will benefit the organisation. So try using the word we. If you are relying on your personal authority and your suggestions are fundamentally self-interested, people are less likely to follow you.

People are constantly assessing whether to trust you or not, so it's also important to mind your body language and your tone of voice. Humans are hardwired to determine whether another person is a friend or a potential enemy. Remember Amy Cuddy's advice, competence is often seen as a threat until people trust you. Your body language is critical to conveying the right message. Standing up straight with your shoulders back helps you come across as confident and commanding. Slouching and looking down at your feet has the opposite effect. Try to keep your arms uncrossed, your hands by your sides, your body open and pointed towards the other person, and look them in the eye. You don't need to stare, but too much eye movement looks deceitful and disinterested.

Leading without authority is all about your ability to have a positive influence on the people around you, in the first instance by making sense of things for them and inspiring them. When you're the person consistently answering the "Why" questions for others, people will begin instinctively to look to you for insights: Why is this project important? Why are we doing it this way? Why do I need to be involved? But if you don't know the answers, then you will first need to lead with questions, so that you can gain a deeper understanding yourself before you articulate it for others.

Leading Through Questions

Anyone who is familiar with Douglas Adams' comic science fiction book *The Hitchhiker's Guide to the Galaxy*[2] knows that the answer to "Universe and Everything" is 42. The problem, as the great computer Deep Thought observed, was that insufficient thought was given to the question. The answer, therefore, is meaningless. In some cases answers to poor questions can be downright dangerous, setting off a chain of events that compound the original problem.

You can of course influence others by providing a clear logic and rationale for your suggestions, laying out the facts, explaining the benefits and reassuring people that it is the right course of action. But unless you are a hitherto undiscovered genius, you will not always know the answer, and when this happens, you should have the intelligence and humility to lead with powerful and considered questions and listen to the answers. Having prior opinions about everything is one of the principal characteristics of poor decision-makers. Victims of ideology or arrogance often talk more than they listen, and fail to acknowledge that on almost every subject, someone else knows more than they do. Good decision-makers, by contrast, listen respectfully and range widely to seek relevant advice and facts before they form a preliminary view. And when they do arrive at a view, they invite challenge to it, before drawing the discussion to a conclusion.[3] Darcy Willson-Rymer also advises that in pursuit of understanding, we "Listen for the principle which is guiding the opposing belief".[4]

You may not even be the one "in charge" but you can still lead with great questions. Try out a few of the following questions and imagine how they might change the course of a conversation or meeting:

- What if…?
- Have we considered…?
- Can you help me understand what you mean when you say…?
- What have we possibly overlooked?
- Who else should we invite to be part of this?
- Is the issue we're talking about here the real issue?
- What must be done first?
- Can we describe what success looks like for this project?

This capacity for great questions becomes even more important as you rise through an organisation. As you move from functional to general management, your narrow expertise becomes less important than insight (Figure 5.2). People will still look to you for answers, but the best leaders don't provide all the solutions. Instead, they inspire curiosity, creativity and deeper thinking in their employees. And that starts with asking the right questions.

Encouraging employees to slow down and explain what they're proposing in more detail is a profound skill of senior leaders. You can use phrases like "I wonder why…" to encourage curiosity and then follow up with "I wonder if things could be done differently". Another extremely simple but profoundly powerful question to ask is: "How can I help"? Not only is this question disarming in its supportiveness, but it also forces colleagues, direct reports and managers to define the problem, which is the first step towards owning and solving it.

Questions also have the advantage of being indirect. They are less likely to be taken as an indication of criticism and challenge and rather in the spirit

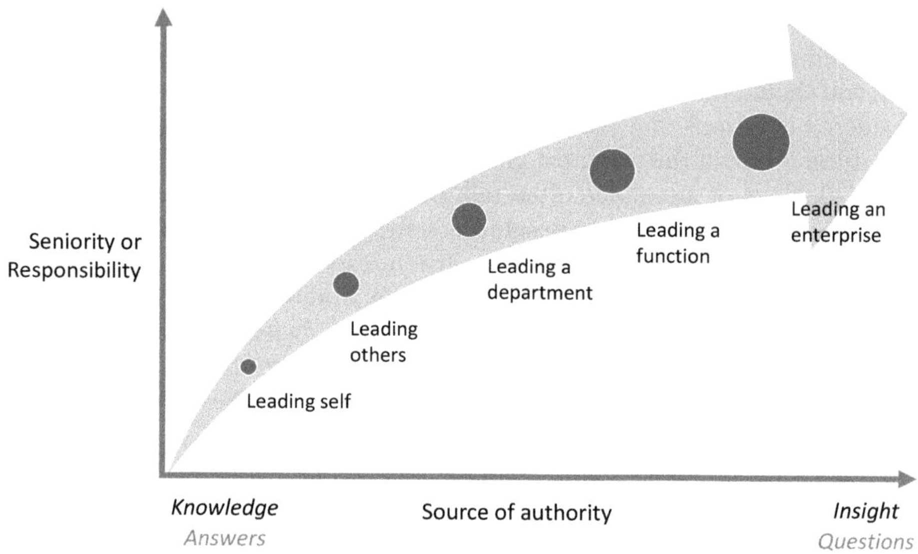

Figure 5.2 Source of Authority – The Role Of Questioning Insight With Seniority.

of understanding and refining. Statements such as… "The plan won't work", "we've tried this before", "the process is broken" can make people feel disrespected, even threatened. But if the same statements are posed as questions: "Can you explain how you will overcome this difficulty"? "We found that didn't work last time, what is different now"?" "What are we trying to achieve so that we can make this process better"? Then they often open a dialogue. Statements tend to set up an "us" versus "them" dynamic, whereas questions require joint exploration. As Jonah Berger observes[5]:

> Questions shift the listener's role. Rather than counter-arguing or thinking about all the reasons they disagree, they're sorting through their answer to your query and their feelings or opinions on the matter. And this shift increases buy-in. It encourages people to commit to the conclusion, because while people might not want to follow someone else's lead, they're more than happy to follow their own. The answer to the question isn't just any answer; it's their answer, reflecting their own personal thoughts, beliefs, and preferences. That makes it more likely to drive action.

The value of curiosity and inquisitiveness is particularly helpful in boundary-crossing work. It's nearly impossible to work across boundaries without asking a lot of questions. Inquiry is critical because what we see and take for granted on one side of an interface is not necessarily the same as what people experience on the other side. Leaders with high levels of curiosity are also more likely to build networks that span disconnected parts of an organisation, because they will seek out colleagues for answers.

Not asking questions is a big mistake many professionals make. Experts want to offer a solution because that's what they're trained to do. And even when we do recognise that we don't know something, we may avoid asking a question out of the misguided fear that it will make us look incompetent or weak. In fact, the opposite can be true. Voltaire, for example, recommended that we judge a man by his questions rather than his answers. Network leaders know how to ask deep and powerful generative questions that disrupt and provoke peoples thinking, questions that capture their attention and generate options and opportunities.

You do need to be careful, however. Do not make it sound like an interrogation, which will only inhibit rather than encourage the development of new perspectives. Questions are key to productive work relationships, but only if they are driven by a genuine interest in understanding another's view rather than a roundabout way of proving your point. It's also important to learn how to request information in the least biased way possible. This means asking open-ended questions that minimise preconceptions rather than yes-or-no questions that can close dialogue. For example, "What do you see as the key opportunity in this environment"? is likely to generate a richer dialogue than "Do you think this is the right opportunity to pursue"?

Bias also plays a part when you listen to people's answers. It is natural, as conversations unfold, to assume you understand what is being said. But what we hear tends to be biased by our expertise and experience. So it's important to check whether you really understand your colleagues' meaning by playing back to them what you just heard by asking confirmatory questions like "This is what I'm hearing … did I miss anything"? or "I think what you said is this … Is that correct"?

Humility, as Jonathan Deacon observes, "Is borne of the ability to talk with anyone at a human level – human scale interaction – not by rank or position".[6] And asking questions conveys the humility that more and more business leaders and researchers are pointing to as vital to success. A leader can make other people feel more comfortable asking questions of their own by openly acknowledging when he or she doesn't know the answer, and that is where its real power comes from. The recognition that problems are increasingly complex and challenging, and if we don't work together, we will end up with answers that make no sense or just create new problems.

Managerial Irreverence

We also think it is important that managers display a due sense of irreverence towards their work and the organisations in which they operate. Managerial

Asking the Right Questions[7]

US President Obama generated a powerful dialogue through good questions when, very soon after taking office in 2009, he was asked by the Pentagon to approve a surge of 40,000 extra troops to Afghanistan. To the military, the answer was obvious: sign up to a surge of further troops into Afghanistan to match the deteriorating situation there. But Colin Powell, a former Chairman of the Joint Chiefs, advised President Obama: "You don't have to put up with this. These guys work for you. Because they're unanimous in their advice doesn't make it right".

Obama went back to the Pentagon and asked what they thought the aim of their efforts was in Afghanistan. This confused the military staffs, for they had an aim that addressed the threat that the military faced in Afghanistan – defeat the Taliban – not what was in the wider interest of the United States. After several months of discussion, with Obama holding his thoughts unseen, a better aim emerged that addressed the wider issues, and that was to provide security for the Afghan people to allow them to develop their broken state in order that the Taliban would be rejected.

Even at this stage, Obama did not agree to a troop surge, although neither did he rule it out. He started to drill down into what the extra troops would be used for without commenting whether the uses were right or wrong. This triggered an important further debate about whether the way to achieve the now agreed aim would be through counterterrorism or counterinsurgency, and if the latter, whether enough troops could be surged into Afghanistan to face down such an insurgency.

Under this latest questioning, the military consensus began to fracture and strong positions were taken. Obama continued to support the Chairman of the Joint Chiefs, but also asked for the views of the NSC Adviser and the individual Service Chiefs. He got different answers from all of them, including his own Vice-President Joe Biden, an articulate supporter of a limited counterterrorism strategy. By this time, all concerned realised that a trivial answer would just not be accepted and a vigorous debate ensued, reaching down into the middle ranks of the military staff. Finally, a completely different package was submitted to the President – one that contained several genuine options.

The result was that the US presence in Afghanistan was more purposeful, with the field commanders having a much better idea of the outcome they were trying to achieve. It led to General Stanley McChrystal, the coalition commander in Kabul, turning the existing approach on its head and eschewing violence in preference to "courageous constraint". It alerted the Pentagon to difficulties that were going to arise downstream, but they were no longer travelling blindfolded.

All this was achieved by a President who had no military experience but with the ability to ask the right questions, supported by an expert military staff capable of debate.

irreverence is not disrespect or discourtesy, but a healthy understanding about what is possible through the formal organisation and the principles of rationality. Butcher and Clarke[8] see it as a perspective essential to political competence, which constructive leader-politicians use to question and challenge from a position of benevolence towards those still caught in the hierarchical and rational mind-set.

The analogy they use is the way children, as they develop, discover their parents to be flawed role models of adulthood. But difficult as this insight may be for some young people to reconcile with the image they hold of their parents, it does not follow that they lose respect for them or for the institution of parenthood. Irreverence and respect can coexist, but respect is no longer unconditional and unquestioning. It is, instead, founded on balanced judgement rather than received values alone. Butcher and Clarke describe this constructive use of organisational politics as the principled use of power.[9]

The key to constructive politics is to act on a personal agenda, your manifesto, in a way that balances self-interest, views and values with those of others. To be ethical, personal gain must be in the service of others. Constructive politics is the process by which diverse interests and stakeholders may be reconciled in organisations, implicitly balancing the need for coherence and diversity. Butcher and Clarke describe four components, which resonate with Network Leadership:

1. Conceptual Understanding: evaluating the complexity of the influence process and the role of motives; evaluating the different barriers to organisational relationships; the mechanisms and value of lobbying formally and informally; and identifying and cultivating pockets of good practice.
2. Social Understanding: stakeholder knowledge, knowing the agendas and motivations of key players; organisational knowledge, knowing who makes key decisions and how; and business environment knowledge, knowing the critical organisational issues.

3. Social Skills: persuasive presentation and developing collaborative outcomes through personal enthusiasm, suggestion, logical connection and disclosure of motives; productive challenge, causing others to analyse their motives; and reading others through continual observation of the motives and actions of others.
4. Self-understanding, in terms of balanced motives, considering personal, collegial and organisational motivations, but critically a sense of "managerial irreverence", which is a healthy scepticism about what is possible in formal organisations.

Such maturity of perspective about the values of rational organisation is essential to political competence, but they acknowledge it is hard won. It clearly requires more than being prepared to adopt an anti-formal organisation stance and engage in cynicism or subterfuge. Radicalism is rarely the answer in organisational contexts because revolutionaries are easily marginalised, patronised and dismissed as incompetents. After all, it is always easier to take an extreme position and vilify your rivals than it is to maintain a strong position while honouring and trusting the intentions of those who oppose you.

The foregoing discussion has attempted to elaborate some of the core skills and attributes of leaders who are able to lead beyond their authority. We now want to investigate how these abilities might be applied in the context of the complex or wicked problems we discussed in Part One.

Notes

1 Winnicott, D. (1960). The Theory of the Parent-Child Relationship. *International Journal of Psychoanalysis*, 41, pp. 585–95.
2 Adams, D. (1986). *The Hitchhiker's Guide to the Galaxy*. London: William Heinemann.
3 Kay, J. and King, M. (2020). *Radical Uncertainty: Decision-making for an Unknowable Future*. London: The Bridge Street Press, p. 179.
4 Interview with the authors 1 Mar. 2021. See Appendix 2 Leader Biographies.
5 Berger, J. (2020). How to Persuade People to Change Their Behaviour. (online) *Harvard Business Review*. Available at https://hbr.org/2020/04/how-to-persuade-people-to-change-their-behavior.
6 Interview with the authors 8 Mar. 2021. See Appendix 2 Leader Biographies.
7 Elliott, C. (2015). *High Command*. London: Hurst & Company, pp. 226–7.
8 Butcher, D. and Clarke, M. (2008). *Smart Management: Using Politics in Organisations*. London: Palgrave Macmillan.
9 Butcher, D. and Clarke, M. (2008) ibid. p. 97.

19
Dealing with Wicked Problems

In *Using the Outdoors for Management Development and Teambuilding,*[1] Creswick and Williams devised a four-box model to describe the relationship between problems and solutions, specifically, problems known and unknown versus solutions known and unknown (Figure 5.3).

Putting this model alongside our own experience and work with leaders, managers and senior teams led the authors to develop a model which attempts to match different leadership approaches with the differing needs of each Box (Figure 5.4).

Box 1 represents the easiest situation to operate in, where both problems and solutions are clearly known. In Box 2, while the problem may be known, the solution is unknown. And in Box 3, we enter an area of maximum uncertainty in which both the problem and solution are unknown, the domain of the "wicked problem" we discussed earlier. Finally, there is the oddity of Box 4, in which the problem is unknown and yet a solution is available. This is

Unknown Solution	2	3
Known Solution	1	4
	Known Problem	Unknown Problem

Figure 5.3 Problems and Solutions.

DOI: 10.4324/9781003092582-29

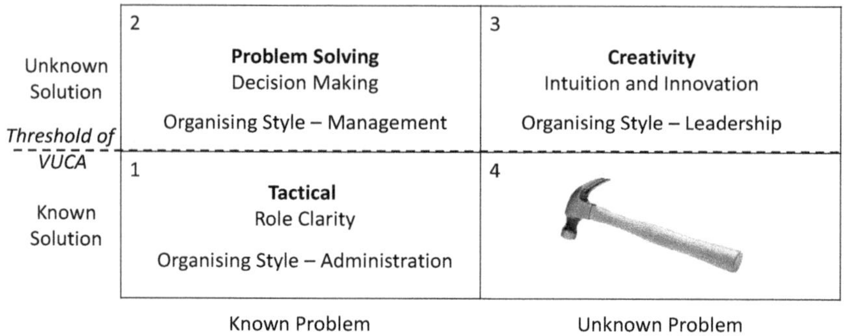

Figure 5.4 Approaches to Problems and Solutions.

intriguing and we liken this to trying to use the same solution whatever the problem, rather like the saying, "If you only have a hammer then every problem looks like a nail".

Box 1, we suggest, requires good administration, placing people and resources against the known elements of a problem. Business and military systems often include repetitive tasks and problems and have a standard operating process in place to reduce time spent reinventing the wheel and more time doing productive work. In Box 2, we need management to co-ordinate the various moving parts and work towards identifying a solution. In Box 3, however, when uncertainty is greatest and neither the problem nor the solution is in sight, innovation, strategic insight and leadership become necessary.

This is not the domain of puzzles, difficulties from which escapes are thought to be known, but of mysteries for which Revan's action learning was intended for addressing problems or opportunities:

> about which no single course of action is to be justified by any code of programmed knowledge, so that different managers, all reasonable, experienced and sober, might set out by treating them in markedly different ways.[2]

Action learning is for intractable or novel situations where there is no single right answer and the biggest danger in such situations is to act on the basis of thinking we know what to do or on the advice of those who think they know, instead of starting with a process of questioning inquiry.

What also becomes apparent is that once above the midway line, above Boxes 1 and 4, leaders and managers cross a threshold of uncertainty and, as they move further towards Box 3, the uncertainty increases. In presenting and discussing the model with a variety of clients, it appears that, as far as possible, our instinct is to drive anti-clockwise from Box 3 to Box 1, from maximum uncertainty to maximum certainty.

Equally, however, true empowerment is only possible when we cross the threshold of uncertainty. Leaders and managers need to have some degree of discretion to be empowered – what can we really be empowered to do if the problem and solution are already known? And at an organisational level, rapidly changing markets, unexpected events and the general quickening of everything means more organisations are reluctantly finding themselves in Box 3.

Smaller companies may be able to cope better in Box 3 because of their ability to move quickly, and with less history, they may be able to extrapolate more broadly than their larger competitors. But increasingly, managers must operate in Box 3, spending time investigating the future to see what it might hold, deciding upon a course of action with imperfect knowledge and then taking their people with them. Leadership is, after all, often about taking people to places they have never been.[3] In the past, organisations could reasonably predict and create their own futures. However, with fewer certainties and fewer ready solutions, the challenge now is to develop leaders and strategies that balance targeted achievement with organisational alignment.

Leaders, followers and organisational structures need to be aligned to enable them to operate in Box 3 when appropriate. Unfortunately, hierarchies, appraisal systems and performance-related pay often concern themselves with only that which is measurable, which tends to be the preserve of Box 1 and, to an extent, Box 2, despite espousing visions and values from Box 3. As previously suggested, leaders could usefully, therefore, spend more time thinking, deciding when and how they should divide their time and energy between the boxes and how to handle uncertainty.

Resolving Wicked Problems

In the first place, wicked problems require holistic rather than linear thinking: grasping the big picture and attempting to identify the full range of interrelationships between causal factors and policy objectives. But for those who work in large organisations, it also requires an understanding of their own structural limitations. As discussed earlier, for reasons of history and efficiency, bureaucracies tend to be stove piped. Going "outside your lane" is frowned upon and protecting those boundaries is often deemed a success. Problematically, resources tend to follow bureaucratic lanes, and even when the need for a holistic solution is recognised, it is often the case that resources cannot be easily transferred to where they would have greatest impact, because groups hoard them in pursuit of their own narrow objectives.

Resolution of such problems therefore means devising a strategy that copes reasonably with the issue (the wicked problem itself) and halts enough of the antagonistic and destructive behaviours (bureaucracy and politics) in order to create a solution that is "good enough" (i.e. more good than bad outcomes). Nancy Roberts, Professor Emerita in the Department of Defense Analysis at the United States Naval Postgraduate School, has identified three such approaches: authoritative, competitive and collaborative.[4]

Authoritative strategies involve putting problem solving into the hands of a few stakeholders who have the authority to define the problem and come up with the solution. This has the advantage of reducing problem complexity, as it eliminates many of the competing points of view, but has the disadvantage that those charged with solving the problem may not have an appreciation of all the perspectives needed to tackle the problem.

Competitive strategies attempt to solve wicked problems by pitting opposing points of view against each other, requiring parties that hold these views to come up with their preferred solutions (essentially going with the flow of organisational politics and stovepipes). The advantage of this approach is that different solutions can be weighed against each other and the best one chosen. The disadvantage is that this adversarial approach creates a confrontational environment in which knowledge sharing is discouraged. Consequently, the parties involved may not have the opportunity or incentive to come up with the best possible solution.

In contrast, collaborative approaches assume a win-win, aiming to engage all stakeholders to find the best possible solution for all. Typically, this will involve meetings in which issues and ideas are discussed and a common approach is formulated. Alliances, partnerships and joint ventures are all variations of this theme. The disadvantage with this approach is that adding more stakeholders increases transactional costs (more meetings, more people and more time to communicate and get agreement). And as numbers grow, so does the difficulty of achieving synergy. In addition, the skills required for collaboration are often limited, especially in hierarchical organisations and systems, and these take time and resources to acquire. Critically, dialogue can turn into debate and positions can harden, turning it into a protracted competitive conflict in which there is no guarantee that the outcome will be satisfactory for everyone.

The key to success, Roberts suggests, is to blend the three strategies, allowing greater flexibility and more effective approaches to achieving "good enough" solutions. But this requires leadership, specifically, leaders who can elicit different solutions (competitive approach), get everyone around the table to agree a "good enough" solution (collaborative approach) and then enforce it if necessary (authoritative approach). In every case, the "solutions" should be adaptive but enduring, recognising the very different interests of the relevant stakeholders, expecting that the nature of the problem will change over time and that success is not assured.

Fundamentally, leaders must get comfortable with relinquishing control and enabling others. Leaders must recognise they can't do and know everything anymore. They need to shift away from being the person who leads and directs everyone to being someone who pulls in information and ideas and shares them, allowing others to accomplish tasks. Progressive leaders rely on their teams' expertise, experience and knowledge. They assign decision-making rights and planning activities to key managers and employees, who are closer to where work gets done. They recognise that organisational agility is a product of empowerment. In the military it is called mission command.

Mission Command

By the 1940s, the British Army was learning from bitter experience that the nature of warfare had changed and a different, more dynamic kind of leadership was needed. They had seen how the exceptional effectiveness of the German army depended not on rigid implementation of battle plans, but rather on decentralisation of decision-making and flexibility amid the fog of war. And the more complex the battlefield, the more important it was to free officers and non-commissioned officers (NCOs) from the constraints of centralised command and control.

The British Jungle Book manual of 1943[5] instructed that command must be decentralised because junior leaders will be confronted with situations in which they must make decisions and act without delay on their own responsibility. In other words, leaders should be empowered to make decisions in the face of rapidly changing situations because they were best placed to see what was happening. Similarly, in the European Theatre of Operations, US General George S. Patton advised his commanders:

> Never tell people how to do things. Tell them what to do, and they will surprise you with their ingenuity.

This contrasted with much extant British military doctrine. British Army success in the Second World War was largely about focusing huge resources on a smaller enemy and wearing them down through attrition. Battles were fought top-down so that everyone knew exactly what was required of them and how to achieve it. In short, everyone knew their place. Montgomery called it "a tidy battlefield" and described the process as the "orchestra of war", with the general conducting and all the different instruments doing exactly what they were told.

This culture of top-down direction continued into the Cold War, not least in the Falklands War of 1982, where the British Army found that soldiers were waiting to be told exactly what to do in circumstances where casualties might have been avoided had they been more proactive. Consequently, during the 1980s, the British Army radically redesigned the way decisions were made and how officers were empowered to make rapid decisions in order to disrupt the enemy, operating at such a high tempo that their cohesion was disrupted and they began to fall apart. And this was achieved by encouraging junior commanders to adjust their response should the situation change, without having to ask for further orders. Which, in turn, relied upon them understanding the commander's intent – the ultimate aim of the operation.

The focus for training was helping commanders to understand how to think, not what to think. How to find a solution, instead of being told what to do, which would not work in a fast-paced environment, where orders from the chain of command might be redundant before they were even delivered. Mission command provided a framework for problem solving and decision-making that outlined the constraints placed upon commanders, such as time, space and the materials provided, but allowed them to be creative within those parameters and adjust should the situation change, as it invariably would.

For example, before Mission Command, a junior commander might have been ordered to "take and hold that bridge by 0400 tomorrow", but with the new orders framework he would be told to "secure that bridge by 0400 tomorrow, in order for the rest of the force to cross the river by the close of day tomorrow". Now, if the situation changes, the bridge is demolished by the enemy, for instance, and the commander knows that his mission isn't over because there may be another way to cross the river. After all, the aim of the operation was to cross the river, not simply take the bridge. With the overriding purpose of the mission in mind, the commander is able to adapt without seeking further orders.[6]

But in order for that to happen, the army had to introduce standardized processes for the way it planned, the way it gave direction and the way it communicated the commander's intent. To become more agile, the Army needed to be thinking the same way and speaking the same language. To do this, the Army focused on mission planning, which is common to all military operations, and came up with a standardised set of seven planning questions across the entire organization.[7] Paradoxically, standardizing mission planning allowed far greater flexibility, because commanders felt confident to make decisions knowing they could trust that everyone else not only understood the aim, but also shared their way of thinking about the problem.

A focus on process, instead of outcomes, is not normally recommended, but when we are confronted by uncertainty or pursuing something so big that we don't even know where to begin, it is helpful to focus on a process that will help us frame the problem and identify possible solutions. A good process, based on sound questions, provides a guide to help us arrive at good enough solutions.

Notes

1 Creswick, C. and Williams, R. (1979). *Using the Outdoors for Management Development and Team Building*. Food, Drink & Tobacco ITB, Gloucester.
2 Revans, R. (2011). *ABC of Action Learning*. Farnham: Gower, p. 4.
3 Kouzes, J. and Posner, B. (1987). *The Leadership Challenge: How to Get Extraordinary Things Done in Organizations*. San Francisco: Jossey-Bass.
4 Roberts, N. (2000). Wicked Problems and Network Approaches to Resolution. (online) *International Public Management Review*, 1(1). Available at https://journals.sfu.ca/ipmr/index.php/ipmr/article/view/175 (accessed 17 April 2021).
5 The Jungle Book, Military Training Pamphlet No. 9 (India), was a military training manual to assist commanders in preparing their units for Jungle Battle in East Asia and Asia Pacific region. The title, as you may have guessed, is a nod to Rudyard Kipling's *Jungle Book* (1894).
6 McKinsey Quarterly. (2019). How the British Army's Operations Went Agile. (online) Available at https://www.mckinsey.com/business-functions/organization/our-insights/how-the-british-armys-operations-went-agile (accessed 17 April 2021).
7 The seven questions are: What is the situation and how does it affect me? What have I been told to do and why? What effects do I need to achieve and what direction must I give to develop my plan? Where can I best accomplish each action/effect? What resources do I need to accomplish each action/effect? When and where do the actions take place in relation to each other? What control measures do I need to impose?

Summary

People who can lead beyond their authority are able to produce change beyond their inner network. It is leadership in the raw, primitive leadership, stripped of hierarchical badges of rank, title and position and depending instead upon who you are, what you know and what you can find out, not what your title says you are. It depends upon your qualities as an individual, your strategic insight to seek out and chase opportunities and, crucially, an ability to connect people and build relationships towards the achievement of shared goals.

There was perhaps a time, if you were in a position of authority, when you could simply announce what needed to be done and assume it would be carried out. But times have changed. Apart from the simplest of challenges (known problem, known solution), it no longer suffices to just tell people what to do. Mysteries, complex or wicked problems, require that we make the most of informal networks of human connection. The alternative, rigidly hierarchical systems that replicate parent–child relationships run the risk of creating dependency. They sap individual initiative and worse yet, authority-based systems are a breeding ground for egotism and the abuse of power, which make them prone to becoming oppressive work environments, sacrificing connective value for a veneer of control.

Leading without relying on formal or positional authority is a higher evolutionary skill. It supports relationships based on mutual objectives and creates work environments grounded in respect for human dignity. Specifically, it is the ability to get people who don't necessarily work for you, those over whom you have no formal, positional or hierarchical authority, to contribute fully to achieving a shared outcome. They may be peers, hierarchical leaders or other stakeholders, it doesn't matter. Whoever they are it requires a different approach to leadership founded on connection and collaboration, not direction and control.

Connection, networking and the development of strong personal relationships are the linchpins of accomplished leaders and successful organisations.

DOI: 10.4324/9781003092582-30

We should not think of networking as a manipulative strategy, the preserve of sycophants and those who take advantage of others' talents, but rather embrace networking as the art of connecting for mutual benefit. The pursuit of your personal manifesto need not be a zero-sum game.

Nothing exists in isolation, least of all human beings, and we live in times of unprecedented technological interconnection, exemplified by the small world connections of social media, such as Facebook and LinkedIn. Network Leaders understand that networks function upon the mutual need for understanding and a sense of identity, and as a result they invest the time and energy required to build trusting relationships that will ultimately pay dividends. Instead of viewing networking as a necessary evil, they perceive it as an opportunity to spread and share best practice and new ideas.

Leadership Questions

Before answering these questions revisit your personal manifesto or think about your purpose and what you are trying to achieve:

1. Where will you find the boundaries and edges?
2. How can you find time to think?
3. What are your "if only" statements?
4. How can you challenge your assumptions and self-imposed constraints to turn "if only" into an active statement beginning with "If I…" or "If we…"?

Part VI

Restless Persuasion

Every great story has a hero who overcomes the obstacles in their path, and it is the obstacles that make the hero. Restless persuasion describes the energy and resilience to keep going despite the obstacles in your path: the micro level barriers thrown up by individual and group dynamics; the meso barriers within organisations and communities, the silos and organisational antibodies that reject change; and the macro, large-scale social processes of stability and change, such as culture and Covid-19.

Restless persuasion has two components: "restlessness' which describes a constant state of agitation and "persuasion" being the ability to encourage and enlist those around you in your endeavour. Great Network Leaders have a dogged energy that keeps them going over, under, through or around obstacles and all the while bringing people with them.

Leaders grow through overcoming challenges, and they may feel uncomfortable and perhaps, at times, scared. But that is how we all grow and develop, leaders included. The distinction is that proven and effective leaders often thrive in the face of uncertainty and setbacks. Restless persuasion also denotes a disposition towards feeling comfortable in chaos, a capacity to revel amid crises and the baffling complexity of wicked problems. Such leaders recognise that interesting things come from the edge; that there is a sweet spot between the known and unknown where amazing things happen; and that they can linger there without panicking. And as leaders, they help others to linger there too, supporting and encouraging people to live, grow and work productively in a context of uncertainty. But they are also impatient.

Leaders are impatient to get things done, the leader's personal manifesto of things they believe to be important, necessary and right. It is a relentless resolve to push the boundaries of what can be achieved. On occasion, such

DOI: 10.4324/9781003092582-31

leaders may wish to do something that it is simply impossible or reckless, and they need the self-control to recognise this, but there are other times when the leader knows something can and must be done, and everyone just needs to embrace their fears and work harder to make it happen. That's when leaders drive their followers to achieve more than they, and the public at large, ever thought possible. Examples abound, think of Mahatma Gandhi, Emmeline Pankhurst, Winston Churchill, Margaret Thatcher, Nelson Mandela and more recently entrepreneurs like Steve Jobs, Elon Musk and Jeff Bezos. Jayne-Anne Gadhia makes a broader point with regard to women when she observes: "Women in power is outside of what is considered normal. Women are dismissed unless they are unreasonable. You only get noticed by being controversial".[1]

Samantha Power became the US ambassador to the UN under the Obama administration. She started her career as a journalist and in 1993 without proper credentials rented a car and drove across the border into Sarajevo to interview Bosnian military leaders. She documented the massacre of civilians and soldiers through the conflict and became a passionate and committed journalist compelled to report and try to prevent genocide. When appointed UN Ambassador by Obama, she notes in her biography that he "seemed to want my perspective and my sense of urgency in the mix".[2] Compelled by an inner sense of justice, she was never afraid to talk, write and campaign. The final words of her book capture the essence of restless persuasion: "People who care, act, and refuse to give up may not change the world, but they can change many individual worlds".

Winston Churchill was notable for his powers of restless persuasion, whether it was pursuing opportunities for military adventure as a young army officer and journalist or throughout his political career in backing the maintenance of free trade; supporting the introduction of general unemployment benefit; advocating on behalf of the Royal Navy; opposing Nazi Germany and his continued calls for British rearmament during the 1930s; and ultimately his unflagging resolve as wartime leader of Britain. All of which were underpinned by deeply held moral beliefs as a libertarian: preaching the values of democratically elected government, the rule of law and the freedom of the individual. As John Keegan observes:

> without his determination, conceived at the conflict's outset and sustained throughout its long and turbulent course, to 'wage war'; without his conviction, during the eighteen months of 'standing alone', that allies would be found to redress the balance of German military power; without his belief that evil would not triumph over good and that his country embodied virtue; without his restless energy and relentless will, the harvest of victory would not have been brought in.[3]

And yet, he was a difficult man. He had few genuine friends, was difficult to live with, made political enemies and was prone to flights of strategic fancy. As General Sir Alan Brooke, his military Chief of Staff for much of the war, observed, Churchill had ten ideas every day, one good, the rest bad and most of Alan Brooke's time and energy was spent discrediting the bad ideas. Churchill could be unreasonable, but he was invaluable as Britain's wartime leader.

Similarly, as Meryn King and John Kay relate,[4] "Steve Jobs failed to conform to the conventional depiction of rational behaviour under uncertainty. Just as Churchill became premier with no specific plan for how the war would develop, Jobs returned to Apple content to wait for 'the next big thing'" and an approach to leadership that was "a confounding melange of a charismatic rhetorical style, indomitable will, and eagerness to bend any fact to fit the purpose at hand". They also shared an incredible resilience to uncertainty and setbacks.

As George Bernard Shaw observed, "The reasonable man adapts himself to the world: the unreasonable one persists in trying to adapt the world to himself. Therefore all progress depends on the unreasonable man [*or woman*]".

Notes

1 Interview with the authors, 22 March 2021. See Appendix 2 Leader Biographies.
2 Power, S. (2020). *Education of an Idealist: A Memoir*. New York: Dey Street Books.
3 Keegan, J. (2002). *Churchill*. London: Weidenfeld & Nicolson, p. 9.
4 Kay, J. and King, M. (2020). *Radical Uncertainty: Decision-Making for an Unknowable Future*. London: The Bridge Street Press, p. 169.

20 Resilience

For most of us, life has become increasingly demanding, presenting us with evermore complex challenges at a relentless pace, fuelled by tools allowing instant communication and working from anywhere. Most employees are now only an email or instant message away from their manager and work is increasingly omnipresent in our lives. With many working from home during the Covid-19 pandemic, managers and co-workers, who were once in the office or down the hall, are now in our living room, kitchen, bedroom or wherever we can find a quiet place to work. Add in personal and family needs and it's easy to feel overwhelmed.

The negative effects of this "always-on" lifestyle were becoming apparent even before the pandemic, with research demonstrating higher levels of stress and burnout, alongside spousal resentment and work-family conflict increasing as work commitments progressively impinged on family time. In their book, *Immunity to Change*, Harvard Professors Robert Kegan and Lisa Laskow Lahey discuss how the increase in complexity associated with modern life has left many of us reeling.[1] The complexity of the world is exceeding our "complexity of mind", overwhelming our ability to cope and still be effective. It has nothing to do with how intelligent we are, but with our ability to make sense of the world and how we operate in it.

While this kind of overwork is not ideal, there are undoubtedly situations in which it becomes a necessity or makes personal sense. But in the longer term, the cognitive impact of feeling perpetually overwhelmed ranges from mental slowness to confusion, forgetfulness, difficulty concentrating or thinking logically and an impaired ability to solve problems. When we have too many demands on our thinking over an extended period, chronic fatigue makes us prone to distractions and our thinking less agile. To survive we need to develop resilience. The difficulty is that being resilient is often mistaken for robustness.

To be robust is to be strong and healthy and rests on the resistance of a system to change but with the crucial addendum – without adapting its initial stable

DOI: 10.4324/9781003092582-32

configuration, think of the Pyramids of Giza, which have survived 4,500 years but look visibly decayed, what will they look like in another 1,000 years? Resilience, however, is about reconfiguring and adapting to change or damage, like bacteria.

When we resolve to be more resilient and mentally strong, we often adopt a robust grit and determination approach. That is, we believe the more we put our noses to the grindstone and endure, the stronger and tougher we'll become. Think of a marathon runner straining themselves over the last mile. But resilience, just like sport, isn't just about endurance during the race, it's also about how you recuperate and recharge between races. Grit and determination without rest and recuperation lead to injury and burnout. To an athlete, rest is as important as physical activity because that is when muscles adapt and reconfigure so they can give of their best when it's required.

Some of the best work we have found on resilience, which resonates powerfully with Network Leadership, has been developed by the Roffey Park Institute.[2] In a research report written by Dan Lucy, Meysam Poorkavoos and Arun Thompson, they identify five key capabilities for building resilience.[3] This was developed in response to an identified need in organisations to equip their leaders with the ability to be more resilient and adaptable in the face of more frequent and disruptive change. It accords extremely well with our views on how to support and enable more effective responses to the ambiguity and turbulence of the modern business world, which they too note has been dubbed a VUCA world (Volatile, Uncertain, Complex and Ambiguous).

Through a survey of over 1,000 managers, they explored how current UK managers perceived their own resilience capabilities, identifying areas of strength and relative weakness. Their results suggested that managers struggled most with managing the boundary between work and home life and taking steps to maintain their levels of physical energy. Drawing upon a wide range of literature about resilience, from developmental psychology through to social neuroscience, they went on to develop a theory of resilience focused on capabilities and the dynamic interaction of the individual with his or her environment. An exploration that culminated in the development of a model of personal resilience. The five key capabilities are perspective; emotional intelligence; purpose, values and strengths; connections; and managing physical energy. Here, we will use them as a backdrop to restless persuasion.

Perspective is the capability to step back from a challenging situation, to "accept rather than deny its negative aspects whilst finding opportunity and meaning in the midst of adversity". Finding opportunity, they believe, "spurs active striving, the setting of goals and the taking of action to achieve them", while at the same time allowing us to expand the range of options open to us.

Perspective empowers us to recognise opportunities rather than being disabled by risk and threat. Crucially, "the act of gaining perspective allows resilient people to focus their efforts on those things they can change and accept those things they cannot".

Emotional intelligence, to which we have already alluded, is first and foremost about being aware of your own emotions and being able to regulate them – "not being overtaken by our emotions but allowing space and time to process them". Resilient leaders, however, are also aware of emotions and needs of others which makes them socially skilled and able to navigate social situations, while also being compassionate towards others as well as themselves. In other words, they recognise when recuperation is necessary, giving time to others and taking time for themselves.

Purpose, values and strengths combine our belief in the importance of a personal moral framework guiding a leader's actions and a clear sense of purpose (a personal manifesto) that is congruent with those values and provides us with the strength to hold to those values "when all around there is change".

Connections is wholly in accord with the power of positive actor-networks, identifying that "leaders who are able to stay resilient in challenging times have a wide network of friends and colleagues to draw on, both to get things done and to provide support". It also recognises "that connections are not only one way … there is a great deal of evidence to support the strength that helping others give us".

Finally, managing physical energy, which discusses "keeping physically fit, eating well, and giving ourselves the time away from work to engage in activities we enjoy and recuperate enables us to maintain our energy levels". A big part of recharging is about finding periods of time for mental decompression. Taking a holiday or at least a day off is ideal, but you can also make simple adjustments at work that will allow you to turn off and recharge your mental energy. Experts recommend a cognitive break every 90 minutes (at least) to allow you to boost your mental batteries during the day. Eating lunch away from your desk can also help, as can taking a walk during your breaks instead of scrolling through the news on your phone.

A key component of these five capabilities is that they can be learnt and they are interrelated. Developing capabilities in one domain is likely to have positive benefits in some or all the other domains. They give the example of connecting with others, which allows us to maintain our perspective and generate options for solving problems that we experience. Equally, engaging in physical activity often provides the opportunity to connect with others. If you are interested, their research has led to the development of an online Resilience Capability

Index (RCI), available through Roffey Park's website,[4] which managers can use to assess their own resilience capabilities alongside practical suggestions on what they might do to boost their capacity for resilience.

Notes

1 Kegan, R. and Laskow Lahey, L. (2009). *Immunity to Change: How to Overcome It and Unlock the Potential in Yourself and Your Organization (Leadership for the Common Good)*. Brighton, MA: Harvard Business Review Press.
2 Roffey Park Institute www.roffeypark.ac.uk.
3 Lucy, D., Poorkavoos, M. and Thompson, A. (2018). Building Resilience: Five Key Capabilities. (online) Available at www.roffeypark.ac.uk/knowledge-and-learning-resources-hub/building-resilience-five-key-capabilities/ (accessed 17 April 2021).
4 Op cit. www.roffeypark.com/rci.

21 Being Comfortable in Chaos

"Chaos isn't a pit. Chaos is a ladder", says Petyr Baelish in *Game of Thrones*.[1] What Baelish means is that where there is confusion, where things become uncertain and formal social structures are fluid and unstable, it is easier to shift your position to a more powerful one. Baelish loves disruption and disorder because it provides him, someone with little formal or positional authority, the opportunity to climb the social hierarchy and gain more power. Now, just to be clear, we do not condone the pursuit of power for power's sake or for selfish gain. However, we do believe that success as a leader requires that you are as adept in the volatile and uncertain world of wicked problems and informal social networks as you are in the formal confines of tame problems and the corporate hierarchy.

Conversely, Ruthanne Huising's study highlighted just how infrequently we recognise how poorly designed and managed many of our organisations really are, we simply do not understand the system.[2] Ironically, this may be a good thing. Not acknowledging the dysfunction of existing routines may in fact protect us from seeing how much of our work is wasted effort. In conclusion, she writes:

> Knowledge of the systems we work in can be a source of power, yes. But when you realize you can't affect the big changes your organization needs, it can also be a source of alienation.

In our experience, the qualities that enable people to lead beyond their formal and positional authority come to nothing if individuals are alienated or uncomfortable operating in the complexity and confusion of the outer and peripheral networks, the informal and often hidden substructures that exist within and around all organisations. In fact, the best Network Leaders are not just comfortable in this environment, they thrive in it. They revel in the turbulence at the interfaces and edges where different people, processes and philosophies

DOI: 10.4324/9781003092582-33

collide. Just as in Poker, almost anything can happen, so a player must cope with uncertainty. The best poker players take advantage of the uncertainty and make it work for them by identifying patterns in the environment (the behaviour of other players). They recognise that bad luck is part of the game and the best you can do is try to make the right decisions given the inevitable ambiguity.

Another way to describe it is that Network Leaders are comfortable in situations of dynamic stability. Most people want stability, but the time of static stability has gone; instead, we must adapt to dynamic stability, in which, like riding a bicycle, you cannot stand still (because you will fall off), but once you are moving it becomes easier. It is not our natural state, but we must learn to exist within it. To use another analogy, the worst thing you can do while white water rafting is to stick your paddle in the water to try and slow yourself down, you will capsize. Instead, stability requires that you go as fast, or faster, than the water that is carrying you while taking advantage of any periods of calm to think and prepare yourself for the next piece of white water which may be just around the corner.

But embracing such instability and complexity is not just a cognitive challenge, it is also emotional. It's about learning to manage negative emotions, such as anger, fear and anxiety, when confronted by complex and uncertain situations. When we move into the fight, flight or fright state (such as crisis), our vision literally narrows, our prefrontal cortex begins to shut down and we become more reactive and less capable of reflection. Reacting to our primal emotions for survival tend to make us one-dimensional and in these moments our attention automatically shifts from focusing on the task at hand to physically defending ourselves or, as is more likely in the modern world, our sense of self and what we believe to be true.

Quite simply, the brain signals threats to our deeply held beliefs in the same way that it signals threats to physical safety. As far as his brain is concerned, you may as well be brandishing an axe when you question your colleague's deeply held beliefs about the appropriate strategy. So tread lightly. But this awareness is also the first step in helping us to modulate our own inclination to attack, blame or scapegoat others and instead turn inward to restore a state of equilibrium and measured thinking.

The Amygdala Hijack

Stress, as we all know, is the confusion created when one's mind tries desperately to override the body's desire to scream, punch the wall or choke the living daylights out of someone who desperately needs it – or words to that effect (there are more precise clinical descriptions available). If you've felt that type of stress, you were in the midst of an amygdala hijack. The term derives from the work of Daniel Goleman in his 1996 book *Emotional Intelligence: Why It Can Matter More Than IQ*,[3] and describes an emotional response to a situation which is immediate, overwhelming and out of proportion to the actual stimulus. Out of proportion because it is a survival response, and these days the threats we face tend to be psychological not physical.

The "hijack" takes place because our emotional brain processes information milliseconds faster than the rational brain and can therefore act before any direction from the rational, thinking brain is received. Which is useful when facing a sabre-toothed tiger, but less so when facing an aggravating problem or an annoying colleague. The problem, as most of us have probably experienced, is that it can lead us to react irrationally and detrimentally, lashing out first and regretting it later or freezing and not acting at all: overwhelmed by events and paralysed with uncertainty. But, as previously stated, the first step to controlling our emotions is to name the problem. Well we've done that and it's called the "amygdala hijack". The second step is to understand it.

The human brain has reached a level of complexity that, as far as we know, is unparalleled in our universe. It has ensured that we have outcompeted all our competitors, including other human species, to become the most successful and dominant species our planet has ever known. But the brain is far from perfect and it suffers from its evolution, which in construction terms could be described as a renovation project rather than a new build. Imagine a building that began as a wooden hut (our reptilian brain), which then had a stone extension attached to it, on top of which was erected a first floor made of brick (our mammalian brain), to which was added a second floor of concrete, glass and steel (our human brain), while running through it are the remnants of older plumbing, heating and wiring systems that have not been replaced, but simply repaired, adapted, extended to accommodate the renovations or simply forgotten.

Consequently, despite our logical, analytical and innovative powers (those aspects of our human brain that set us apart from other species), we still share the primal and emotional instincts of other animals. Of which the primary concern is survival. To ensure our survival, the amygdala, which sits in our mammalian or limbic middle brain, is constantly scanning the environment for threats, and if it detects one, it takes over the rest of the brain. It cannot, however, differentiate a 50,000 BC threat from a 21st century one like our rational, thinking "human" brain can.

For the limbic brain, the identification of a "threat" leads to the triggering of one or more avoidance emotions (fear, anger, disgust), which provoke an avoidance/threat response (denial, attack, paralysis or withdrawal), which, in turn, takes our thinking brain off-line, leaving us unable to use our higher brain functions until equilibrium is restored. The danger is that when someone becomes, in effect, a threat, our emotions rule our reactions without the benefit of logic or reason.

Regaining self-control is therefore essential and it turns out that counting to ten does help. It helps because it distracts our emotional brain, giving time for our rational thinking brain to kick back in and equilibrium to be restored (it is no coincidence that neuroscience now tells us that it takes about six seconds, the time it takes to count to ten, for chemicals stimulating the amygdala to dissipate). So, in the first instance, pause and take a deep breath. Simply focusing on long deep breaths takes you out of your head and into your body, away from the amygdala and back towards physiological and emotional equilibrium. You can also do something as simple as getting up from your desk and making a drink (tea perhaps rather than a gin and tonic – so accessible when WFH) or going for a short walk.

This will not only give you more time to get your rational brain back online, but it will also help you to avoid potential misunderstandings and launch into immediate but ill-judged solutions. The key is to take time to try and understand the problem or situation in all its messy complexity. And if you still don't feel in control, then give yourself more time, ask questions and try to objectify the problem. Recognize that you will not always be able to manage your feelings and delaying thought is better than allowing impulsive reactions to cloud your judgement or have a negative impact on your decision-making or relationships. So, take the time to step back and refresh your perspective. But of course, it's not just about you.

Beyond our inner network, boundaries are more fluid and the further we go beyond our formal authority, the messier it gets. In these spaces, we will need to collaborate, accommodate, persuade and influence, constantly adjusting our approach to deal with different characters and context. Command in the inner circle is relatively straightforward and can happen in an instant, and influence in the outer circles can be tortuous and takes time. We need to take a collective step back to try and understand some of the external complexity that plagues us.

Makers and Breakers

As Thomas L. Friedman observes, at a fundamental level, technology and globalisation are empowering both political makers, who want to remake autocratic societies into more consensual ones, and political breakers who want to bring down governments in order to impose religious or ideological tyranny.

Unfortunately, as he pithily observes, it is easier to turn an aquarium into fish soup than it is to turn fish soup into an aquarium. The evidence so far suggests that social networks make it much easier to go from imposed order to revolution than to go from revolution to a new kind of sustainable, consensual order.[4]

In other words, while it is becoming easier to gain freedom from dictators, micromanagers, hotel chains, department stores and supermarkets, to live the way you want as an individual it is necessary ground this freedom in the broader collective of consensual societies, which are anchored in free and fair elections, the rule of law and government. Fundamentally, it requires a recognition that our individual rights as citizens need to be balanced by the collective duties and obligations of citizenship, not least participation in the democratic process and respect for the rights, beliefs and opinions of others. All of which are culturally artefacts and therefore take time to develop. In short, "freedom from" can happen quickly, but "freedom to" takes time and requires trust.

Niall Ferguson charts this same dynamic in *The Square and the Tower*, in which he attempts to find a middle way between mainstream history, which has tended to understate the role of networks, and the conspiracy theorists, who exaggerate them. Instead, he proposes a new historical narrative in which major changes, dating back to the Age of Discovery and the Reformation, are understood as disruptive challenges posed to established hierarchies by networks. Because of their relatively decentralised structure, because of the way they combine clusters and weak links and because they can adapt and evolve, networks tend to be more creative than hierarchies. Consequently, innovations have tended to come from networks more than from hierarchies. The problem is that networks are not easily directed towards a common objective. Like Friedman, he challenges the confident assumption among some commentators that there is something inherently benign in this network disruption of hierarchical order.

Ferguson goes on to argue that the global impact of the internet has few better analogies in history than the impact of printing in 16th-century Europe. Both became transmission systems for all kinds of manias, panics, sects and conspiracy theorists. And both led to an erosion of territorial sovereignty and intervention in the domestic affairs of other nation-states. Russian hackers and trolls pose a threat to Western democracy just as Jesuit priests posed a threat to the English Reformation, a threat from within sponsored from without. However, there are three major differences that make modern networks an exponentially different challenge.

First, our networking revolution is much faster and more geographically extensive than that of printing. Disruption took centuries after 1490, it took just decades after 1990 and, unlike printing, literacy is no longer a barrier to connection. Second, the distributional consequences of our revolution are quite different from those of the early modern revolution. The printing press created no billionaires and no oligopolies emerged in the realms of either hardware or software. In Ferguson's view, the old truth stands – corporations will pursue monopoly, duopoly or oligopoly if they are left free to do so, and social networks allow this freedom because they are inherently unfair and exclusionary by nature. Third, the printing press disrupted religious life in Western Christendom before it disrupted anything else. By contrast, the internet began by disrupting commerce, then politics and finally religion by giving a voice to fundamentalists, most notably within Islam.

Ferguson concludes that networks are more likely to lead to an anarchic dystopia rather than a collective utopia, so some form of hierarchy or structure is required to control and direct them. He advocates a top-down approach, a new alliance of great powers who need to recognise their common interest in resisting the spread of jihadism, criminality and cyber-factionalism. Friedman, however, offers a bottom-up approach. For him, the fundamental problem in our efforts to combat radical Islam is that we treat it as an organisation (hierarchy), not a movement (network). Just as General Stanley McChrystal realised in confronting Al Qaeda in Iraq. Organisations can be penetrated, broken and their leadership destroyed, but this does not work for a movement (or a networked insurgency). The only thing that might work is to challenge it at source. The only way to eliminate violent Islamic movements is for Muslims to do it. It takes families, friends, neighbours, teachers, religious leaders and communities to deter a breaker of this kind. In other words, it takes social networks and trusted sources of authority.

Polarisation and silos are driven by human behaviour, and while social networks improve our ability to connect, we need to recognise that it is no substitute for organisation, culture and leadership. What Friedman and Ferguson can agree on is that the fundamental Leninist insight holds true: nothing can be done without some form of organisation, and this takes time. In essence, it is the same discussion we have been having about organisations: how to align the formal hierarchy with the informal social network and rational strategy with emotive politics and elusive cultures. Primarily, how can leaders and mangers gain trust, legitimacy and connections in order to get stuff done when volatility, uncertainty, complexity and ambiguity render formal structures and authority inadequate.

Dealing with Ambiguity

We live in uncertain times and uncertainty is unsettling. Extremists, communists, fascists, religious fundamentalists all play on our fears and attempt to unlock the complexity of human behaviour by offering simple answers. Democracy, however, recognises complexity and our need to live within it. At work, it is no different; leaders must resist the "easy but wrong" over the "hard but right". Above all, managing complexity and dealing with ambiguity requires resilience: the willingness to sit in the discomfort of uncertainty and let its rivers run through us.

Resilience is about more than just keeping calm and carrying on; it's the ability to experience something stressful without letting it destroy your ability to think rationally and shatter your resolve and sense of purpose. Just like the resilience of a material is its ability to return to its original shape after being compressed or stretched, like a spring that is stretched beyond its elastic limit. For a person, it is the ability to deal with pressure and change without getting bent out of shape. But unlike materials, the right degree of stretch makes us stronger and more capable. Stepping out of our comfort zone is uncomfortable, so much so that we may seek to avoid these types of situations altogether, but it's only by challenging ourselves that we grow and improve.

For humans, being resilient is fundamentally an emotional state that allows you to acknowledge and process negative feelings instead of locking them away or being overwhelmed by them. In other words, it is important to our sense of balance, whether that's work-life balance or our ability to navigate challenging situations successfully. It helps us feel like we can control how we respond to events, even when we don't control the events themselves, and it acts as a buffer against anxiety and depression. There's even evidence to suggest that resilience helps support the immune system. Stress hormones such as cortisol are involved in triggering the immune system response. However, the immune system can build up a tolerance to cortisol when levels stay elevated for long periods of time, thereby leaving us more susceptible to illness. Cultivating emotional resilience helps regulate your stress levels and therefore keeps your immune system responsive.

When confronted with a situation weighed with anxiety and ambiguity, like a pandemic and/or frightening news about the economy, it's difficult to think positively. We are in danger of being overwhelmed by events and descending into an uncertain and unproductive state of mind. But there are people who manage to see their way through and find a positive path forward. Some even manage to make uncertainty work for them: the innovators and entrepreneurs, who can navigate turbulent times and uncover potential opportunities. And while part of that capacity to deal with the unknown is probably innate, a significant portion is learned by acknowledging your fears and stepping into the arena of anxiety.

One of the first things to recognise is that what happens to you isn't solely down to your actions. The only thing you can truly control is your response.

In the words of psychologist and concentration camp survivor Victor Frankl, "Everything can be taken from a [person] but one thing: the last of human freedoms – to choose one's attitude in a given set of circumstances, to choose one's own way". The serenity prayer advises a similar approach: God, grant me the serenity to accept the things I cannot change, courage to change the things I can and wisdom to know the difference.[5] The world is getting more complex not less and we therefore need to suppress the notion that we are able to control everything.

The second thing to acknowledge is that in an uncertain and ambiguous world, we will never have all the information we need for absolute certainty. It is pointless therefore to wait for that final bit of hard data that will tell you what to do because it will likely never come. You need to get the information available, make the best decision you can and act on it. At times, it makes sense to act on the 70% solution today rather than waiting for the 90% solution tomorrow, because by then it may be too late. In the face of continued uncertainty, follow Churchill's directive for "Action this Day", which during the Second World War he had stamped in red on all directives requiring a speedy resolution.

The third element is humility. Having made the best decision you can, realize that it might be wrong. Sometimes a wrong decision is better than no decision (and not acting is also a decision, albeit by default). Ambiguity means that you will make wrong decisions, but don't let that put you off. Being a leader is about making more right decisions than you do wrong. So get comfortable with making mistakes by looking at them as learning opportunities. Allow yourself to feel the frustration, but then ask what you can learn from it. This will allow you to be flexible in the face of setbacks.

In dealing with crises and wicked problems, flexibility is also key. As Eisenhower observed, "The plan is nothing, but planning is everything". Or as Mike Tyson more colourfully put it: "Everyone has a plan until they get punched on the nose". This is sage advice and reiterates the far older military maxim of Field Marshal Helmuth Karl Bernhard Graf von Moltke that "No plan of operations extends with any certainty beyond the first contact with the main hostile force". So you need to be willing to change course as more information comes to light and don't let pride delay you in correcting that course. Ambiguity can reveal facts at any time that are going to affect even your best decisions, so be willing to accept fresh evidence and make the necessary changes.

The alternative is cognitive closure, the desire to reach a decision quickly and an aversion to ambiguity and confusion. This is the antithesis of being comfortable in chaos. Individuals with a strong need for cognitive closure rely heavily on early information cues, dislike multiple points of view and struggle to change their minds as new information becomes available. Consequently, they produce fewer ideas and alternative explanations, which paradoxically makes them more confident in their own initial and potentially flawed beliefs. Individuals who, however, resist the need for cognitive closure tend to be more thoughtful, more creative and more comfortable with competing narratives. They are also better at handling crises.

Notes

1 Just in case you missed it, *Game of Thrones* is a fantasy drama television series created by David Benioff and D. B. Weiss for HBO. It is an adaptation of *A Song of Ice and Fire*, George R. R. Martin's series of fantasy novels, the first of which was *A Game of Thrones*, published in 1996.
2 Huising, R. (2019). Can You Know Too Much About Your Organization? (online) *Harvard Business Review*, December 4. Available at https://hbr.org/2019/12/can-you-know-too-much-about-your-organization (accessed 17 April 2021).
3 Goleman, D. (1996). *Emotional Intelligence: Why It Can Matter More Than IQ*. London: Bloomsbury.
4 Friedman, T.L. (2017). *Thank You for Being Late: An Optimist's Guide to Thriving in The Age of Accelerations*. New York: Penguin Books.
5 The Serenity Prayer was written by the American theologian Reinhold Niebuhr.

22
Leading in a Crisis

The Covid-19 pandemic was/is an unprecedented event in modern history and yet the experience of managing through it is not necessarily unique. Although there is no precedent for the magnitude of this crisis, it does have parallels with previous disasters, such as the Ebola pandemics, Hurricane Katrina, the Gulf of Mexico oil spill, the global financial crisis and 9/11. Principally, crises make people feel uncertain and uncertainty triggers nervousness, anxiety and fear, with people wondering what it means for them and their families. In the context of work, the role of the leader is to first help them make sense of the situation. As Rosabeth Moss Kanter observes, in recovering from a crisis the right tone must be set top down:

> In the best turnarounds and disaster recoveries, leaders stress open communication and a spirit of accountability. Even before solutions are clear, they offer assurance that they are guided by values and a sense of purpose. They put the same information in front of everyone, using evidence to guide their decisions. They encourage frank communication, act decisively, admit what they don't know, and make clear when and how they will communicate. They empathize with victims and recognize acts of heroism. They make investments that signal their belief in their mission and their people, putting this ahead of financial considerations.[1]

As Kanter goes on to explain, crises are crises because they affect people. But leaders can instead become fixated on the daily metrics of share price, revenue and costs. These are important, but they are the outcome of the coordinated efforts of people. She concludes with the classic "how-not-to-do-it" example of the then BP CEO Tony Hayward, who, following the Deepwater Horizon explosion and oil spill in the Gulf of Mexico, was widely reported to have said, "I'd like my life back", instead of expressing compassion for the people whose lives and livelihoods were threatened or lost.

Crises, which are necessarily fast moving, complex and unpredictable, require both the compassion and far-sightedness of leadership and the hard-nosed

DOI: 10.4324/9781003092582-34

calculation of management. Addressing the urgent needs of the present is the work of management. You need to make immediate choices and allocate resources. The pace is fast and actions are decisive. Leading, by contrast, involves guiding people to the best possible eventual outcome over the longer arc of time. The focus needs to be on what is likely to come next and readying to meet it. That means seeing beyond the immediate to anticipate the next three, four or five obstacles. The best leaders navigate rough waters deftly, saving lives, energizing organisations and inspiring communities. But, again, as Kanter observes, crises tend to be over-managed and under-led.[2] Inverting Henry Mintzberg's observation that the business world tends to be over-led and undermanaged.

In the first place, the human brain is programmed to narrow its focus in the face of a threat. It's an evolutionary survival mechanism designed for self-protection. The problem is that our field of vision becomes restricted to the immediate foreground just at the time when leaders need to intentionally step back and look up, opening their mental aperture to take in the bigger picture: taking a broad, rounded view of both the challenges and opportunities, understanding the many possible unfolding scenarios around the crisis, such as business continuity issues, the economic and social health of affected communities, legal concerns, political fallout, environmental impact, inter-agency coordination and more. For the leader, the most pressing concern is not managing the response to the crisis itself, it is leading through the wicked tangle of possible implications and unintended consequences, creating the space and top cover for the operators on the ground to succeed.

Second, for leaders who have risen through a single organisation or industry, micromanagement is a real danger, the result of managers returning to their comfort zone either because it's what they really enjoy doing or because it feels easier than the job they have been promoted into. Either way, it's not a good idea. The same can happen in a crisis. Managing a crisis can be thrilling, and when the adrenaline spikes, leaders are often drawn back to their operational comfort zone, managing the action and experiencing a tangible sense of adding value. But leading through a crisis requires a longer view, not just managing the present.

Leaders need to devote a portion of their time to thinking beyond the crisis to anticipating what comes next in order to prepare the organisation for the changes ahead. They need to delegate and trust their people as they make tough decisions, providing proper support and guidance based on their experience while resisting the temptation to take over. This is perhaps easier in organisations in high-risk industries, such as energy and aviation. From bitter experience, they should have established and robust health, safety, security and environment (HSSE) functions to help them cope. But for organisations without these processes in place, leaders are in danger of being drawn into micro-managing the response and disrupting the operating rhythm of the managers who are actually responsible.

Kanter cautions that leaders must resist the urge to over-centralise the response. Risk and ambiguity increase during a crisis because so much is uncertain and volatile, and the trap for leaders is trying to control everything by creating new layers of approval for minor decisions. This only makes the organisation less responsive and frustration grows with each new constraint. The solution, she suggests, is to "seek order rather than control". She describes order as people knowing what is expected of them and what they can expect of others. Leaders, therefore, must acknowledge that they cannot control everything, determine which decisions only they can make and delegate the rest, establishing a clear framework of values and principles while foregoing the temptation to do everything themselves. The same applies to the complexities of strategic management.

In a seminal paper on business strategy, Henry Mintzberg and James Waters distinguished between deliberate strategy, which is intentional, and emergent strategy, which instead consists of the company's responses to a variety of unanticipated events.[3] Mintzberg's thinking was informed by his observation that managers overestimate their ability to predict the future and to plan for it in a precise and technocratic way – to control it. By drawing a distinction between deliberate and emergent strategy, they were not dismissing deliberate strategy but wanted to encourage managers to watch carefully for changes in their environment and make course corrections in their deliberate strategy as required. Not least because of the dangers of sticking to a fixed strategy in the face of substantial changes in the competitive environment.

The fundamental difference between deliberate and emergent strategy is that the former focuses on direction and control – getting intended or desired things done – whereas the latter seeks a sense of order in which "strategic learning" can take place. Defining strategy as the completion of intended outcomes, they argued, effectively precludes the notion of strategic learning. Once intentions have been set, attention is riveted on realising them, not on adapting them, and messages from the environment tend to get blocked out.

Their insight, adding the concept of emergent strategy based on a definition of strategy as that which is realised rather than what is intended, opened the process of strategy to the notion of learning. Emergent strategy, by its very nature, implies learning from what works and acting iteratively, one step at a time, in search of a viable pattern. Emergent strategy does not mean that it is chaotic or out of control, only that it is open, flexible and responsive – it is willing to learn. Such behaviour is especially important when an environment is too unstable or complex to comprehend because it enables management to act before everything is fully understood, to respond to an evolving reality rather than focusing on a stable fantasy.

Emergent strategy also benefits from mission command. Enabling senior leaders, who are not close enough to a situation or know too little about the varied activities of the organisation, to surrender control to those who do and allow them to shape strategy within the bounds of overall intent as the situation changes. That is not to say that deliberate strategy has no place. When the necessary information is available and can be largely understood and predicted, then it may be appropriate to suspend strategic learning for a time to pursue intentions with as much determination as possible. They conclude that strategy formation:

> walks on two feet, one deliberate, the other emergent … managing requires a light deft touch – to direct in order to realize intentions while at the same time responding to an unfolding pattern of action.[4]

A deft touch is also required in the art of being unreasonable with a smile.

Notes

1 Kanter, R.M. (2020). Leading Your Team Past the Peak of a Crisis. (online) *Harvard Business Review*. Available at https://hbr.org/2020/04/leading-your-team-past-the-peak-of-a-crisis (accessed 17 April 2021).
2 Mintzberg, H. and Mangelsdorf, M.E. (2009). Debunking Management Myths. (online) *MIT Sloan Management Review*. Available at https://sloanreview.mit.edu/article/debunking-management-myths/ (accessed 17 April 2021).
3 Mintzberg, H. and Waters, J.A. (1985). Of Strategies, Deliberate and Emergent Waters *Strategic Management Journal*, 6(3, (Jul–Sep), pp. 257–72.
4 Mintzberg, H. and Waters, J.A. (1985) ibid. p. 271.

23
Being Unreasonable with a Smile

Matt Ridley writes that "innovators are often unreasonable people: restless, quarrelsome, unsatisfied and ambitious".[1] In discussing Amazon at the turn of the millennium, when it was set to lose a billion dollars in the next year and was predicted to be on the point of failure, he quotes a colleague of Jeff Bezos, saying, "As usual it was Jeff against the world", fighting his colleagues for ideas they thought were ludicrous and defying analysts who misunderstood his appetite for experiment and tolerance for failure as ineptitude.[2] It wasn't. He was being unreasonable, but only by the standards of what was then widely assumed to be reasonable.

If management is the science of getting the right people in the right place at the right time with the right equipment to get the job done, then Network Leadership could be described as the art of doing what the science of management says is impossible. When, as is often the case, there are not enough people or resources and time is not on our side. When reasonable people say it is impossible, at times we need leaders to act unreasonably to get things done – and that requires courage. The morale courage to do what they believe to be right in the face of pressure from others to do something different or nothing at all. It is the ability to transcend the group, which, taken to its logical conclusion, means accepting that on occasion leaders may wish to disobey or withdraw entirely from a project or organisation.

As previously discussed, this requires personal resilience, a capacity to feel comfortable in chaos and the capability to lead in a crisis, but it also requires an ability to push others to achieve targets that appear impossible, to do things that they think are beyond them and to accomplish tasks that leave them feeling drained and exhausted. But they cannot break them. A spring stretched beyond its elastic limit will never function as a spring again, and from a moral and practical perspective you cannot do that with people. That said, unlike a spring, humans improve and grow stronger when they are tested and pushed to their limits. It is akin to the notion of Progressive Load – increasing the total

DOI: 10.4324/9781003092582-35

capacity in a system by gradually increasing demand on the system, prompting the system to adapt to the new demands over time. In other words, developing its resilience.

For people with the right mind-set, disruptive, demanding and stressful experiences are often opportunities for individual growth,[3] but they can also spur organisational change, creating new opportunities for people to voice their ideas on how to do things better together. And as we are forced to take on new challenges, face new uncertainties and recover from mistakes in the Covid-19 era, it reminds us that our abilities and those of our peers are not fixed, but are open to development and improvement. It is a growth mind-set that will likely serve us well during the next inevitable crisis.

The challenge for leaders in all this is to strike a balance between pushing people too hard and not pushing them hard enough. We use the notion of the Zone of Proximal Development (ZPD) to illustrate this point. The ZPD describes a sweet spot or Goldilocks moment (not too hot and not too cold) between overloading a person's capacity to cope, leading to demoralisation and burnout and the experience of optimal experience which helps people to grow and develop. It can be related to the psychological concept of "Flow", first developed by Mihaly Csikszentmihalyi[4] (Figure 6.1).

Csikszentmihalyi describes "Flow" as a highly focused mental state conducive to productivity and well-being, which exists in the space between a job that is mundane and too easy, leading to boredom, and a task that is too difficult, leading to stress and anxiety. In a state of flow we experience joy and are so utterly immersed in the task or experience that time passes without us noticing. It is a time at which we are at our most creative and there is an exhilarating feeling

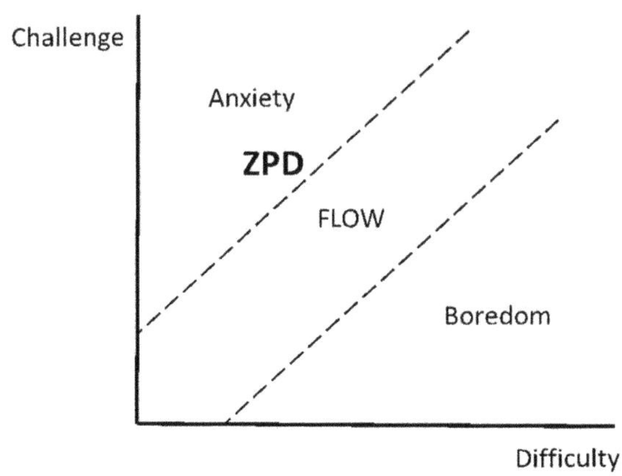

Figure 6.1 The Relationship between ZPD and 'Flow'.

of self-transcendence and control. In sports, it is often described as being in the zone. We identify the ZPD existing at the upper edge of "Flow", marking the point at which we leave our comfort zone and are challenged to do more than we currently feel capable. It describes the place in which we confront anxiety.

The term ZPD is taken from the work of Lev Vygotsky (1896–1934), a Russian psychologist, known for his work on psychological development in children. He was particularly interested in the social context of a child's learning, believing that a child's cognitive development is driven not only by its biological maturation, but also through its interaction with others. In short, children learn through problem-solving experiences shared with "experts", people more knowledgeable than the child such as parents and teachers. This begins with shared dialogues, but progresses with the skills of mental representation to an inner dialogue or reflection on the part of the child. And the ZPD is where this cognitive development takes place. A place beyond what the child can do now but not too difficult that it cannot be accomplished with help. In effect, the expert offers a hand across the divide, the ZPD, which exists between them and the child, in the same way an expert manager/leader/coach offers a hand across the skills and knowledge divide to a less experienced member of staff.

This means that as well as being unreasonable, making the learner reach for the hand, a leader must also show compassion, which requires the emotional intelligence to understand when a person is capable but stretched and when they are utterly out of their depth and likely to "drown". It is a judgement call and requires leaders to understand that the very strengths that make them fearless can, when overplayed, be their greatest weakness – that they are vulnerable to a lack of compassion. In the heat of the moment, they forget that not everybody is as strong and resilient as they are. And being blind to this fact, they are unable to relate to their employees empathetically and instead assume that they are not trying hard enough or have chosen to fail. And from here it is only a small step to contempt and blaming them for their weakness, something you cannot allow to happen. You cannot let this kind of amygdala hijack control your actions and you cannot judge others based solely on yourself.

For the ZPD to work successfully, you must also create a zone of psychological safety for the learner. Don't be so quick to judge them as failures. In the first place, you may have no idea what else may be going on in their lives or what they have to offer if you give them the opportunity and support. And remember, some of your strength and resilience may be inborn, so you can't take credit for that. Empathy involves making an extra effort. Holding out a hand to where the other person is, trying to see the world from their point of view and then helping them see yours. You may find that they weren't weak after all and together you can figure out a better way forward. Allow them to fail, as long as they learn, but don't make them failures. Growth requires that defeat is turned into victory.

Defeat into Victory

Field Marshal Viscount Slim is not a household name like Nelson or Wellington or even as well-known as his contemporary Montgomery, but he was nevertheless a brilliant and hugely admired leader, and he wrote one of the best memoirs of a serving general *Defeat into Victory*, which covers his time in Burma during the Second World War. His approach to leadership exemplifies the balance required between restless impatience to get things done in a crisis and the necessity for compassion and empathy.

Slim was promoted in March 1942 to command Burma Corps and subsequently commanded the longest retreat in British military history, over 900 miles. Yet he managed to turn a disorderly panic into a controlled military withdrawal and was consequently promoted again, taking over Eastern Army (later renamed 14th Army) in October 1943. On taking command, he found himself confronted by three major problems – supply, health and morale, to say nothing of a highly competent and until then victorious enemy, the Imperial Japanese Army.

Supply was a problem of weather, terrain and distance. He tackled it by giving a trusted subordinate, Major General AJH Snelling, the men he wanted and a "free hand" to carry out his plans. A great example of mission command, what the management literature would call empowerment. He tackled the health issue, with the practical application of the latest medical research; forward treatment of the sick and wounded to deter soldiers from feigning sickness in the hope of being sent back to the comparative comfort of India; air evacuation of serious casualties, to reassure soldiers that they would be treated as quickly as possible; and discipline – he sacked three commanding officers for failing to enforce the taking of malaria tablets, which were rumoured to cause sterility. As he observed, "by then the rest [of the commanding officers] had got my meaning".

But it was his approach to poor morale on which we wish to focus. The 14th Army was suffering from a record of defeat against the Japanese; lack of elementary amenities; the discomfort of life in the jungle; and feelings of isolation and homesickness (it is no coincidence that they are known to history as the "Forgotten Army"). In response, Slim gave great thought to what he felt were the foundations of morale. He decided they were threefold: material, intellectual and spiritual.

First, from a material perspective, he felt strongly that a soldier must feel that he will get a fair deal from his commanders and from the army generally. That he must, as far as humanly possible, be given the best weapons and equipment for his task and that his living and working conditions must be made as good as they can be. Second, intellectually, a soldier must be convinced that the objective can be attained, that it is not out of reach. That he must see too that the organisation to which he belongs is an efficient one. He must also have confidence in his leaders and know that whatever dangers and hardships he is called upon to suffer, his life will not be lightly flung away.

Third was what he called the spiritual dimension, by which he meant that there must be a great and noble object whose achievement must be vital. The method of achievement must be active and aggressive, and the soldier must feel that what he is and what he does matters directly towards the attainment of the object. But he did not stop there; this was not a philosophical exercise in leadership theory, it was fundamental to his strategy. So he also thought very carefully about how he might put his ideas into practice. He was, without a doubt, a reflective practitioner.

His approach to the material foundation was to begin by being honest. He admitted to the shortages, but he told his soldiers why that was so: because the German Army was better equipped than the Japanese and the strategic priority was Europe. Second, he stressed that all his commanders would do their utmost to rectify the shortages, otherwise they would improvise or simply do without. But he emphasised that no one would be asked to do something unless they had the minimum level of equipment required. Furthermore, while the supply problems persisted, he instituted half rations for everyone, irrespective of rank, including himself and his staff, and stipulated that there was to be no distinction between race and caste in regard to treatment. This was significant because 14th Army was a multicultural force comprising soldiers and auxiliaries from Britain and the Commonwealth, including substantial numbers of Indians and Africans.

From an intellectual perspective, he began by emphasising the small wins, beginning with a significant Australian victory. He also ensured that fighting patrols and minor operations were carried out with overwhelming strength to ensure success. As well as improvements in supply, he emphasised the importance of sharing information throughout his command and began a news journal that was issued to all troops. Reinforcement camps were also improved to allow genuine recuperation, but at the same time discipline was enforced, the soldiers were not to be allowed to develop bad habits before returning to the frontline. He also ensured that officers were carefully selected for command. Those found not up to it were sacked.

Spiritually, he adopted a direct approach, visiting as many units as possible and speaking to groups of men. He asked all his officers to do the same and to talk "the same stuff with the same object". As he later observed:

> one did not need to be a great orator to be effective. Two things only were necessary: First to know what you were talking about and second, and most important, to believe it yourself … I found that if one kept the bulk of one's talk to the material things the men were interested in, food, pay, leave, beer, mail, and the progress of operations, it was safe to end on a higher note – the spiritual foundations – and I always did.

The context and the times may have changed, but human nature hasn't. Slim knew how to strike a balance between the hard-nosed drive to achieve objectives and the compassion to recognise that people work best when they are as well treated as possible and kept informed.

Slim recognised that good process is important, and that people must believe the organisation to which they belong is an efficient one. Similarly, they must have confidence in their leaders. Passion and energy are all very well, but people quickly lose patience with incompetence. Slim ensured that officers were carefully selected for command and those found not up to it were sacked.

How you lead under pressure is the hallmark of a good leader and sets the tone for how your followers respond in a crisis. It is not unusual however for managers under pressure to become emotional, controlling and close-minded, which can have a hugely negative impact on their team's morale and productivity. To lead effectively under pressure requires that we step back and look up, considering the team dynamic we want to build over the long term and then considering how our stress-driven actions support or undermine that dynamic. We know that in normal circumstances, it is counterproductive to motivate people with fear or threats or get angry and shut down difficult conversations, so don't let stress keep you from listening to others and engaging thoughtfully.

People want decisiveness in a leader. But refusing to show any sign of compromise is counterproductive. It's not a tragedy if you change your mind later in the light of new information and acknowledging your mistakes builds trust, but at the same time you don't want to panic people or lead them to believe the situation is hopeless. Leaders are role models and in this case it is about creating an environment for effective dialogue, which includes a capacity to change your own mind, on the basis that to change others you must be prepared to change yourself: humility to listen and learn, to keep an open mind.

But what Slim recognised, above all else, is that for leaders to be role models they need to be seen. Slim made a special effort to visit the units under his command, not only the frontline units but also the admin and supply units. Not only did this allow him to role model the behaviours he expected, it also gave him direct contact with people down the hierarchy so that he had unfiltered information about people's actions and states of mind. This is especially critical when people are working in disparate geographical locations or remotely. Such interactions can help leaders understand how employees are coping, identify areas where the risks of siloed behaviour are more likely and establish links among people so that they are better able to support each other. And in all his communication he was honest.

Slim's approach to the material foundation was to begin by being honest. He felt strongly that a soldier must feel that he is getting as fair a deal as possible from his commanders and from the army generally, but at the same time he needed them to recognise that the strategic priority was Europe and why that was so. He resisted the temptation to gloss over bad news and harsh realities because while trying to alleviate people's anxiety is understandable, in the long run it does no one any favours. When you sugar-coat things, you can come across as someone who's out of touch or untrustworthy. The facts of the situation will become apparent over time and softening hard truths can backfire. When the truth comes out in dribs and drabs, it degrades trust.

Slim acknowledged the uncertainty. He knew the genuine concerns of the soldiers: their record of defeat against the Japanese; the lack of elementary amenities; the discomfort of life in the jungle; and the feelings of isolation and homesickness. He didn't carry on, regardless, he acknowledged that these concerns were very real and could not be ignored or marginalised. Instead, he addressed them directly, openly acknowledging that things seemed chaotic and unpredictable. At the same time, however, he only commiserated up to a point, he had to avoid a negative spiral of despair. He acknowledged how people were feeling, but then moved on to talk about how he wanted them to act going forward. He was also consistent in his messaging and asked all his officers to do the same: to talk "the same stuff with the same object".

Small Wins

At an intellectual level, Slim recognised that soldiers, like any other human being, must be convinced that the objective can be attained and that it is not out of reach (it is within their collective ZPD). So he adopted what is now regarded as a classic principle of change management. He began by emphasising the small wins, beginning with a significant Australian victory. He also ensured that fighting patrols and minor operations were carried out with overwhelming strength to ensure success, which was then widely communicated.

As Kotter emphasises in *The Heart of Change*,[5] leaders of successful change efforts create short-term wins. Without early wins that are visible, timely, unambiguous and meaningful, change efforts invariably run into serious problems. In successful change efforts, leaders focus first on tasks that can quickly achieve results. Actions and results that provide feedback about the validity of their visions and strategies; give those working hard to achieve a vision a pat on the back and an emotional lift; build faith in the effort, attracting those who are not yet actively helping; and take power away from the cynics. Without these micro achievements, large-scale change rarely happens. And for this to happen, focus is essential.

A change effort may require hundreds of projects, and when people feel the urgency and are empowered to act, they can easily charge ahead on all fronts, but with scattered attention, you might not achieve your first win for months, even years, and by that time it may be too late. Kotter advises that we focus instead on a handful of projects that are likely to get results. And when they do, make sure that everyone knows about them. The more visible the victories, the more they help the change process. Too often, we create wins that we can see but which others do not, at least not to the same degree.

The order of projects is also important in large-scale change efforts. The temptation is to target problems in a logical order, but he counsels that instead we should focus on those that generate quick wins and build momentum. Kotter gives the example of a company vision for globalization, which rationally entailed work on a manufacturing plant before marketing. The problem was that building a factory in Frankfurt could easily take two years, cost a $100,000,000 and then another year to determine whether the company could handle its first German manufacturing facility. During this time, wins would be hard to find. A less obvious but better choice was to sell the product and then build it. So the company put together a marketing plan for Germany and implemented it at minimum cost with a product from Chicago, which achieved clear success in less than a year. It was visible, meaningful, unambiguous and quicker.

Higher Purpose

The spiritual dimension, by which Slim meant that there must be a great and noble object whose achievement must be vital, can be equated to the modern understanding of organisational purpose. Slim's objective in aligning people to a common purpose was to reduce resistance. He recognised that we people are more resistance to change when it's done to them. If, however, people feel in control and have some stake in the destiny of the organisation, then that makes change a lot easier. He knew that he had to give the 14th Army something to work for collectively.

On the one hand, he recognised that soldiers needed to feel that what they did mattered directly towards the attainment of the ultimate objective, the defeat of the Axis Powers. But on the other hand, he understood that not only does a belief that their work fulfils a higher purpose motivate people to act, it also helps them to think and act in a more collective and collaborative fashion. Understanding the situation and the business goals helps people see how their own knowledge contributes to, but doesn't fully satisfy, the complex needs of the organisation. They understand the plan and crucially their part in it, which necessitates that they not only do their job but help others to fulfil theirs.

Collaboration

Crises like Covid-19 highlight the importance of effective collaboration for long-term organisational success. Wicked problems and crises require innovation, critical thinking, creativity and commitment to find a collective way forward. They demand that we challenge many of the traditional constructs which exist, such as organisational rivalries, competition, protectionism and societal boundaries. In a crisis, organisations need to pull together experts with unique, cross-functional perspectives to solve rapidly changing, complex problems that have long-term implications. Harnessing diversity of experience allows them to see risks and opportunities from different angles so they can generate new solutions and adapt dynamically to changing situations.

However, we also know that anxiety makes people risk-averse and provokes a tendency to fall back on actions and solutions that worked in the past rather than seeking out different approaches and perspectives. The desire to bring things under control leads to a narrowing of focus, and as resources dwindle, people often focus on self-preservation. They erect walls around their projects, jealously guard their clients and hoard knowledge, which further diminishes collaboration. If unaddressed, occasions to share existing opportunities and identify new ones diminish. As a result, collaboration across an organisation can break down.

Instead, as uncertainty and stress increase during a crisis, leaders need to encourage the expansion of networks across functional and industry silos, increasing and not decreasing the numbers of colleagues we work with. Leaders must be willing to pitch in on others' projects; team up with trusted colleagues to identify and pursue new opportunities, even if it means getting less personal glory; work on a wide variety of clients or projects; and involve people with a wide variety of skills to tackle novel and complex problems that would elude individual experts.

Notes

1 Ridley, M. (2020). *How Innovation Works*. London: 4th Estate, p. 196.
2 Ridley, M. (2020) ibid. p. 319.
3 Dweck, C. (2007). *Mindset: The New Psychology of Success*. New York: Ballantine Books.
4 Csikszentmihalyi, M. (2002). *Flow: The Psychology of Happiness*. London: Random House Group.
5 Kotter, J. (2002). *The Heart of Change: Real-Life Stories of How People Change Organizations*. Brighton, MA: Harvard Business Review Press.

Summary

Organisations have had to change in the face of crises before; Covid-19 is just one example. The future, however it may turn out, will require us to change again, we cannot hold on to everything as it was and simply hope things will return to the way they were pre-crisis. Things have already changed, with some organisations investing heavily in these changes and feeling the pain of sudden transformation. People are coming to terms with new patterns and contexts, which should lead us to consider new opportunities. In our experience, the people who experience the most success in the world are the people who accept the uncertainty and fear as best they can, learn from their experiences and keep trying new things.

Rather than resisting, preserving and maintaining, Network Leaders encourage us to be pattern-breaking and then rebuild, focussing on creating, collaborating and supporting. The human tendency in the face of uncertainty, to narrow our focus and fall back on what we did before, requires unreasonable leaders: those who are willing to challenge their own approach and ours. We won't always get the progress we hoped for, but we should be reflective about that, not fatalistic. As Matthew Syed observes, much of modern performance psychology is about mitigating the fright, flight, fight response. It is about "managing the chimp", by which he means the amygdala hijack and controlling our inner demons. An alternative method is to redefine the word failure. Failure is central to life and learning, it is how you grow, develop and ultimately flourish. Syed quotes Michael Jordan: "I fail. But that is why I succeed".[1] Failures, just like crises, are opportunities to learn and develop and we need unreasonable leaders to remind us of that.

Network Leaders can be unreasonable with a smile. They have no-nonsense views on the situations they face. They aren't overly optimistic and they don't deny reality. They intuitively understand the balance between push and pull; how to push people to achieve more than they thought possible and, at the same time, creating an emotionally safe space for performance; incrementally building the resilience of the leader and the led.

DOI: 10.4324/9781003092582-36

Resilient people find meaning in what happens. People who bounce back devise theories about their challenges to create some sort of meaning for themselves and others. Overcoming obstacles means having to improvise a solution to a problem when you don't have what you want. Resilient people make the most of what they do have. Fundamentally, it is a shift from "if only" to "if I/we".

Leadership Questions

1. How will you manage and maintain your energy to give to others in pursuit of your manifesto?
2. Who do you need to persuade?
3. What are the opportunities across your network to enlist others?
4. How and when will you be "unreasonable" in pursuit of your personal manifesto?

Note

1 Syed, M. (2017). *The Greatest: The Quest for Sporting Perfection*. London: John Murray, p. 52.

Conclusion

The world is changing at a faster pace than ever and despite, or arguably because of, our advances in computing and communication, it is becoming more uncertain and less predictable. The acronym VUCA, describing a world of volatility, uncertainty, complexity and ambiguity, was first coined towards the end of the 1980s based on the leadership theories of Warren Bennis and Burt Nanus, and was subsequently taken up by the United States Army War College to describe the multilateral complexity of the world that emerged after the end of the Cold War and has subsequently been given fresh impetus by 9/11, the 2008 financial crisis and Covid-19. Each episode reminding us how unpredictable the world is and that none of us are immune.

That is a problem because we humans don't like uncertainty. We prefer a definitive yes or no; right and wrong; left or right. Most of us like to paint by numbers and have the next steps laid down in front of us; do A, then B and so on. Our brains aren't wired to cope well with the psychological impact of events that leave us not knowing what the future holds. In the case of Covid-19, we are left worrying about a whole list of unanswered questions: will it happen again, will there be another lockdown, when will there be a vaccine, when can I safely go back to the office, will I lose my job and so on? This is challenging on two counts: first, we don't know what's coming; second, we can't do much about it. It turns out that most of us would rather deal with the certainty of bad news than the anxiety of not knowing. Even if it's bad news, knowing what we're dealing with at least gives us some sense of agency. But uncertainty just leaves us scrabbling to regain some sense of control. And it will probably come as no surprise that this stems from our primitive brain.

From an evolutionary perspective, being intolerant of uncertainty has survival value, but it's of no use to us as babies or very young children understanding where danger is because we can't do anything about it. What is useful is recognising signs of safety and that means learning to identify people and places that keep us safe and, conversely, being suspicious of ones that aren't familiar.

DOI: 10.4324/9781003092582-37

And that instinctual search for safety stays with us as we grow. Most of us like to have a place we call home and to create social networks of people like us, people who make us feel physically and mentally safe, and critical among them are those who help us make sense of the world and reduce the uncertainty. In our search for greater certainty we turn to leaders.

Leadership is a critical success factor for groups, communities, organisations, societies and nation-states. Sometimes leaders wear a badge to help us identify them, but often not. Instead, and certainly in the absence of formal leadership, we turn to people with personal authority, those whom we describe as Network Leaders, leaders who have a thorough understanding of their network and an ability to connect and energise it around a personal manifesto of what they believe and what they are trying to achieve. They position themselves to form connections between individuals and groups, enabling collaborations to evolve through trust and the identification of common aims, in order to regain a measure of control and get things done. It is an approach that is always open to possibility and opportunity: reforming networks and ideas as projects unfold and reconfiguring to deliver, but always remaining true to a positive moral framework of core beliefs.

For some, this ability to bridge the gaps between different organisational and social contexts appears innate, but most of us must learn how to do it. In which case, the complexity of contemporary organisations and the volatility of the environments in which we live and work call for a playbook of how to operate in our networked world. A clearly articulated approach to working across organisational and external boundaries, with the potential to deliver a collaborative advantage leveraged through engaging internal and external networks, this book has been our attempt to make a start on that playbook.

The genesis of the book emerged from a recognition that what constitutes personal authority and the style of leadership that grows from it is not fixed. Many of the attributes of leadership, what makes others follow, vary over time and space. What works in South Africa may not work as well in south London, what worked in Elizabethan England may not work in post-Covid Britain. Equally, just as social leadership suggests, the mantle of leadership can be taken up by different people at different times, depending upon who is best suited to lead in that context. The football manager who got his team into the Premiership may not be the leader to keep them there, the wartime leader may not be the right leader in peacetime and the CEO who saved the company from financial ruin through hard-nosed cost-cutting may not be the leader to reinvent the company and take it in a new direction.

However, we have found that whatever the context and whatever the challenge, the best leaders demonstrate the four aspects of Network Leadership.

They have a thorough grasp of the context in which they operate – they understand the system. They have something to say that is worth listening to – they have convening power. They make things happens, with and without a formal leadership position – they can lead beyond their authority. And finally, they have incredible reserves of energy and an impatience to get things done – they display restless persuasion.

Understanding the System

Social networks represent the natural inclination of humans to develop social relations and ultimately societies. We have social instincts and come into the world with predispositions towards learning how to cooperate, how to discriminate the trustworthy from the treacherous, to commit ourselves to earning a good reputation and to exchange goods and information for mutual benefit. However, there is a darker side to our social nature, a tendency for humanity to fragment into competing groups and tribes, with minds all too ready to adopt familiar prejudices and, at an extreme, pursue genocidal feuds.

As human beings we are distributed across networks, actor-networks and social networks, which inextricably combine our inner world or consciousness with our external social world. Alva Noë, Professor of Philosophy at the University of California at Berkeley, describes consciousness as something we do, enact or perform in dynamic relation to the world around us. Consciousness, in other words, happens within a context.[1] In effect, we are as much a part of our networks as our networks are a part of us.

From a leadership perspective, actor-networks challenge the idea of the single super leader, compelling us to rethink leadership as something embedded in and constituted through networks. It reinforces the notion of post-heroic or shared leadership, highlighting that a key component of better leadership performance is understanding and exploiting our leader-network to greatest effect. And, through an examination of Social Network Analysis (SNA), we sought to help that understanding by making explicit the networks in which we exist, enabling us to "see" how they form and evolve, how we influence them and how they influence us.

Furthermore, we have examined how to think critically within the networks in which we find ourselves. Networks shape what we perceive and lead us to construct personal models of how the world works. These models are unique to us, no one can see the world quite the way we do, nor can we see how others perceive the world. Awkwardly, our networked consciousness is so fundamental to who we are that it is often hard to fully comprehend these networks and to realise how we are influenced by them and how much is hidden from us. And without such knowledge it is hard to lead effectively. As Ed Catmull, co-founder of Pixar and president of Walt Disney Animation Studios, observes:

> If you don't try to uncover what is unseen and understand its nature, you will be ill-prepared to lead.[2]

It is a difficulty compounded by the nature of knowledge, which in itself is profoundly problematic, being contextual, perishable, imperfect, competitive and increasingly abundant. On the one hand, understanding is hampered by the sheer volume of data and information, and on the other by the sheer anarchy and lack of veracity among multiple individual and collective perceptions, biases, interpretations, prejudices and preferences. That together creates the social echo chambers in which we exist.

At a personal level then, we have investigated the requirement for healthy critical self-awareness: a grasp of why and how you know something, interrogation of what you think you know, awareness to ensure you have sufficient sources of relevant knowledge and an ability to consider them from a variety of perspectives. An individual capacity that corresponds well with Donald Schön's notion of the "reflective practitioner", an individual who is able to cope with change and uncertainty by interpreting and responding to the peculiarities of the circumstances in which they find themselves.

Understanding is foundational to any form of leadership, but it is absolutely explicit in our formulation of network leadership, and in our experience network leaders understand four things. First, they understand that we all exist within networks (we are all connected, no individual is an island) and that these networks determine how we perceive the world with all its biases and prejudices. Second, they understand their own network, the system or context in which they live and work, including a recognition that it is dynamic and continually evolving. Third, they have developed the individual capacity to act efficiently and effectively within that context. And finally but most critically, they know how to lead others within this context.

Network Leadership requires not only knowledge of your social network; it requires this deeper level of understanding, what we might call wisdom, the wisdom to place knowledge in its wider context, thus providing the background for a more nuanced appreciation of leadership, more sophisticated problem solving and insightful decision-making. The analogy we used is chess. Knowledge is about recognising where the pieces sit on a chessboard and how they move, but understanding is having the foresight to anticipate how the game could and should develop. Understanding supports the development of effective strategy and efficient planning through an appreciation of the environment and the actors within it, which, in turn, informs the application of power and our capacity to influence behaviour and the course of events. Without understanding, leadership flounders.

Network Leaders can see across the whole system/network in which they operate with a view to making the sum of the interacting parts greater than the whole, which, in part, is about recognising who has what and who needs what in terms of knowledge, skills and resources. But crucially, it is about recognising that opportunities and threats do not come neatly parcelled to fit the organisational teams, departments, divisions and sectors into which we have arranged ourselves.

Convening Power

Network Leaders not only understand the system in which they operate, coping individually with change and uncertainty, they shape it. Returning to our chess analogy, while understanding is having the foresight to anticipate how the game could and should develop, convening power is about shaping the system, shaping and developing the game itself, adding your own rules and pieces (just as chess has evolved over time), creating the network conditions that are required for success. In this sense, the role of the Network Leader is to enable the right environment. And the first step in that endeavour is having something to say that is worth listening to. Having a personal manifesto, a declaration of intent made public through your words and actions, has an attractive power to gather people around you. Broadly speaking, this takes two forms.

Either you powerfully articulate an existing idea, appealing to a constituency of fellow travellers, who have yet to coalesce around a shared mandate for action but are able to do so around you, or you have something new to say, an idea or approach that attracts people with its freshness, vibrancy and explanatory power. But in both cases, you become the hub of a newly forming network, which, with skilful application of power, is yours to craft and grow.

Leadership is a function of power, but our focus is on the power derived from your person not your position. We recognise that formal and positional power often helps, but principally we are concerned with how personal power is used to persuade or influence the behaviour of others, which in itself is often used as a definition of leadership. To illustrate this, we adapted a clinical behavioural model that describes influence in terms of certain key elements: convincing people that your idea is of value to them; that it is achievable and worth their effort; and that it is within their ability or potential. It also requires the creation of a conducive environment for behaviour change and the opportunity to see others doing and achieving positive results because of that behaviour.

To do that, a network leader's personal manifesto must, in the first instance, be well told. Stories and narratives appeal to our base emotions and compel action in a way that often defies rational argument. As Maya Angelou, the American poet and civil rights activist, famously observed:

> I've learned that people will forget what you said, people will forget what you did, but people will never forget how you made them feel.

This is a hugely powerful capability, and with such power must come responsibility. No discussion of leadership can proceed without considering ethics. Leadership is neutral; it can use fair means and foul and be directed towards ends that are either noble and self-effacing or repugnant and self-serving. Examples of both abound. But we firmly believe that the mantle of leadership and all that means in terms of the hope and trust placed in leaders demands that they act ethically and towards ends that are morally justifiable, right and true. At the very least, leaders should seek to fix problems, not exploit them for selfish or political gain. It also demands that leaders have the moral courage to speak out when they see others acting unethically.

At an organisational level, this means we cannot ignore organisational politics, which is effectively the informal network made explicit: the alliances, the deals and informal connections that make things happen. But the use of personal power and influence for political gain should not be a prescription for fighting dirty and behaving unethically. Rather, it is a prescription for being smart, one that recognises both the practical and ethical implications of each action you take and its implications for the organisation and its people. In business, as in war, the line between the ethical and unethical should never be crossed. Integrity and self-discipline on the part of the community leader, the military commander and the business leader are paramount.

Some people say they don't do politics, but the hard truth is that rational, logical argument and doing a good job will only get you so far. Leaders need to be able to operate within the messy reality of organisational politics, but to do so constructively, positively and for the collective good. And to act morally is a sound practical approach, because so much of effective leadership depends upon trust. Trust is the only foundation on which to build a personal manifesto worthy of others' support and is a powerful source of alignment.

Alignment is crucial in any collective endeavour and Network Leadership highlights the value of connective power, not only in the ability to understand the network and know what is required of it, but the capacity to connect it towards the achievement of what is required. In short, great leaders are great connectors. They understand the dynamics of how to grow, nurture and enable effective networks through mapping, weaving and building to the point where the network is not only sustainable but can grow without them.

These are not superficial networks of business cards and contacts, but networks of relationships directed towards specific goals. Networks give us all strength when we are wavering and question us when we are perhaps being overconfident. Networks give us new learning and new ideas, but ultimately networks help us to implement our passions and our ideas.

Leading Beyond Authority

In its purest form, leading beyond your authority is about turning your ideas, your personal manifesto, into action without recourse to formal or positional authority. Fundamentally, it is about making powerful connections across your inner, outer and peripheral networks, and it recognises that as we move from our inner to peripheral network, our formal authority diminishes until all that is left is our personal authority. It becomes leadership in the raw, deriving from our personal power, an ability to connect and the insight that leadership is something we give, not something we get.

Network Leaders have the ability to simultaneously see two perspectives: their place in the hierarchy and the network that surrounds them. They choose not to be constrained by either, but instead are guided by their own belief, sense of personal authority and ability to navigate between the two systems.

Personal authority is about you. It is a combination of your ideas, intelligence and expertise. The things you know about the business and its sector, the expertise with which you utilise this knowledge, but also the disparate ideas you are able to draw upon. A key part of the leader's role is to be strategic. To maintain perspective and see things in a wider context rather than being caught in the moment. It is all too easy to be reactive rather than proactive, to be driven by events. A wise leader learns to distinguish between the urgent and the important. They learn not to be confused by different advice and information, but to use it instead as a series of reference points to orientate themselves and then synthesise the conflicting views into a coherent way forward.

Thinking strategically sets leaders apart from managers, from those who execute and implement plans. It is the ability to appreciate the bigger picture, the broader environment in which you work. We described it as being T-shaped, the capability to place your deep technical expertise and knowledge and that of your team within the broader context of what the organisation is trying to achieve. This also requires leaders to be polymaths with a sound understanding of what their colleagues and peers do in other functions and departments, how they contribute together and apart.

Thinking strategically speaks directly to the work of Ibarra and Hunter[3] about making the transition from functional to general management, but more broadly it is an ability, at any level in an organisation, to step into the uncertainty of problems with no easy solution or any firm solution at all. It requires a capacity for reflection, an ability to broaden your vision beyond day-to-day operational and tactical concerns. To sit back and look up, to ask what happens next. To seek patterns, identify opportunities, make choices (often based on incomplete data) and align stakeholders around your strategic insights.

But this also requires receptive power: your ability to listen, admit your mistakes and absorb new ideas. This is imperative because, as previously noted,[4] a group of individuals whose collective behaviour is controlled by a single individual cannot behave in a more complex way than the individual who is exercising control. Consequently, once the complexity of demands is beyond that of a single individual, a new approach is needed, one that mirrors the interactions and mechanisms of the network which it is trying to control. Leaders therefore must have a capacity to learn, grow and develop collectively, and help others to do the same. And ultimately, this growth is towards an appreciation of the context in which you operate and an ability to enable collective action.

This is leading through facilitation, essentially creating a conducive environment for people to listen, learn and grow, both individually and collectively, and to see what can be achieved together. And this is made possible by leading with ideas and an inspiring vision. In essence, it is about giving people a reason to follow you, and if you don't think that you have original ideas, then seek them out. Develop the weak ties in your network that will take you to the edge, the interface between networks where disparate people, processes and philosophies collide, the place where great ideas happen, ideas which, with thought and reflection, you can adapt to your own context.

And if you're still at a loss, you can always lead with questions. Socrates, one of the most influential figures of all time, led with questions. Curiosity is a wonderful way to open yourself to new ideas, but it is also a way to open a space for others to have new ideas and think differently, gently challenging people's assumptions and prejudices, asking why we do things like that around here. Leading people into a space where they are able to question their view of the world and consider alternatives.

The contexts in which leadership is enacted vary, but as we have made clear, network leadership is suited to a VUCA world and to handling Wicked

Problems, where both the problem and solution maybe uncertain. And in our experience, leadership in this environment is more about enabling than directing; more about influence than control; more indirect than direct. It is leadership understood first and foremost as a social process that creates rather than forces direction, alignment and commitment. It is less about formal and positional authority and more about personal power and influence, and that takes more time and energy than simply telling people what to do.

Restless Persuasion

There is nothing new under the sun and Network Leadership is no exception. We do, however, believe that significant aspects of the energy and resilience required of leaders has been somewhat neglected, particularly that network leaders develop a capacity to thrive in chaos and need a degree of unreasonableness and impatience to get things done. There will be times when network leaders are a pain in the neck, pushing their peers, colleagues and followers where they do not believe they are capable of going or towards outcomes that appear impossible. But this is vital.

In part, Network Leaders have such energy and resilience because they are comfortable in chaos. They relish complexity and the challenges and opportunities it provides. They delight in wicked problems and the challenge of gathering a constituency of the like-minded to take on such problems. They step into such situations with an assurance that provides comfort and confidence to those around them, those who might otherwise walk away from such ambiguity and uncertainty.

If you want to lead in complex environments, you have no choice but to develop a similar capacity to cope, if not thrive, in situations of uncertainty. But let's face it; no one becomes a better leader by avoiding difficult situations. As the old saying goes: a boat in harbour is safe, but that's not what boats are for. Network leaders recognise that crises can also create opportunities and they are therefore better able to position themselves to prosper when others falter and anchor themselves in a set of unshakeable values and beliefs. As we mentioned, Ignatius Loyola, founder of the Jesuit movement, captured this aspect of network leadership well, in describing the ideal Jesuit as "living with one foot raised".[5] An individual always ready to respond to emerging opportunities but grounded in core beliefs and values that are non-negotiable, providing a foundation for purposeful change as opposed to aimless drifting in pursuit of the next best thing. But to lead in this environment also requires emotional intelligence, a capacity to recognise that for most people uncertainty is uncomfortable.

As a rule, we humans like to know where we are and where we are headed, but our networked world and the innovation and creativity it demands require that we spend time on the edge and travel paths that lead who knows where. Covid-19 and events like it present organisations and individuals with challenges to health, well-being, income and future employment. In times like this giving people the support they need requires leaders with empathy and understanding. Leaders who appreciate the personal change curve and can diagnose, with absolute honesty, where they and their people are on that curve, whether they are in shock, denial, experiencing anger, feeling depressed, exploring possibilities or committing to new ways of operating.[6]

A leader must be a container of their followers' anxieties, but also the spark igniting activity and the fuel rekindling and sustaining it. However, just as in Stephen King's book *The Green Mile*, where the hero takes away the pain of others but suffers physical pain and exhaustion as a result, this requires uncommon powers of determination and mental toughness. It is also a difficult balance to strike. The problem with a nanny state, like a helicopter parent, is that it breeds dependence. Coddled children are not only unable to think for themselves, but they are also less likely to think about others. Just as Network Leadership requires you to grow and build self-sustaining networks, it also requires that you help other people to live and work productively for themselves in a context of uncertainty: balancing compassion with, at times, impatience and unreasonable determination.

When reasonable people say there are not enough people, resources or time to get a job done, leaders may need to act unreasonably and that requires courage as well as energy. The morale courage to do what they believe to be right in the face of pressure from others to do something different or nothing at all. It is the ability to transcend the group and what is mistakenly assumed to be reasonable. But they must do so without breaking people, the empathy to understand that not everyone is like them and we used the notion of the Zone of Proximal Development (ZPD) to illustrate this point. Creating an environment that enables people to achieve their best in pursuit of shared objectives.

Finally

Our context is changing and those you lead are watching you. More is expected of leaders in times of change and uncertainty. On the one hand, leaders are still expected to get the job done, to push things to a conclusion and get results, but on the other, they must also connect things, they must bring people together, developing and maintaining collaborative activity in pursuit of shared goals and nurturing individuals to give of their best. Leaders cannot choose one or the other, they must choose both. Network Leaders achieve this balance.

Unreasonableness, impatience and setting a demanding pace is an important element of leadership, sometimes it is just what is needed, but it won't provide lasting improvements unless you balance it with compassion. Always pushing on at a relentless pace will eventually find you pushing on alone with nobody following. You and they will eventually burn out. But the answer is not necessarily to reduce the pace, it is also to have strategies to support those we lead in coping with the pace, to be a coach and confidant as well as a pacesetter.

The best leaders must be extremely challenging, but alongside this, they need to show that they welcome challenge themselves. They need to role model an open and engaging style of leadership, encouraging their teams to question their thinking, going out of their way create an environment in which it is okay to question and quiz them. Equally, great leaders are curious. They ask questions and genuinely listen to the answers, because they don't believe they have all the answers. They involve their staff in crucial decisions and encourage them to test new ideas.

The role of leaders is to do the best they can to improve their operating environment and this, of course, means that there is competition within and between organisations, often expressed though organisational politics. While perhaps being unfashionable to admit it, organisations need competition as well as collaboration. Competition stops us from being complacent and keeps us on our toes, but without collaboration, all we will get is greater variation in quality. Some will get better and do well, but others won't and overall the system will not improve. The right kind of collaboration is key, though it's not about huddling together and mindlessly endorsing each other's views and practices. It needs to be inclusive but also focused on outcomes, on raising the collective bar and achieving real solutions for improvement.

Above all, Network Leaders can adapt their leadership to different circumstances. They are capable of asking themselves whether the leadership approaches that have worked for them in the past are still going to work for them in the future in a world that is likely to be different from the one we have now, whether we like it or not. As the whole system shifts and turns, more than ever before, we need leaders who demonstrate personal authority, pace and a commitment to systems that work, combining competition with inclusivity, collaboration and contextualisation – leaders who can step up to create and lead self-improving networks.

This feels like a defining moment, characterised by unprecedented levels of uncertainty, politically, economically, socioculturally and from local to global. However, as unprecedented as many of these events may be, humanity has been through similar crises before. Inevitably, we are not entirely in control of our own destiny, we never have been nor likely ever will be, but unlike other species we do have a degree of agency and a capacity to influence events and impose some form of order. That capacity resides in Network Leaders, in anyone with the grit and determination to step up and make a stand, to gather people around them and get things done; leaders who seize the opportunity to redefine our world and work relentlessly towards positive outcomes for us all.

Leadership Questions

You are now at the end of the book but at the beginning of your next step in leadership, so take some time to reflect. Update Your Leadership Questions (LQs), which provide your personal guide to Network Leadership, and reflect on what you have learnt:

1. Has it changed how you think about leadership? If so, how?
2. How have you or how might you use Network Leadership?
3. What's next for you as a Network Leader? Make at least one commitment to action!

Notes

1 Noë, A. (2009). *Out of Our Heads: Why You Are Not Your Brain, and Other Lessons from the Biology of Consciousness*. New York: Hill & Wang.
2 Catmull, E. (2014). *Creativity, Inc. Overcoming the Unseen Forces that Stand in the Way of True Inspiration*. London: Bantam Press, p. 169.
3 Ibarra, H. and Hunter, M.L. (2007). How Leaders Create and Use Networks. *Harvard Business Review*, 85(1): pp. 40–7.
4 Bar-Yam, Y. (1997). Complexity Rising: From Human Beings to Human Civilization, a Complexity Profile. [online] Available at: https://necsi.edu/complexity-rising-from-human-beings-to-human-civilization-a-complexity-profile (accessed 17 Apr. 2021).
5 Lowney, C. (2003). *Heroic Leadership: Best Practices from a 450-Year-Old Company That Changed the World*. Chicago: Loyola Press.
6 The change curve, now often used in diagnosing the effects of change on people in organisations, was developed from the original work of the psychiatrist Elizabeth Kubler-Ross; see Kubler-Ross, E. (1969). *On Death and Dying*. New York: Macmillan Publishing.

Appendix 1: A Brief History of Social Network Analysis[1]

Arguably, the study of networks dates to the mid-18th century and the East Prussian city of Konigsberg. Among the sights of the city were seven bridges across the Pregel River, which connected the two river banks and two islands in the middle of the river. A familiar conundrum for the inhabitants was whether it was possible to cross all the bridges in a single walk without re-crossing any of them. In 1735 Leon Euler demonstrated why such a walk was, in fact, impossible, and in the process invented network theory.

Social Network Analysis emerged from the social science disciplines of psychology (specifically Gestalt psychology and social psychology), sociology and social anthropology, each of which offered unique approaches to the study of social networks, but historical accounts tend to agree that the field started through the efforts of Jacob Moreno, a student of psychiatry from Vienna, who immigrated to the United States in 1925 and developed the field of "sociometry", widely considered to be the precursor to social network analysis. Moreno was influenced by Gestalt psychology, which argued, in contrast to the behaviourist school, that human perceptions could best be understood in the context of the mind as a whole rather than its individual parts. While a student at the University of Vienna, he also became interested in how the psychological well-being of individuals was linked to the social relations in which they were embedded.

Working with Helen Hall Jennings, they developed sociometry, which used quantitative methods to study the structure of groups and the positions of individuals within those groups. The approach also used "sociograms" to depict individuals (or any social unit) and their relationships to others in the group. The individuals were portrayed as points (nodes) and the relationship linking them as lines (ties or edges).

Sociograms were first presented to the public in 1933 after Moreno helped to explain the spate of runaways from a reformatory school in New York, which he illustrated was explicable in terms of the girl's social networks.[2] The sociograms

DOI: 10.4324/9781003092582-38

generated a great deal of interest and public attention. Much of their appeal stemming from the simple yet powerful way in which they communicated a new way of conceptualising social relationships. However, despite this initial success and the publication of a journal called *Sociometry*, by the 1960s and 1970s, interest had largely drifted elsewhere and the journal changed its name to the *Social Psychology Quarterly*.

Working at much the same time was Kurt Lewin, another European trained scholar who had also been influenced by Gestalt theories. He too brought this knowledge with him when he immigrated to the United States in the 1930s, although there is little evidence for Moreno and Lewin actively working together or citing each other's work.

Lewin is best known for developing the theoretical framework called "field theory", which describes and explains human behaviour and perception from a structural perspective. Lewin saw behaviour embedded within a "field", which he defined as "the totality of coexisting facts which are conceived as mutually interdependent". He argued that to truly understand perception and behaviour, one needed to understand this larger context of coexisting facts. In 1945, he became director of the Research Center for Group Dynamics at Massachusetts Institute of Technology (MIT), where he influenced Alex Bavelas, Dorwin Cartwright and Leon Festinger. Unfortunately, he died shortly after and his research team were split between MIT and the University of Michigan.

Alex Bavelas led the Group Networks Laboratory at MIT and designed several experiments centred on issues of communication and information diffusion in small groups, focusing in particular on which kinds of network structures affected the speed and efficiency of information diffusion. This, in turn, led to the development of centrality and cliques, key concepts in social network analysis. Social psychology continues to influence network theory through Friedkin's social influence theory and Cook's social exchange theory.

The irony of the history of social network analysis, particularly in the early days, is that many researchers were working separately from each other without knowledge of each other's existence. Thus, while Moreno and Jennings were developing sociometry, social anthropologists in Britain and the United States were also exploring new ways of studying social issues.

A particularly influential figure was Alfred Radcliffe-Brown, who argued that society could be seen as a "complex network of social relations" that he labelled a "social structure" and could be used to move beyond abstract categories of culture and class, towards direct observation of the connections between individuals, in other words an empirical method of studying culture.

One of Radcliffe-Brown's protégés, W. Lloyd Warner, collaborated with Elton Mayo in the Harvard Business School to widen the scope of Mayo's study of the psychological characteristics of workers in the Western Electric company to include a concern for the social context and structures surrounding workers. Together they led an anthropological study on interpersonal interactions among 14 workers at the Hawthorne factory (1931–32). It was the first major study, within a natural setting, to use a sociogram to describe the relations observed by field workers.

Warner also launched a second study in a New England town based upon a conceptual framework, in which he describes society and communities as composed of "a group of mutually interacting individuals", whereby each relation is "part of the total community and mutually depended upon all other parts". Despite having little direct impact on social network analysis until the 1950s, ideas relating to social networks were also present in early sociological thought and had an impact on the work of Radcliffe-Brown and Warner.

Emile Durkheim, for example, argued that any social phenomena (what he referred to as social facts) could only be understood in relation to others and to the wider social context. In his famous study on suicide (1897), he argued that suicides were less frequent amongst those individuals who were well integrated into society, and as such, suicides were an example of how one particular social phenomenon (in this case suicide) could only be understood by looking at how individuals were embedded within a larger social system.

Georg Simmel used similar arguments to contrast his theories with those of macro level theorists such as Weber and Marx. In Simmel's view, macro level structures and social phenomena could be understood by focusing on micro social interactions among individuals or small groups. In his work, *Philosophy of Money* (1900), he discussed the distinction between a dyad (a relationship between two persons) and a triad (a group formed of three persons), noting that the simple addition of a third person transforms the social dynamics in crucial ways and that understanding this could shed light on society at large and how larger structures constrain individuals.

With dyads, each individual still maintains his or her own identity, yet this situation changes with the introduction of a third member. With a triad, a group effect or structure is more likely to occur, and in doing so constrain or undermine the individuality of each person. Triads introduce the possibility of alliances and group pressure and illustrate how larger structures, such as institutions and cultures, could dominate and constrain individuals.

It was in fact another sociologist, George Homans, who described and synthesised all the techniques, methods and theoretical insights that were currently in use. His book, *The Human Group* (1950), was the first comprehensive account of small group research combining insights from psychology and social anthropology and went on to influence other theories in the field, including James Coleman's *Foundations of Social Theory* (1990), theory of social action and social capital, which, in turn, has been widely cited in the more recent work of Ronald S. Burt (1995) and Robert Putnam (2000).

But it was Harvard's sociology department that became the centre of social network analysis under the leadership of Harrison White, where he established a research programme combining social network concepts with mathematical techniques and the testing of empirical data. His years of teaching at Harvard influenced and shaped a generation of social network scholars, including Mark Granovetter, who developed the concept of weak and strong ties (1973).

Notes

1 A fuller version can be found in Prell, C. (2012). *Social Network Analysis: History, Theory & Methodology*. London: Sage Publishing.
2 Fortunately for Jazz music, the study came too late to prevent a 15-year-old girl called Ella Fitzgerald from escaping.

Appendix 2: Leader Biographies

Caroline Naven

Caroline has led public sector multi-agency, multidisciplinary teams in London and the West Midlands sector for 25 years. She has set up new innovative services in community safety and neighbourhood management and is currently the Head of Preparation for Adulthood at Birmingham City Council. Previously, she has worked with a plethora of public, private and voluntary and community sectors which has required her to lead beyond authority. A compassionate, curious leader, she is governed by the mantra of agitate, educate, organise and empowers her teams through the application of a distributed leadership model. A former lecturer in law, she utilised her legal training to work as a volunteer on the Release helpline providing advice about substance misuse. She currently sits on the Board of trustees for St Anne's hostel for homeless men and their canine companions as well as being a governor at Langley Secondary School.

Darcy Willson-Rymer

Darcy was appointed Chief Executive Officer (CEO) of Card Factory in March 2021. Prior to this appointment, he served as CEO of Costcutter Supermarkets for eight years. During his time at Costcutter, Darcy successfully steered a nationwide multisite owned and franchised convenience retail business through a period of significant change and led the brand transformation of the business. Prior to this, Darcy held a range of roles in international branded businesses, including Starbucks Coffee Company, Unilever and Yum Restaurants International. He is Chair of Stop the Traffik, an NGO committed to ending modern slavery, he believes passionately that we should not live in a world where people are bought and sold.

DOI: 10.4324/9781003092582-39

Dame Jayne-Anne Gadhia DBE

Jayne-Anne has more than 30 years of experience in finance and banking. She is the Founder and Executive Chair of the fintech Snoop that helps customers to better manage their money. She is the founder of Gadhia Consultants. As one of the original directors of Virgin Direct, she launched the Virgin One Account in 1998. Following the acquisition by Royal Bank of Scotland (RBS) of the Virgin One Account, she went on to lead a number of RBS business units, ultimately joining the RBS Retail Executive Board where she was responsible for RBS's mortgage business. She returned to the Virgin family in 2007 and became the CEO of Virgin Money until its sale to CYBG in 2018. Jayne-Anne is a firm believer in the importance of businesses making a positive contribution to society. She won Leader of The Year at the Lloyds Bank National Business Awards in 2018 in recognition of her personal impact on the culture and success of Virgin Money as a force for good in the banking industry. From 2016 to 2021, she was the UK Government's Women in Finance Champion and continues to support and promote the Women in Finance Charter as an advisor. In November 2020 Jayne-Anne was appointed the new Chair of the Her Majesty's Revenue and Customs (HMRC) Board. She was previously the CEO (UK and Ireland) of Salesforce. A committed supporter of The Prince's Charities, she is a Trustee of the Tate and has previously served as Chair of Scottish Business in the Community and the Chair of Dumfries House.

Professor Jonathan H Deacon PhD

Jonathan is Professor of Marketing at the School of Design, Digital and Marketing at the University of South Wales, where he leads research with a focus on how entrepreneurial firms "create markets" and how SME's can "go to market" in the era of digital platforms and technically literate consumers. He consults with business and government bodies on several strategic projects, business development initiatives and the digital economy. However, Jonathan's career prior to academia was within business – he launched and grew several successful businesses and has a working knowledge of high growth businesses and new venture starts. Jonathan is an acknowledged global "thought leader" at the interface between Marketing, Design Thinking and Management. He is an experienced non-executive director (NED). Jonathan is also Vice Chair and UK board member of the European Marketing Confederation and is an appointed member of the Royal Anniversary Trust's Readers Panel for the

Queen's Anniversary Awards. Jonathan retains an interest in business and sits on the boards of a number of "not for loss" companies. For relaxation he "enjoys" adventure sports!

Ruth Dearnley OBE

Ruth Dearnley OBE became Chief Executive of the charity for STOP THE TRAFFIK in May 2008 having participated in its formation in 2005. The charity aims to disrupt and prevent human trafficking and exploitation worldwide. With a law degree and background in education, she inspires and enables people to transform the world around them, starting in their local community. Ruth believes that STOP THE TRAFFIK's working model demonstrates the unique power of bringing people and technology into a harmonious relationship for good for all, imagining a different future where good can prevail. Ruth was honoured with the award of an OBE in the 2014 British New Year Honours.

Index

Note: **Bold** page numbers refer to tables; *italic* page numbers refer to figures and page numbers followed by "n" denote endnotes.

For Product Safety Concerns and Information please contact our EU representative GPSR@taylorandfrancis.com
Taylor & Francis Verlag GmbH, Kaufingerstraße 24, 80331 München, Germany

www.ingramcontent.com/pod-product-compliance
Ingram Content Group UK Ltd.
Pitfield, Milton Keynes, MK11 3LW, UK
UKHW022010010526
470621UK00020B/1096
9780367552541